WHAT YOU NEVER LEARNED IN GRADUATE SCHOOL

A Survival Guide for Therapists

Also by the Authors

Jeffrey Kottler

The Language of Tears
Finding Your Way as a Counselor
Growing a Therapist
Beyond Blame: A New Way of Resolving Conflicts in Relationships
The Heart of Healing: Relationships in Therapy
    (*with Tom Sexton and Sue Whiston*)
Classrooms Under the Influence: Counteracting Problems of Addiction
    (*with Stan Zehm and Richard Powell*)
Introduction to Therapeutic Counseling
    (*with Robert Brown*)
On Being a Therapist
Teacher as Counselor
    (*with Ellen Kottler*)
Advanced Group Leadership
On Being a Teacher
    (*with Stan Zehm*)
Compassionate Therapy: Working with Difficult Clients
The Compleat Therapist
Private Moments, Secret Selves: Enriching Your Time Alone
The Imperfect Therapist: Learning from Failure in Therapeutic Practice
    (*with Diane Blau*)
Ethical and Legal Issues in Counseling and Psychotherapy
    (*with William Van Hoose*)

Richard Hazler

The Emerging Professional Counselor: Student Dreams to Professional
    Realities
    (*with Jeffrey Kottler*)
Breaking the Cycle of Violence: Interventions for Bullying and
    Victimization

A NORTON PROFESSIONAL BOOK

WHAT YOU NEVER LEARNED IN GRADUATE SCHOOL

A *Survival Guide for Therapists*

Jeffrey A. Kottler, Ph.D., and
Richard J. Hazler, Ph.D.

W.W. NORTON & COMPANY • New York • London

Copyright © 1997 by Jeffrey A. Kottler and Richard J. Hazler

Printed in the United States of America

First Edition

For information about permission to reproduce selections
from this book, write to
Permissions, W.W. Norton & Company, Inc., 500 Fifth Avneue,
New York, NY 10110.

Composition by Bytheway Typesetting Services, Inc.
Manufacturing by Haddon Craftsmen, Inc.

Library of Congress Cataloging-in-Publication Data

Kottler, Jeffrey A.
    What you never learned in graduate school : a survival guide for
therapists / Jeffrey A. Kottler and Richard J. Hazler.
        p.   cm.
    "A Norton professional book."
    Includes bibliographical references and index.
    ISBN 0-393-70242-1
    1. Psychotherapy—Vocational guidance.   2. Psychotherapy—
Practice.   I. Hazler, Richard J.   II. Title.
RC480.5.K683   1997
616.89′14′023—dc21   96-41947   CIP

W. W. Norton & Company, Inc., 500 Fifth Avenue, New York, N.Y. 10110
                    http://www.wwnorton.com
W. W. Norton & Company, Ltd., 10 Coptic Street, London WC1A 1PU

                1 2 3 4 5 6 7 8 9 0

Contents

Preface

Therapists had every right to expect that what they learned in graduate school would serve them well during a lifetime of service to others. Certainly some theories would be revised; even a few new ones would come to the forefront. Research and practice would continue to evolve, but at least in a form that was remotely recognizable to those who have been in the field for a while. Who could have ever imagined the kinds of changes that would take place in the last decade or two?

Practicing therapists, and even those currently in graduate school, were not prepared to deal with the new order of things, a world where "managed care" has replaced compassionate healing. There have been shifts not only in the transition of therapy from a profession to a business but also changes in: (1) the ways we do treatment planning, (2) the paradigm shifts from single theory allegiance to broad schools of thought, (3) the prevalence of politically correct beliefs that are officially sanctioned, (4) the call for greater moral responsibility on the part of clinicians, (5) the demands for greater cultural and gender sensitivity, (6) the widespread use of computers and technology, (7) the resurgence of qualitative research methodologies, (8) the increased preference for pills to cure maladies, and (9) the increased popularity of short-term interventions rather than long-term relationships. It is this last change that has been most dramatic, considering that most therapists have been prepared to do a kind of work that is now being called obsolete.

Therapists and counselors are not only struggling to adapt to the changing landscape of the profession, but also to a number of other demands that are directly related to professional and personal success. Graduate school didn't teach us quite a number of critical skills and attitudes that we have to learn on our own, through trial and error, and through an underground network that provides us with useful information, as well as inaccurate gossip. As just a few examples, we were not sufficiently warned (1) about the negative side effects of being a therapist, (2) that life is not a multiple choice test where there is one right answer, (3) that even with advanced degrees we would still not be taken seriously by our families, nor feel that we know enough to do our jobs, (4) that our feelings of ineptitude and fears of failure would continue to persist, (5) that there are personal reasons we chose to enter this field that we didn't confront, (6) that we take ourselves far too seriously, (7) that the answers to our most important questions are not found in books, (8) that there is a lot of hypocrisy within our ranks and absurdity in what we do, and (9) that we will never, ever feel good enough.

What You Never Learned in Graduate School is written primarily for three groups: (1) practitioners of social work, psychology, counseling, marital and family therapy, psychiatry, psychiatric nursing, and other mental health disciplines, (2) advanced students in these professions, and (3) intelligent readers who are interested in learning about the inner world of therapy and the changes this field is undergoing.

While this volume satisfies the demands of traditional scholarship, it is written in an unpretentious, accessible style that engages the reader on a personal level. Citations have been held to a minimum in favor of an author's voice that speaks directly to the reader about subjects that have all been ignored.

The focus throughout this book is on themes, issues, and critical areas that were rarely addressed in formal educational experiences. The first section is conceptual and provocative in nature, addressing seismic shifts in the field, the limits of professional training, and a review of the most critical areas for which practitioners are not prepared. The second then focuses on the practical areas where even experienced therapists need additional growth to maximize their potential: mastering new conceptual paradigms and cutting edge technology, learning innovative forms of therapy responsive to the marketplace, preparing and delivering speeches and lectures, doing professional presentations, the process of mentoring and supervising therapists, publishing books and articles, dealing with organizational politics, sustaining a private practice, dealing with the media, transforming oneself through travel and risk taking, and planning for the future. Each discussion provides specific ways to better meet your professional future successfully.

WHAT YOU NEVER LEARNED IN GRADUATE SCHOOL

A Survival Guide for Therapists

SECTION I

More than You Bargained For

CHAPTER ONE

Seismic Shifts

To say that the fields of psychotherapy and counseling are undergoing rapid changes hardly does justice to the magnitude and scope of what has been taking place during the past decade. There once was a time when preparing to be a professional therapist held promise of a stable and prosperous future, one in which you could expect to earn a decent salary and enjoy the benefits of being part of a very exclusive club. All the sacrifices you have made to join this profession—the money you have spent, the time you have invested, the humiliation you may have suffered, the anxiety and pressures you have survived, the hard work you spent reading books, writing papers, taking exams, gritting your teeth through certain classes, competing with the best and the brightest—all seemed worthwhile as long as you would have your prize at the end. Throughout all the hoops you were made to jump through, the rites of passage you earned every step of the way, there was always that dream waiting for you at the end.

Now you sit in your perfectly appointed office. You had spent hours while dozing in boring classes fantasizing exactly what this space would finally look like. You selected your furniture carefully, pondered exactly how you would arrange things in the absolutely perfect configuration guaranteed to make the most reluctant clients open their hearts to your compassionate scrutiny. During particularly tense or slow times in class, you would lapse even further into the most minute details of what your new lifestyle would be like. You thought about how you would arrange your books, where to put your diplomas, who you would associate with, how you would market yourself and your wonderful new skills.

It has come as quite a shock to learn that the world you had every right to expect would be waiting for you upon graduation is nowhere near what it once was.

NOT WHAT IT USED TO BE

There once was a time, not too long ago, when all therapists needed to begin practicing their craft was a quiet room, a few good referral sources, an appointment book, a phone, and an answering machine. This was during that era, a mere decade ago, when the public had insurance policies that subsidized psychotherapy in such a way that most people paid a nominal fee and could easily afford to come a few times per week as long as they liked. The only justification that was required was our certification that a person was indeed undergoing some sort of adjustment reaction, marked by anxiety or depression, or perhaps a combination of both. We were not asked how long our treatment would take and it was perfectly reasonable to assume that this person could keep coming as long as he liked and was getting something from the experience.

It must be awfully strange for newcomers in the field to hear these stories about the good ol' days, kind of like the claims by our parents or grandparents that they had to trudge three miles to school every day, braving snowstorms and any number of obstacles along the way. Indeed, it does seem like there is a different world for therapists today.

Comparing what was once needed to practice our profession, it is staggering to consider the requirements today. The comfortable chairs and diplomas are certainly still in evidence, but computers and support staff are virtually a requirement (or soon will be) to process the mountain of paperwork needed to gain and maintain approval for our services. There have been seismic shifts not only in what is required to conduct our business but also in a myriad of other ways.

END OF THE GOLDEN ERA

There has been a fundamental change in the role of a therapist, from that of a dependable confidante to a temporary consultant. There once was a time when we would contract with our clients to be available for them throughout their lifetimes. Especially for those who were suffering from deep-rooted intrapsychic struggles, those who were suffering narcissistic or borderline personality disorders, or those individuals who were interested in understanding the nature of their life-long issues, there was an assumption that treatment would last just as long as both of us wanted it to.

We are not speaking of the Woody Allens, the extreme cases of neurotic, "professional clients" who would visit a therapist several times a week for 10, 20, or 30 years. Rather, we are referring to what used to be the typical length of a therapeutic relationship, not only for psychoanalytic practitioners, but also for most clinicians. During this golden era, most insurance companies would subsidize our treatments to the tune of 80–90% of whatever we would reasonably charge, for as many sessions as we felt necessary and for as long as was considered appropriate — 6 months, 1 year, even several years when it was indicated.

The whole method of compensation has changed as well, from a fee-for-service basis to other alternatives such as capitation and limited reimbursement. We might very well feel that our time is valued a certain amount per hour, but the marketplace is no longer based on free enterprise in which we will actually be paid what we think we are worth. Many managed care organizations now pay a standardized rate of, say, $50. "Take it or leave it" is the attitude, and don't you dare try to collect anything else from the client!

DOC IN THE BOX

Sprinkled liberally around most communities today are little clinics that offer the public medical services in the same spirit as department stores or chain restaurants. Gone are the times when you had a personal physician, one who knew your family and history intimately. Now you show up at one of these mini-medical centers (no appointment needed), take a number, and then take your chances that the doctor on duty is someone who knows something about what is ailing you. Forget about anything resembling personal service: Their job is to administer medicine cheaply and efficiently, not to deal with you as a human being.

The public is growing so used to this doc-in-the-box mentality that when it comes time to see a professional for some personal concern or emotional difficulty, they don't even flinch at the prospect of choosing a random name from a published list of "approved providers." One therapist is as good as another, they reason. The important thing to consider is: Can I see this professional who is covered on my plan?

These are the days of managed care, health maintenance organizations, employee assistance programs, and preferred provider networks. If the concept of private practice is not being systematically eradicated, then it is at least being altered to the point where therapists are working more hours, for less money, doing homogenized treatment for prescribed intervals. It is not just the solo practitioner who is losing autonomy; any community agency or mental health service that has to deal with third party reimbursement companies has had to change the ways it operates.

More and more articles have been appearing in professional journals, urging practitioners to think about such things as economic risks, cost effectiveness, market research, sales strategies, program marketing, and computer systems analysis. In one such advice column, Butler (1994) explains that aggressive self-promotion goes against the grain of all we have ever learned about what it means to be a professional with integrity and class: "Selling yourself to a managed care company means adapting to a new role and learning new social skills that graduate schools—and seeing clients—don't teach" (p. 29).

It is predicted that the changes taking place within the field are going to evolve at an alarming rate. If the trends continue, it appears that we will have less autonomy in what we choose to do with our clients and how we prefer to do it. The emphasis seems to be on doing therapy as briefly and efficiently as possible, dealing only with the original presenting complaint, and being accountable to large, impersonal organizations that have no investment in a client's welfare. In one instance, a psychiatric nurse was appalled that benefits were cut off for one patient who was determined to have made "substantial progress" because now he felt only 4 snakes crawling around inside his belly instead of the 20 with which he first entered treatment.

Although this situation certainly sounds bleak and discouraging, rather than giving in to the inevitability of increasingly managed mental health care, therapists are having to learn new skills in order to survive and flourish. These include such things as increased computer literacy and marketing sophistication, but also a more proactive stance to organize ourselves so that we take back control of our own profession instead of letting services be dictated by utilization and review boards that are run by physicians and corporate executives. Sometimes this even involves hiring "practice consultants" to help organize billing systems and marketing strategies (Lawless, 1995).

The major problem seems to be the degree of competition rather than cooperation that now exists between members of the therapeutic community. The truth of the matter is that between social workers, psychologists, family therapists, counselors, pastoral care workers, psychiatric nurses, and psychiatrists, not to mention all the paraprofessional mental health workers operating without licenses and primary care physicians functioning outside of their specialties, there are too many of us in the marketplace. It is now survival of the fittest.

Economic and political realities have turned one profession against the other, and even within specialties practitioners undercut one another, outbid one another for contracts, and act as if we are all fighting for a limited number of customers, which in a sense we are. This is especially ironic when we consider that the waiting lists at community mental health centers, veterans hospitals, and charitably funded agencies are staggering. Unfortunately, these underprivileged clienteles can't pay for services. The government continues to cut back funding for their mental health needs, leaving the poor and homeless without support. The result of this calamity is that more and more therapists are leaving the field during a time when the need for their services is greater than ever.

The most difficult part of these changes for experienced practitioners is letting go of the past. Things will never be the same that they once were, when therapists could see clients as often as they liked, for as long as their clients could conceivably profit from continued sessions, and with a minimum of paperwork or interference from insurance companies.

This situation has indeed caused considerable resentment and frustration, but it has also had some constructive impact. The call for increased accountability by the insurance industry has motivated us to increase our effectiveness. Clients are profiting from more efficient methods of symptom alleviation even if they are being cheated out of opportunities to explore deeper issues of meaning in their lives (okay, it is hard for us to be all that convincing when lapsing into rationalizations and complete denial). It is also true that more and more middle class working people are able to afford to seek our services now, even if it is for the merest tease of what might be possible if we had more than a half dozen sessions.

Finally, it is only right that our profession be expected to ante up in the effort to control spiraling health costs that have resulted from decades of abuse by a few irresponsible individuals. In one such case from recent memory, a social worker who worked within a private practice group would bring in large extended families, see them together, but then bill their insurance company for individual sessions, sometimes even 90 or 100 billing hours per week! In another case within the same agency, a psychologist would simultaneously schedule two or even three clients at the same time just like doctors do. He would then run back and forth between each room, giving clients assignments or tasks to complete while he would alternate every few minutes between each of the sessions. Naturally, he would then charge different insurance companies for the same hour, knowing that they would not compare their records to discover what he had been doing. We are certain that most of you can think of a few similar examples of your own. It is no wonder that strict controls have had to be implemented as a way to prevent abuses such as these!

PROZAC GENERATION

First there was Carter's Pills, then Valium. Now Prozac is being heralded as the new miracle cure for everything from depression, for which it was originally intended, to shyness, chronic gambling, sociopathy, lower back pain, obesity, premenstrual syndrome, fear of public speaking, lack of confidence, or even a lackluster personality. Over a million prescriptions for this drug are written every month, most of them by general practitioners who spend less than three minutes talking to their patients about their problems.

Writing about how Prozac has become "as familiar as Kleenex and as socially acceptable as spring water," Cowley (1994) interviewed long-time users of the drug (and its cousins, the other serotonin reuptake inhibitors like Zoloft and Paxil), who proclaim that it "gives them an edge," makes them more open and able to make people laugh, sharpens their thinking, even helps them to sport a more "buoyant personality." Marathon runner Alberto Salazar claimed that his return to champion form occurred largely through this regimen of Prozac, which balanced his body chemistry. Ironically, it supposedly does all this but is still no more effective for treating depression (60–70%) than plain old tricyclics like Tofranil and Elavil.

After the publication of such books as *Listening to Prozac* and *Prozac Nation*, the public became even more convinced that relief is just a swallow away. Designer drugs (so-called because they are intended to work on a single neurotransmitter) are becoming so popular that in a small town in rural Washington one practitioner coerced over 700 of his patients to take Prozac. His defense: "There is a huge amount of unrecognized depression out there. I was just a little bit early in making the diagnosis" (Roberts, 1995, p. 16). We guess so!

Prozac does not represent so much a medical breakthrough as it does an interesting cultural phenomenon (Jaret, 1994). It demonstrates just how desperate the public is for a new generation of Carter's Pills that will cure everything that ails them. Best of all, such a wonder drug would imply that their maladies are not within their own control, not their fault, and they don't have to do invest any time or energy to heal themselves.

Prozac has become a metaphor for quick relief. People are impatient. They want instant results. If it is absolutely necessary, they will even come back for a second session if we can't cure them of their life-long suffering in a single interview. Don't we have some sort of pill we can give them? Isn't there some chemical we can introduce into their system that will save them the hard work of having to take charge of their own lives?

Nonmedical therapists, who have only their powers of persuasion as their primary tools, are facing stiff competition from psychiatrists (and primary care physicians who prescribe the vast majority of antidepressant and antianxiety medications) who are offering the public chemical alternatives to alleviate what bothers them emotionally. What is a therapist to do when a client presenting symptoms of panic attacks or depression believes that symptom relief is only a few weeks away by taking a few pills each day? Sure there are a few annoying side effects, but what is a little insomnia, nausea, jitters, or lack of sex drive compared to immediate changes in one's demeanor, or even a wholesale personality transformation?

The initial promise that all psychological ills could be cured by the new generation of psychotropic medications is now being reevaluated. After an extensive meta-analytic review of outcome studies related to the administration of antidepressant drugs, it isn't altogether clear what results are generated by the chemicals versus placebo effects related to the doctor's belief that the pills would be helpful (Fisher & Greenberg, 1995). It's pretty obvious that even if these medications could deliver what they promise, their impact is heightened, if not dependent, on the interpersonal context in which they are administered. In other words, it seems to take a skilled therapist to help a client to capitalize on the potential benefits of Prozac and related compounds.

The debate that has raged for decades between relatively long-term, insight-oriented practitioners and more behaviorally-oriented clinicians who are after short-term symptom alleviation has now become a moot argument. While there has been no definitive resolution as to which is the superior treatment, both therapies offering something unique, the sheer luxury of being able to delve into a client's past indefinitely is now a thing of the past.

Whereas once upon a time we could think in terms of spending the first month, at least, getting to know the client, learning something about his background and values and family history, goals and aspirations, before we ever had to come up with a definitive diagnosis and treatment plan, now we are actually expected to have already cured the person by that time! Furthermore, the concept of spending a year or two or three engaged in a therapeutic relationship designed to resolve intrapsychic troubles, deep-rooted unconscious issues, or themes of personal meaningfulness, is all but obsolete except for the wealthy segment of the population who can afford this indulgence.

The most popular therapies today are those that promise results in a matter of a few weeks, even if those troubles were thought to have taken years to resolve in the past. Solution-focused therapies, brief therapies, narrative therapies, family therapies, even single-session interventions, are becoming increasingly popular to satisfy the consumer's demand for "magic pills," the managed care industry's requirements for efficient treatments, and even the practitioner's preference to see observable results in a short time.

What is also likely is that we will continue to see better living through chemistry. The pharmaceutical industry will continue to develop new designer medications that will alter personalities, wipe out undesirable emotions, or promote a feeling of inner well-being that people may confuse with happiness. Prozac has now become our greatest competition, and unless we can develop the means to provide satisfactory results in a shorter period of time, we will soon be out of business.

QUICKER. SWIFTER. FASTER.

For the new generation of therapists, who have never known anything else, thinking of their therapeutic role as a technician rather than as an artist may not be all that troubling. For the rest of us, who view the practice of therapy as a kind of poetry in motion in which each session is a co-created work of art, the shift in role is disorienting at best, and more often deeply disturbing.

What was once learned in graduate school, and still is dominant in many institutions, is a kind of therapy in which medium-term or even lengthy relationships are established in order to address psychodynamic features, entrenched dysfunctional patterns, existential themes, and other content that lends itself to prolonged, deep-level investigations of self. Certainly, pills or brief forms of therapy are not the best choice for everyone; there will always be a market for inquisitive people who want to learn about themselves and the ways they relate to others. In our society, where people are increasingly feeling alienated, disenfranchised, and marginalized, there is a desperate need to feel understood.

After completing a series of workshops over a year's time covering the latest innovations in brief treatments, as well as immersion in the literature,

I (JK) had been eager to try out my new skills and techniques in solution-focused therapy, narrative therapy, strategic interventions, eye-movement-desensitization, Ericksonian hypnosis, and a few other innovations I have now already forgotten. I couldn't wait for opportunities to move my clients along a faster route toward deliverance. After all, I have long been far more attracted to dramatic confrontations than I have to more low-key interpretations—not because I believe they work better but because they satisfy my own impatient need for progress.

I had been working with one woman for some time, making modest progress, but certainly not by the standards of my problem-solving colleagues. I felt like a dinosaur still resorting to the "primitive" ways of working I had been practicing for years—listening carefully and compassionately, slowly building a solid alliance, exploring deep issues of freedom, personal responsibility, love, and breaking free of the past.

Clearly it was time to get to the "bottom line." This relationship had been "dragging on" for months now and I was feeling a little guilty that I was not meeting the contemporary standards of what is expected. I interrupted my client on several occasions, especially proud of the deftness with which I introduced an "externalization," "deconstruction," "paradoxical maneuver," and even an old-fashioned direct confrontation when I told her that I thought she might be needlessly stalling the pace of things in order to avoid facing the world on her own.

The tears that had been streaming down her face abruptly stopped. I could see anger in her eyes and in cords of muscle in her neck. "Kottler, what is your problem?" she asked none too politely. "In case you haven't noticed, I have not felt that many men have ever listened to me in my life, not my boss, my father, my brothers, my ex-husband, or certainly my current husband, and not even my own son. I am used to being interrupted. I have never been taken as seriously as I deserve.

"I had hoped that with you I might feel a little understanding. After all, I am paying you to listen to me. Now I wish you would stop trying to fix me and just listen. I want you to understand, I want *someone* to finally understand who I am and what I want."

She actually said all that. I, of course, immediately protected myself from this censure by telling myself that this "intervention" clearly worked: Look at how assertive she had become, and all because of my technique of challenging her. While patting myself on the back, I also felt confusion settle over me. I realized that in my urgency to move more quickly, I had focused more on technique than on the person in the room with me.

Any therapist, whether practicing traditional psychoanalysis or the briefest solution-oriented approach, must demonstrate a high degree of sensitivity, patience, and subtlety. Any therapy, Lipchik (1994) reminds us, can be delivered poorly or well, depending on the clinician's ability to move as slowly or quickly as the client needs at any moment in time.

PROVE IT

There is not only an imperative to move more quickly in our work, regardless of what the client wants or needs, much less what we believe is appropriate, but also a mandate that we must measure the results of our efforts. And we damn well better be able to prove that what we are doing is consistent with what the managed care organization's own research shows is most efficient with this presenting complaint. It makes little difference whether solution-oriented therapy is appropriate for a given case or whether you even practice that sort of intervention; that is what you are ordered to do because its results can be easily measured. It is sort of like an insurance company telling a doctor that it will not approve the heart transplant for a needy patient because it is too expensive but they will permit a gall bladder operation.

Medical personnel and corporate executives who make up utilization review boards can't fathom the work that we do, where we can't show them the offending tumors or body parts that we have excised from the patient's body. They are not even certain that things like depression and anxiety even exist in the real world, nor are they convinced that there is anything we can really do to help these people. On one level, it *is* absurd that we make people better by simply talking to them.

People are constantly looking over our shoulders and they are not the sort of benevolent supervisors who actually care about client welfare, our continued professional development, or such matters as autonomy, confidentiality, and quality of service. Quite often, the person who approves our treatment and decides whether we are allowed to continue seeing a client is not even another therapist who understands what we do. Such a case manager or utilization review worker may be a practical nurse, a general doctor, or even a corporate executive who is consulting computer data and graphs but has never, ever even spoken to a person like our client.

Nevertheless, if we expect to continue doing business with the handful of organizations that will one day control all health care in this country, we must be able to document exactly what we did, what effects it had, and what results are likely if they should be kind enough to grant us another few sessions. This is not an unreasonable request if you are talking about engineering or even traditional medicine. The problem for us, however, is that if we are really honest we would have to admit that most of the time we don't really know what it is that we said or did that had the greatest impact. Oh, we can make stuff up, and we *do* have our theories that we are quite fond of. Nevertheless, when a client improves or gets worse we delude ourselves that we think we know why. It is always a humbling experience to do a follow-up years later and have clients tell us what they found to be most helpful, often things that we don't remember saying or doing, or even things completely unrelated to our treatment.

CONSEQUENCES OF INDUSTRIALIZATION

After the first two centuries of being a quaint group of trade professionals, we have now been industrialized with the rest of health care professionals. The consequences of any industrial revolution, Cummings (1995) points out, is that (1) those who create the goods or services lose control over the production process, (2) labor becomes cheap, both in terms of reduced income and minimal qualifications, (3) less efficient practitioners become weeded out, spawning a survival of the fittest, (4) competition becomes severe among all members of the guild, (5) quality of service becomes more reliable and predictable as the diversity of options is significantly reduced, and (6) a consolidation takes place in which a few mega-organizations will control all service within the industry.

The bad news, of course, is that what was once viewed as a form of poetry and artistry is now offered to the public as an assembly line industry—get them in and get them out. The good news is that what was once restricted to a small segment of the upper middle class is now becoming accessible to a wider population. Neurotic, angst-ridden, wealthy people used to be the mainstay of the therapist's practice; now it is filled with the full spectrum of socioeconomic diversity. Those who can afford to pay for our services out of pocket still have the option of doing so, however, now factory workers, as well, have the option of seeing a therapist for a limited time.

Industrialization may not make it any easier to do our jobs, and may not make it any more satisfying, but it has motivated us to extend our services to those who had previously been closed out. We now offer a cheaper product at a cheaper rate. Unfortunately, that may make us feel cheap. At the same time, extending our services to a wider population has increased our cultural and gender sensitivity.

CULTURAL AND GENDER SENSITIVITY

Our increased sensitivity to language began as a way to correct injustices that were perpetuated against the underclass, particularly with regard to cultural and gender inequality. Change the way we speak and then we change the ways we think about the world, or so goes the reasoning of many who have fought long and hard to alter the speech patterns of our society.

In just seven years, from 1987 to 1995, the number of times the term "politically correct" was mentioned in the *Washington Post* increased from 9 times to 292 (Morley, 1995). One outcome from this dramatic cultural change has been increased sensitivity on the part of therapists to cultural and gender differences. Whole new systems of feminist therapy and culturally responsive treatments have been spawned as a result, attempting to minimize the extent to which members of a traditionally white, male, middle class profession "colonize" those who have been marginalized.

Sensitivity to differences in the ways that women learn and develop (Gilligan, 1982), as well as think and communicate (Belenky, Clinchy, Goldberger, & Tarule, 1986), have irrevocably altered the landscape of our profession. Similar changes were initiated with the publication of works that dealt specifically with adjustments we need to make when working within different ethnic and cultural groups (McGoldrick, 1989).

If there has been a single movement within the field or society at large that has had a greater impact, it has been the emphasis on cultural diversity. No longer is it a simple matter to help a client to become more independent and autonomous, as was once a common therapeutic goal just a few years ago. Now we must consider the client's gender, remaining sensitive to the fact that the whole concept of independence as a good thing is incongruent with the more natural tendencies of women to value relatedness, attachment, and connection over the traditionally male deification of power, control, and assertion (Josselson, 1992).

In a similar vein, universally encouraging clients to develop greater self-control and personal power without regard to their ethnic values is now seen as ethnocentric rather than laudable (Kottler, Sexton, & Whiston, 1994). Whereas in Western culture we may view individuation, achievement, assertiveness, and self-reliance as highly desirable characteristics that will lead to success and happiness, this is not the case among many indigenous peoples of North America, nor in other parts of the world. In Asia or Africa, for example, it is considered far more appropriate to strive for dependence, approval seeking, and reliance on others.

Even with a token class on multiculturalism in graduate school, we were hardly equipped to handle the variety of challenges we must now consider. In the words of one practitioner:

I was simply never prepared for the incredible diversity I would have to deal with. When I learned to do this stuff, we were taught to pick a theory we liked (preferably one our professors and supervisors approved of) and aim for consistency in its application. Help the clients learn the language and concepts. Teach them to be the ways we need them to be in order to help them.

Nowadays, there are so many exceptions I can't figure out the rules. (Kottler et al., 1994, pp. 65–66)

Indeed, the number of exceptions that we must face is staggering. The increased popularity of "social constructivism" now has us thinking in terms of how can the client and therapist together create a view of the world, of his or her problems and concerns, in such a way that the therapeutic solution will be consistent with the value of his or her gender and culture? This is quite a lovely change, actually, one that only increases our flexibility in customizing helping strategies to fit individuals, and especially to be responsive to not only who they are as individuals but also members of a "tribe."

This seismic shift in our thinking, however, presents a number of difficulties in making the transition from the traditional models of helping in which we were originally trained. Whether your teething as a therapist began by following the tenets of psychoanalytic, existential, rational emotive, gestalt, narrative, strategic, or one of a hundred other theories, the internal process remained essentially the same. We introduced to our clients a language and conceptual system that permitted them to view their current predicaments in terms that were suitable for our work that would follow. Thus, we may have helped them to realize that the reason they were floundering was due to unconscious dysfunctional patterns or virulent irrational beliefs or scapegoating within the family or unexpressed feelings or even a chemical imbalance in the nervous system. We believed in our heads and in our hearts that everyone who came to see us had this essential problem.

The next step, after convincing our clients what was really wrong with them and what they needed to do about it, was to employ our favorite modus operandi to reach those objectives. Our tendency was to become proficient in a few strategies that we liked very much and to use them until it was clear that something else would have to be tried instead. This was consistent with what we learned in graduate school where our supervisors and instructors demonstrated a frightening degree of passion and commitment to their favorite theories and didn't show the slightest willingness to alter these views in the face of contradictory evidence.

As one such example, for decades I (JK) had been used to beginning graduate seminars by asking participants to introduce themselves briefly by revealing something meaningful that others present would not know about them. This has worked for me in a variety of circumstances so I had not the slightest doubt that it seemed like an appropriate way for me to begin the first class during a teaching assignment in New Zealand.

Things started out predictably enough, with the first 6 or 7 students sharing some aspect of their personal lives that they felt was important and relevant for others to know. The next volunteer was a man of Maori descent, the indigenous people of New Zealand who were recently experiencing a resurgence of cultural pride. He began innocently enough, telling us about his family origins in the traditional Maori way of greeting. When 10 minutes had passed I realized that unless I did something to cut off his speech, none of the other students would have the chance to speak. Unsure of the cultural conventions under such circumstances, I let things continue a few more minutes until the man then began addressing everyone in his native language.

I could see the rest of the class becoming increasingly uneasy so I had no choice but to interrupt the student and plead a lack of time. This seemed like a reasonable intervention and I took great care to soften my voice and manner so it would not sound like a rebuke. Big mistake. Big, *big* mistake. I could see immediately that I had done something very wrong when the student backed his chair out of the circle and turned his body away from us. The rest of the class began to shuffle their feet nervously. Nobody would meet my eyes.

I never did get an adequate explanation from the student I offended, from the others in the class, or from several colleagues I consulted about the incident afterward, about what exactly I could have done differently. What I found most interesting about this experience was the passion with which I defended my actions. My theory was sound, I reckoned. My methods had been refined after decades of practice with a very large sample. Things didn't work this time but that wasn't my fault, I reassured myself unconvincingly.

Like so many of us who had practiced for years, just like we had learned from our mentors who had been so passionate about their own favorite theories, I had relied on a process in which I expected my students and clients to accommodate themselves to what I was offering. If a client didn't like the way I worked, then fine, he or she could go elsewhere, or so I said when I didn't need any new referrals. When I was feeling a bit desperate to fill gaping holes in my schedule, I adopted quite another attitude that was considerably more flexible: I started with what the client wanted and then adjusted my style accordingly, at least until I could convince him or her to my way of thinking at a later time.

Little had I realized that this strategy born of desperation would later prove to be the direction the field was moving toward. It is now evident that we can no longer expect male and female clients to respond in the same way to our helping efforts, nor can we realistically anticipate that working with someone who is Lebanese would respond to the same therapeutic style as someone who is Cherokee, Inuit, Mexican American, or Cambodian. No longer can we simply make minor adjustments in our favorite theory in order to accommodate the diversity of our clientele. It is now clearly evident that the developmental patterns and learning styles of various cultures are so diverse that it often takes dramatic revisions of our cherished assumptions in order to respond to the differences. Furthermore, the variations within a given culture are often greater than those between them.

The implications of these realizations are that we can no longer afford the luxury of subscribing to a single model for promoting change. If we can discover a conceptual framework that is broad and flexible enough, we must account for human differences in ways that have been unprecedented. We could even make the case that the best predictor of therapeutic effectiveness would be the clinician's willingness and ability to respond sensitively to the client's perceptions of self, of the world, and all within it, so that constructive changes can be implemented in ways that do not compromise or sabotage the essential cultural worldview.

Although new training models have been developed to help therapists be more culturally sensitive and responsive (Ridley, Mendoza, & Kanitz, 1994), and most of us had some exposure to multicultural training, we were never prepared for the extent to which we would have to make adjustments in our methods. Our whole diagnostic system is hopelessly flawed and rife with biases toward those who are not part of the majority culture. Such clients are more often overdiagnosed or misdiagnosed, and then mistreated accordingly (Sinacore-Guinn, 1995).

We pay lip service to the multicultural movement and engage in public displays of politically correct language and behavior, but the simple truth of the matter is that we don't do nearly as good a job with those who are not like us in background and values.

CALL FOR GREATER MORAL RESPONSIBILITY AND SPIRITUALITY

The subject of morality has rarely been dealt with in our profession except for a few notable contributions (Doherty, 1995; Holmes & Lindley, 1989; London, 1986; Rieff, 1961; Wallach & Wallach, 1983). Family therapists such as Cloé Madanes have been introducing the morality of shame into their sessions, even urging perpetrators of violence to beg their victims for forgiveness. We have long been told that morality is something that belongs in a seminary, or at least in a philosophy department, but not in the secular study of therapy. And spiritual dimensions of being a healer? That is completely out of the question! In a scientifically based discipline such as the practice of therapy which is advocating greater precision, measurement of outcomes, and reliability of interventions, what place is there for something as soft and ethereal as spirituality?

Doherty (1995) claims the therapy profession is suffering a crisis of confidence not because of our inability to help people, but due to our failure to take a stand for what is obviously right. Granted, what is "right" is often open to debate, but in some cases therapists have gone to such absurd lengths to avoid dealing with the moral implications of behavior, they have lost all credibility. One such example occurred during the Woody Allen–Mia Farrow child custody dispute in which the expert witnesses refused to take a position that it was wrong for the comic to have a secret affair with his stepdaughter. After all, they "were caught in a web of psychotherapeutic discourse which has been stripped clean of moral barnacles like right and wrong" (Doherty, p. 4).

We learned in graduate school about the importance of neutrality, being nonjudgmental, detached, unpolluted. Taking a moral stand was equated with a loss of objectivity and professional judgment. It was evidence of overinvolvement at the least, and more likely a case of raging transference. Professionals who lapsed into dimensions of morality would be seen (sometimes quite correctly) as highly unprofessional in trying to impose their notions of right and wrong on others. It is for this very reason that we were warned consistently in graduate school to be very careful about taking any such moral stand in which clients, who are already overly concerned with what we think, might adopt our values wholeheartedly before they ever had the chance to develop their own beliefs.

In spite of these dangers, moral issues are unavoidable in our work. What are we to do with a client who confesses that she had physically abused her child in the past, and while there have been no reoccurrences in the previous year, she feels the need to deal with the issues openly with her daughter?

By law, we are required to report this mother to protective services even though the abuse has stopped, the child no longer appears to be in danger, and there is a magnificent opportunity to heal family wounds. The ethical codes are just as clear; it is not our place to decide whether the mother should or should not be punished.

What about our moral position? The consequences of reporting the abuse is that there is likely to be an investigation that will disrupt the newfound family stability. The therapy will be sabotaged with trust irreparably breached; in fact, they may never be willing to open up to a professional again. Yet by not reporting the incidents, the therapist will place the child in jeopardy should the abuse be resumed. What if the abuse never actually stopped in the first place but both mother and daughter are only revealing part of the story? And what of the professional vulnerability the therapist places herself in? If things should later come out that she knew of a prior history but did not report this to the authorities, she could very well have her career ruined forever.

Issues such as these are so thorny we tend to stay away from them during our training years, focusing instead on clear mandates from our ethical codes. Furthermore, we don't want the responsibility of taking a moral stand and suffering the consequences. We barely know what to do with our own lives, much less what others should do with theirs.

Yet there is nowhere for us to hide when clients bring us their conflicts that are fraught with moral implications:

"I'm bored in my marriage and I want out. I don't know if it's best for everyone else or not but this is best for me."

If we act like neutral therapists we will make some benign interpretation or reflection of feeling: "You are really struggling with your obligations to yourself versus those you feel toward others."

If, however, we become more like what Doherty advocates as a "moral consultant," we will push the client harder to examine the moral nuances of her decision: "That's a good question. Let's look at the consequences of your options, both for you and for others."

Our roles become even more complex and confusing. On the one hand, the public is asking us to be more morally responsible in our actions, and to help our clients to do the same. Such a discourse takes time and involves a series of discussions that rely less on specific interventions than they do on a therapeutic posture that is consistent with our historical legacy as respectful and patient confidantes and consultants. On the other hand, legislative and legal actions are taking away more and more of our freedom. We are cautioned by our professional associations and state licensing boards to be more conservative and cautious than ever, more compliant to the strictest norms for professional conduct. Both the frequency of malpractice suits and complaints to ethics boards are skyrocketing due to a change in public sentiment, more assertive consumers, and more aggressive lawyers who work on commission. The issue has no longer become whether a therapist has done anything wrong, but rather whether his malpractice insurance will settle a nuisance suit for the price of a threatening letter.

FROM INDIVIDUALS TO FAMILIES TO GROUPS

Most therapist preparation in the past, and to a lesser extent in the present, dealt with conducting individual sessions. There were several courses in group therapy and family therapy, but these were mostly viewed as specialties that would be used on occasion. Now individual therapy is no longer seen as cost effective. The role of therapist is changing from that of individual consultant to psychoeducational program expert.

Whereas once 90% of our caseload involved individual therapy sessions, the latest prediction is that in the future less than 25% of our work will take place in this modality while 25% will take place in group and family therapy, and the rest will involve structured mental health programs (Cummings, 1995). Individual interventions we learned in graduate school will become less important than a whole new range of therapeutic skills that will take place in group settings. The ability to lecture persuasively, organize people into structured, therapeutic programs, lead groups, fund grants, and other skills discussed throughout this book will become far more useful than the interpretations and reflections of feelings that were once our bread and butter.

TREATMENT PLANNING

It boggles the mind to consider how rapidly what we once learned is quickly becoming obsolete. The types of presenting complaints that we were used to working with seem to have transformed themselves into new maladies. Nowadays, if you don't know much about dissociative disorders, eating disorders, or ritual sexual abuse, you are guilty of gross negligence. It is not so much that these are necessarily "new" disorders as the fact that they are being diagnosed with greater accuracy.

Likewise, what we do with clients has changed dramatically over the years. Even among practitioners who identify strongly with a particular theoretical orientation, it is difficult to ignore the innovations in technique that have been developed in the past decade. In fact, conceptual purity is now quite difficult to maintain in the face of new research and clinical improvements that are being made across a wide range of disciplines and schools of thought. We are all becoming more alike, converging toward the center, as would be predicted in a profession that is maturing into its second century of evolution.

The mental health profession is also being revolutionized by advances in psychotropic medications, changes that we rarely learned about in graduate school. Since it is not considered to be part of the specialty of doing therapy, practitioners receive little education about what psychopharmacology can and can't do for their clients. It is not even all that unusual that we end up being the ones who "prescribe" the medications, if not legally than at least functionally.

The scenario often unfolds as follows. As a courtesy, we call the primary care physician of a new client to inform her that we are also working on the case, to coordinate our treatment, and to find out any relevant medical information. "Oh, by the way," we mention, "what do you think about a trial of antidepressants given this patient's family history and previous lack of responsiveness to therapy alone?" "Seems like a good idea to me," the doctor responds. "What have you found works best in cases such as this?"

Just as often are those times that clients come to us with prescriptions already in hand. It becomes immediately apparent to us that these medications are probably not needed, that they were offered routinely by a doctor who didn't know what else to do with someone who was feeling anxious or upset. Again, we end up recommending a course of action to the physician which, more often than not, is actually followed. The problem, of course, is that we have not received systematic training in psychopharmacology so we are not only practicing without a license but also without adequate preparation. This may very well change in the future if the movement continues for nonmedical therapists such as psychologists to receive prescription privileges.

NO PLACE TO GO

Many more people who would have been seen in the controlled environment of a mental institution in the past are now on the street. Deinstitutionalization has produced an army of walking wounded, wandering neighborhoods, living under bridges and in parks, hallucinating nightmares that are no worse than what they must face every day just to survive.

It was a beautiful, crisp spring morning, just perfect for a walk before I (RH) went to the office. The city can look dirty and unwelcoming many times, but on that day it seemed to be fresh and new. The clean feel of the cool air made all my problems seem smaller and gave me hope that I'd have real success with my clients.

It was getting late but I still slowed down when I got to the park. Grass was spouting everywhere, trees budding, a symphony of smells wherever I turned my head. Some kinds of plants were popping out in what would likely turn into flowers and I had my regular regret at such times that I wouldn't take the time to learn more about flowers so I knew better what to expect as they grew. I promised myself, again, that I would read some books about plants tonight, but I knew I wouldn't. I would be tired and want nothing more than to have a drink, make small talk with my family, and wait for unconsciousness to overtake me.

As I approached a tree, a man who had apparently been leaning on the other side fell over. I was startled because I hadn't seen him and because he fell like a dead weight banging his head. My immediate reaction was to move toward him but I stopped when I saw the empty Jack Daniels bottle and the dirt that covered him from head to toe. He wasn't dying; he was homeless and drunk.

I began to walk quickly away, thinking that the homeless and the drunk are just part of the unfriendly landscape of the city. Certainly not my problem: I give at the office. In fact, I was feeling quite proud of my noble efforts to see seven clients that day, mostly all professionals or members of middle-class families.

Before I had walked a few steps, something made me stop as if an invisible hand had grabbed me by the back of my belt. My legs were spinning but I wasn't moving. I turned and looked at the man who had rolled over. He opened his glazed eyes, tried to focus on my fuzzy form, and then reached out his hand. I'd go broke giving away money to drunks every time they begged for it. I'm not sure it helped them anyway. So I turned and walked away even though I continued to be haunted by his outstretched arm and pitiful, broken form.

This man had more problems than all the clients I would see that day put together. The insurance companies that served my clients would subsidize their care, but nobody was ready to help this man. The closest thing he would get to professional attention would be when the police came by to move him on.

We've devoted our lives to helping people, feeling a bit smug and self-satisfied with our altruism. Yet seeing a mentally ill, homeless person roaming the streets reminds us of the ways we have chosen to help based on our own terms and preferences, rather than what may actually be needed. The fact of the matter is that most practitioners prefer to work with people who are like themselves and tend to shy away from those who are economically disadvantaged, an underclass that is becoming more and more vocal.

No longer can the role of therapist be restricted to the confines of well-appointed offices. If we truly expect to serve the needy, as well as those who may easily afford our services, adaptions must continue to be made in the ways that we work, the methods we employ, and the context for our interventions. The starting place to understand the seismic shifts that have been taking place, and will continue to rumble along, is to take note of the changes within ourselves.

RIDING SEISMIC WAVES

The seismic shifts in our profession produce a wave-like motion similar to those that move along the ground during an earthquake or the ocean's waves caused by the shifting tides and winds. The waves form a continuous series of ups and downs which humans have no way of stopping. The secret to riding the waves is to focus all attention and skills on rolling with the swells, riding the crests, and exploring the troughs. The end will come only when the wave chooses or when you wipe out for lack of concentration, inadequate skills, or not adapting enough to the immediate situation.

There is always great discussion about when, where, and why these professional seismic waves may end yet there is no reason to believe they ever will. One wave follows another in an endless progression of challenges. Spending time thinking about the shore at the end of the ride almost assures you'll not get there in the way you want. What you can deal with best is the visible crest or trough that now demands your complete attention. Once you recognize the pattern of the waves, the task becomes one of finding the ways to match it with your unique strengths, limitations, and abilities to learn and adapt.

The shifts in therapeutic practice described in this chapter will change even as this book is published and they will be followed by others that will be both similar and far different. No final set or level of your accomplishment will assure success and satisfaction because another set of waves will follow even before you feel like the current ones have subsided. The secret is to concentrate on continuously reevaluating the environment and yourself in order to select and then act on making necessary regular adaptations.

The next four chapters focus heavily on evaluating therapist motivations, skills, training, weakness, as well as the most current theoretical models that can influence your ability to adapt to the future. The sample questions below are likely to be ones you've considered before and answered thoroughly enough to get you to your present level of success. To maintain and expand that success, they will need to be considered again in the context of a very different therapeutic world than the one you found in graduate school:

• Who am I compared to other therapists?
• What motivates others and me?
• What are the most and least productive aspects of myself and my work?
• Where has the profession passed me by and is it possible to catch up?
• How do I manage the unending amount of information and details that emerge each day?
• How do I separate what will be the lasting changes in the profession from the "theory of the week" variety?
• How did I get this way and what can I do about it?

Increased understanding of yourself and the changing therapeutic environment is necessary, but insufficient to keep you smoothly riding the neverending seismic waves. Knowledge of the practical skills and means of implementing them is also critical to making the most of this changing professional world. Later chapters help match up the realities of your changing self and environment with the tasks, skills, and attitudes necessary for effective seismic wave surfing. Another series of immediate and practical questions will emerge from these needs:

• What old work do I need to do differently?
• What new work do I need to learn to do?

- Why and how should I expand my clientele to fit the changing professional world?
- What will it take to build the best relationships with future professionals and to avoid the worst ones?
- How can I keep myself in one physical and mental piece with all the turmoil going on around me?

The changing professional environment and all its related pressures are far too complex and everchanging for one simple set of answers. The questions we need to answer, on the other hand, tend to remain relatively constant. The trap we often fall into is believing that having once answered a question, it can be stored away as a permanent fact. Unfortunately, when our situations change, those adaptations that once appeared to be fact can then become counterproductive myths that we hold onto with a deadly grip. Staying out of that trap necessitates continuous attention to new information from the outside world as well as from the personal world inside you. Locating the ways to act on that information and then pushing ourselves to apply it is then necessary for completion of the growth cycle. It's an easily ignored cycle that must be given our full attention in order to maneuver effectively amidst continuous professional turbulence.

CHAPTER TWO

Walking on Water

Therapists are godlings. We walk on water. We can read minds and predict the future. We know all the answers. We even know a few of the questions. Whatever we don't already know, we can easily figure out by *consulting the literature*. This mythical body of wisdom contains all the knowledge we could ever want to unlock the mysteries of the soul and cure human suffering. Such is one of the things that we learned in graduate school—there is truth, it resides in a single form, and it can be unearthed quite easily if only you know the right combination of search modifiers in the data bases.

ARE WE REALLY HELPING ANYONE?

We graduated school as professional therapists convinced that we were prepared to deal with practically anyone or anything that might stroll into our offices. After all, we had a masters degree. When we found that wasn't nearly enough, we tried a doctoral degree as well. The more degrees we accumulated, the more workshops and lectures we attended, the more journals and books we read, the more hours we spent in supervision, the more we heard over and over again that we were indeed qualified to do this strange job of helping others deal with their demons.

People, very intelligent people at that, have been telling us for a long time that we must know what we're doing. "After all," they ask us with a little too much intensity, "your clients get better don't they? You must be doing something right." Sure, we nod in agreement. "Of course our clients improve, and rather quickly at that."

Perhaps we also hear a little voice in our heads, one that sometimes whispers quite loudly, "You don't believe that crap do you? Do you really think that you are helping anyone with that primitive level stuff you try to do? Do you think people actually get better by just talking to them? And even when they do improve, do you actually believe that you had something to do with that? Heck, they got better in spite of you, not because of anything you said or did."

Ridiculous, we think. We learned in graduate school a long time ago that if we build the right kind of relationship, diagnose client concerns accurately, and match our interventions to the specific requirements of the case, we will promote more healthy functioning. We have been practicing just this strategy for a long time and it sure seems to work. We think of all our satisfied customers. We recite case after case in which crippled people walked out of our offices throwing their emotional crutches away forever, or at least until the last time we checked on them. . . .

That's another thing. Maybe they only pretend to get better for our benefit. No, that is insanely narcissistic. Okay then, perhaps it was just a temporary improvement. Or even more likely, maybe they only do well when we are watching them; once we turn our backs, they revert back to their old, destructive ways.

No, we remind ourselves firmly. We are therapists, professionals. We learned in graduate school that as long as we follow the time-honored recipe, all will work out for the best: (1) listen carefully, (2) interpret what we hear and see, (3) structure opportunities for learning and growth, (4) help create alternative realities that are more beneficial, and (5) be patient. The ingredients may change a bit from year to year but basically the process remains the same.

Armed with such confidence, reinforced again and again in The Literature and by our professors' and mentors' voices that still talk to us during times of doubt or need, we often feel like we can conquer the world. We know stuff that most people don't seem to realize. We can get to the heart of things in a matter of minutes sometimes. We can talk in silky and soothing voices, utterly convincing the client, if not ourselves, that a particular course of action is righteous. We learned this from our professors, who learned it from their professors; it all looks easy if you believe in what you are doing. Thus so armed, we have gotten ourselves in trouble a few times when we forget that what we learned in graduate school isn't exactly what happens in reality.

A SLAP IN THE PROFESSIONAL FACE

Almost everyone knows that therapists walk on water, at least during sessions. After all, we embody the best in human beings, all-knowing and all-loving creatures. Clients always see us in a good mood, endlessly patient and wise; we've got the perfect response for every situation, an answer for every question.

I (JK) learned in graduate school that I was expected to be strong, to be a model of composure for others. I also learned how important it was to distance myself from other people's pain; to do otherwise would be to condemn myself to a life of vicarious misery. Nobody ever told me, however, the consequences of this therapeutic stance—that I would cut myself off from my own feelings, that I would begin to see my clients as cases rather than as people, that I would become addicted to relationships in which I was always the one in charge, that I would become a know-it-all. I had begun to believe in my own omnipotence, so much so that I had the misguided belief that I really could do anything, even walk on water.

What a slap in the professional face it is to confront our doubts, to face our imperfections, to own up to our mistakes, to acknowledge our limitations. And yet how freeing such honest revelations are, helping us to face our failures, and in so doing, teaching us humility, prompting greater flexibility, improving our frustration tolerance, promoting reflection, increasing resolve, providing useful feedback on what works and what doesn't (Kottler & Blau, 1989).

I (RH) am racked by such doubts much of the time, even though my job as a therapist educator requires me to appear far more confident than I actually feel. Whether I am presenting a lecture or a workshop, supervising a therapist, advising a student, or writing a chapter, I feel considerable pressure to act as if I really know what I'm doing. After all, would someone really pay for my services if I admitted to them that I wasn't really sure about what I was doing?

It is among my worst fears that people would find out how little I know, how unprepared I feel to deal with situations that come up every day. Yet I realize that students and clients get me at my best when I own up to my doubts and fears of failure. In many ways, I end up working far harder than I would normally. I prepare carefully for each new client or presentation. I give extra attention to all the little details that might come up, not because I think I can prevent inevitable mistakes, but because it is easier to live with myself afterward knowing that I did all that I could.

The confidence derived from this preparation is generally productive for all concerned. Clients get my best since I work so hard on their behalf. I end up learning far more than I would otherwise, pushing myself to learn as much as I can. What is interesting, however, is that as I begin to feel successful and confident, I become increasingly lax in my preparation and efforts. I'm simply not as effective in the fourth, fifth, or twentieth sessions as I was in the beginning because there is less at stake for me. I've gotten over my self-imposed probation and relax now that I know the client believes in me.

This process obviously creates some difficulties, not only for our clients who sometimes aren't getting the best from us, but for ourselves when we stubbornly refuse to forgive ourselves for being imperfect. It is one thing for clients to believe that we are omnipotent; it is quite another for us to see ourselves in this light.

Of course, we know where this myth first got started. We spent years watching our professors field questions with deftness and authority. We watched videotapes of the masters demonstrating their magical skills, without ever seeming to be at a loss for words. We felt surrounded by other professionals who, even if they didn't always know what they were doing, were certainly good at pretending they were. It is no wonder we have felt so much pressure to be perfect, and why often we may feel like impostors (Clance, 1985).

This client thinks I'm a genius because I can read his mind when really all I did was repeat back what I heard him say.

The group members believe I am amazing just because I keep things moving. I shudder to think what I must look like to someone who really knows this stuff cold.

My supervisor thinks I did okay on this case but that's because I didn't give her the whole picture.

Sure, I helped them a bit. Mostly, they got better in spite of me rather than because of anything I did.

The impostor phenomenon rests on our fears that we can't repeat what we've done before. Sure, you've helped clients before, but maybe that was an accident or coincidence or good luck or simply a one-shot deal. Or perhaps you once had the power to heal, but now you've lost your magic. We are haunted by doubts because there is so much at stake.

BEING A SAVIOR

We work in a profession where people come to us in pain and ask little else except for us to take it away. It is a simple request, a straightforward one as well. We have been told many times that we are not godlings, that we don't really have the power to heal people or save them from their suffering. We nodded obediently after these admonishments. It is one of our most private secrets, however, that deep down inside many of us really believe we can save people from themselves.

There is a noble tradition to these heroic expectations, a legacy passed on from generations of healers, doctors, nurses, ministers, and others who attend to human suffering. If only we are pure of spirit, clear in mind and body, well-intentioned and well-informed, in harmony with the forces of the universe, then we ought to be able to work a little magic here and there. Logic and reason may tell us that there are indeed limits to what we can do, that so much rests upon client motivation and factors outside of our control. We often believe, however, that if we study a little more, work a little harder, attend another workshop, or read another book, maybe that will make the difference for the next client.

As a professional guild, we embody the ideal of the ancient Greeks, heroes walking on this planet with super powers. These fictional powers weigh heavily on therapists' shoulders like an invincible, magical force so that we find ourselves walking around with unrealistic expectations of perfection.

Fears of failure and being an impostor are natural company for the challenge of reaching greatness. Clients and society at large expect us to be pretty wonderful folks, raising the stakes beyond the standards supplied by our own profession. We try to walk on water because others expect us to. Ironically, it is by joining our clients *in* the water, rather than by walking on top of it, that we really are able to work some magic, if not saving people from drowning, then at the very least teaching them to swim.

WHEN EDUCATION IS OBSOLETE

It is sheer arrogance to believe that we have the power to fix people, that we are exempt from the same maladies that befall mortal beings. We learned in graduate school that hard work would pay off for us, that "A's" in life come to those who study carefully, prepare meticulously, and unravel the game that is being played so that we can provide the correct answers. What we didn't learn until after graduation was that certain beliefs that we inherited from our instructors may not actually reflect the realities of our jobs.

Even though there have been such dramatic changes in the ways therapists operate today, there have been precious few alterations in therapist training. Many institutions are still preparing clinicians to do primarily relationship-focused, insight-oriented work with middle-class clients in a private practice setting. Beginning therapists are still being told decade-old clichés to "try to be yourself" or "take your time to get to know the client before you attempt any interventions." While this is still legitimate advice, it hardly fits within the parameters we must now operate. When you've got four sessions with a client, utilization review members breathing down your back wanting to know your outcomes and how you will measure them, and a desk full of paperwork waiting to be processed, it is darn hard to be yourself.

These omissions, misinterpretations, and maladaptive lessons were hardly the fault of our professors who did the best they could (it seems important to mention this now that we are professors launching others into the world). Coursework and curricula were also structured as best they could be at the time to provide us as much useful training as possible within the time constraints. Regardless of where fault is placed, in the system, in our mentors, or in ourselves, there are several glaring holes in our preparation for which we have paid a dear price.

Practicing Therapy Is More than a Job

Somewhere along the line, we got the distinct impression that being a therapist is like being any other professional — an accountant, a lawyer, or a doctor. We would learn our lessons well, become duly licensed, and then enjoy the fruits of our labor in a well-paying job that would give us the security, respect, and satisfaction that we have longed for throughout most of our lives.

Little did we realize that after all the sacrifices that were made in order to become a therapist, we might very well end up feeling the same ways about our work as we did in previous careers or even part-time jobs. Although we may be trained professionals, there is no guarantee that we can find employment that feels as satisfying as we had hoped.

It is not that finding meaningful work is not possible, or even likely, but that the boundaries between our work and personal lives are not quite as clear as we were told they would be in our texts, lectures, and supervision sessions. To therapists practicing in Los Angeles or New York, it is certainly possible to arrange your life so you never run into a client when off-duty. Furthermore, in large cities, you also have career options that would not be available if you are committed to staying in other geographical regions.

One therapist who works in a small town describes the predicament this way:

I don't know who writes ethical codes but I did notice that the authors of my texts were all from big, urban universities. They talk a lot about maintaining boundaries, and separating work from family, and maybe some therapists can do that easily. What am I supposed to do, though, living in a town where I am one of the only therapists around for miles? I see my clients in my kids' school. I see their parents in the store or post office. I serve on a commission with one ex-client; another is the mechanic who works on my car; still another has been my son's teacher.

Being a therapist for me involves far more than what I do in my sessions. People watch the way I handle myself in public, the ways I parent my children. Nobody would ever seek my services unless they thought I was a person of honor and integrity.

We need not live in a small town to face similar pressures surrounding our image in the community. Maybe a doctor can get away with smoking cigars or a lawyer can be an eccentric crank, but it is not altogether paranoid to insist that people are watching us carefully for signs of instability and immorality. Most of us were never prepared for this responsibility, or even warned that practicing as a therapist is not simply a job but a calling.

The Illusion that We Are Omnipotent

This myth is one that we are actively engaged in helping to spread: the idea that we are magical wizards who can read minds, predict the future, and change behavior through the power of our incantations. Although we often deny that we have special tricks, that we hardly have the market on truth cornered, our behavior often communicates quite different messages. We pretend to know things that we do not. We act like we have things thoroughly under control during times when we are feeling on the edge of panic. We rarely admit to mistakes or misjudgments. We present ourselves to clients and the public as being all-knowing and all-loving, when in fact we often act quite cruelly and stupidly. We specifically design our actions, and even the setting in which they take place, in such a way to maximize our powers of influence, not unlike the Wizard of Oz.

There are good reasons for spreading this myth that is designed not so much for personal gain as to empower our therapeutic efforts. Even so, there are more than a few clinicians walking around who seem to believe their own exaggerated images, contributing to a level of arrogance and narcissism that is staggering. Clients and students are expected to bolster our fragile egos, and they seem to need to do this as much as we need to hear it.

Everyone wants us to know it all! Our clients expect the answers that will lead to a better life. The public wants reassurance that we do know the best ways that they should parent their children, talk to their spouses, explain their maladies, and justify their existence. Members of our esteemed guild are constantly taking to the airwaves, dispensing truth and wisdon in measured doses that coincide with the limited attention span of the audience.

Instructors in graduate school taught us to be experts by reinforcing the idea that there are, in fact, right answers. Just to be certain we heard them correctly, they tested us to see if we could select the best choice among four alternatives. In all fairness, on some levels we also willingly entertained this illusion of truth since we so desperately wanted to reduce our self-doubts, uncertainties, and intolerance for ambiguity.

The most obvious truth of all is that we don't know nearly as much as we pretend to understand. Even the information we do have at our disposal is so flawed that we can't reliably predict, to the extent that we would prefer, which interventions are going to be most useful with which people.

Clients come to see us. Many improve significantly. They leave as satisfied customers. However, we are never really certain what we did, if anything, that made the most difference. We have our suppositions and theories, of course, but they are hardly definitive. Was it the empty chair technique that caused the client to leave the office with a new zest for life today? Perhaps confronting him with the realities of his present actions was the reason for his new outlook? Did he recognize the faulty logic in his selection of actions and make a conscious decision to make more reasonable choices? Was it the unconditional positive regard and acceptance that allowed him to look more closely at himself? Maybe his more productive behaviors at home were reinforced at work this week and that was the driving force behind his new action plans?

The myth that we are experts is predicated on the assumptions that we know stuff that others do not, and that we can do things that are beyond the reach of mere mortals. As wizards and magicians and healers have noted for centuries, in many ways this makes our job far easier. Quite a number of the ingredients that make up our therapeutic "stew" involve nonspecific factors like the placebo effect and client expectations in which what we can do for people is based on what they believe is possible.

It is not necessarily a bad thing that the public believes our expertise far exceeds what can reasonably be expected. And the truth of the matter is that we *do* understand a heck of a lot about subjects that are even more mysterious to those without the benefit of our training and experience.

You Still Don't Feel Good Enough

Becoming credentialed as a therapist was supposed to bolster our sense of competence and earn us respect. Certainly this is the case to some extent, but not nearly enough as we had hoped. Most of our personal doubts, our insecurities, our core issues are still in residence even if they are relegated to the outermost suburbs of our souls.

We remember seeing our professors and supervisors as the embodiments of all that we wish to be. They seemed to know everything, to know just what to do in any situation. They were so articulate and poetic in the ways they would explain themselves. They appeared calm and unconcerned during situations in which we would feel utterly panicked. There was an implicit promise in our contract together: If we would study hard, read the books they recommended, practice the skills they introduced, adopt the values and attitudes that they modeled, we would sometime be like them.

They lied. They lied not in their promise that we could someday be like them, but in the ways they presented themselves to us in the first place. Deep down inside they were not any more secure and confident than we feel now. They interpreted their jobs to act like they knew what they were doing all the time even though they were just faking it, just like most of us do now. They lied by telling us all about their wonderful successes and neglecting to tell us about their failures. They lied by revealing their strengths in all their glory while covering up their weaknesses. Indeed we all eventually become like our mentors and it is not nearly enough.

Pressures of Failure

In graduate school, case studies seemed like fairy tales: They almost always had a happy ending. We got the impression that if only we did everything just as we had been taught, positive outcomes were virtually guaranteed. If for some reason a client did not return for a visit, improve rapidly, or sing our praises, we thought, "It can't be the methods we are using; it must be us who are somehow lacking."

Since failure was a topic that was so rarely discussed in our textbooks and class sessions, even in the workshops we attended upon graduation to fill in the missing gaps, it is no wonder the secret of our own ineptitude and imperfections had to stay underground. In many job settings, and among most groups of colleagues, it is simply not safe to admit that we don't know what we are doing or that we don't have a clear idea of where to do go next. Instead, we act like the previous generation, our mentors, pretending a degree of confidence and expertise that we hardly feel.

Only after graduation did we learn that we can do good therapy, according to standards and practices that almost everyone would agree are sound, and some clients still won't improve. They don't seem nearly as compliant and cooperative as they did on the training videos we watched. You can do everything perfectly, follow a formula that was supposed to be fool-proof, and you will still encounter resistance as the rule rather than the exception.

There is an underground conspiracy to talk only about what is working quite well and to sweep the failures under the rug, or at the very least, to explain some clients away as "poor risks," "borderlines," or similar labels that imply it is their fault for not cooperating with our best intentions. It is rarely safe for us to admit to ourselves, much less to anyone else, that much of the time we are flying by the seat of our pants, improvising, ducking incoming shrapnel, trying to keep as level as possible considering that most of the time we feel lost. Those clinicians who do seem to exhibit such total confidence that they always know exactly what they are doing and where they are headed are downright frightening: That either means that we are really incompetent or that they are deluding themselves in a certainty of truth that doesn't exist.

Because our professors, authors, and supervisors seemed so poised and in control, know-it-alls who were rarely thrown for a loop, we got the distinct impression that this is how we would one day feel as well. We don't know about you, but we are still waiting for this day of deliverance from our doubts.

Practicing Therapy Has Negative Side Effects

Would we be where we are now if we had been warned about the hazards of our profession? A number of sources have highlighted the perils of practicing therapy (Farber & Heifetz, 1981; Freudenberger & Robbins,

1979; Guy, 1987; Kottler, 1993, 1995; Sussman, 1992, 1995). The dangers that have been mentioned most often (*after* we graduated, of course) include the following:

- a sense of isolation: a feeling that we are alone in the world bearing the burdens of other people's secrets
- narcissism: an inflated sense of self in which we begin to believe that we really do know what truth is, that we really are important people
- emotional depletion: our life force becomes sucked out of the marrow of our bones as a result of coming so close to other people's pain
- one-way intimacy: becoming used to the kind of relationship in which we are always the one in control
- boredom: the inevitable result of doing basically the same thing, in the same place, the same way
- cynicism: seeing clients no longer as people but as "cases" or "border-lines" or "4:00 sessions"
- countertransference: personal issues are triggered or aggravated as a result of getting so close to others who are struggling with themes we have yet to fully resolve
- burnout: general malaise, disinterest, or disengagement that often occurs as a result of not maintaining spirited enthusiasm for the work

Would we have become therapists if we had known that the consequences would be that we would have to get even closer to the dragons that lurk within us? Certainly we had been warned that we might have to examine personal issues a bit, perhaps muck about in a countertransference or two, even do a few rounds as a client (for educational purposes, of course), but did we honestly believe that we would have to deal with our worst nightmares on a regular basis? We could either learn to hide from our own raw vulnerabilities, at the expense of cutting ourselves off from our deepest feelings, or even more painful, to stay intimately connected to our clients, keeping our hearts open to their stories, and in so doing, setting ourselves up for many sleepless nights.

We suppose the ultimate question involves asking therapists if they like what they have become after practicing for a few years. One practitioner responds in a balanced way:

It's not that simple. I like parts of what I've become — being more sensitive to nuances in behavior, being more analytic in the ways I approach problems, feeling more in control of myself. There are other parts of me that I don't like. Ignorance is a kind of bliss and I don't like knowing some of the things I know about what people do with their lives. I don't like that I can't seem to turn my brain off anymore—it is always racing, whirling about thinking of strange ideas, going over cases, plotting future actions, making up new theories to explain things that I don't understand. I wish I could just turn my mind off.

Another therapist describes her transformation as similar to what happens to police officers after they've been on the street for awhile:

How can you see sexual perpetrators and their victims for more than a few years and expect to be the same afterward? I am not nearly as trusting as I once was. I am beginning to question whether any relationship can ever work out.

There are far more positive consequences to becoming a therapist than there are unexpected hazards. The problem is not that there is a price to pay for the privilege of helping others, but that most of us were unprepared, through neglect or denial, to address these issues in constructive ways.

The Real Reasons You Became a Therapist

Fess up: What drew you to this field in the first place? Skip the altruistic part of trying to save the world and get to the part where you are trying to save yourself.

In his study of unconscious motives for entering the helping professions, Sussman (1992) concludes that at the top of the list is certainly the desire to work through one's own emotional conflicts. There was the initial hope that perhaps going to graduate school would equip us with the knowledge and skills we could use to cure ourselves so we wouldn't have to resort to the embarrassing, time consuming, and expensive alternative of actually going to see a therapist as a client.

Once it became clear that whereas we could make some inroads in our own self-treatment but not cover nearly as much territory as we had hoped, the next plan involved using our sessions with clients to continue explorations into the land of the forbidden. This strategy actually works quite well as almost every day someone walks in our office who is struggling with an issue that we haven't yet fully resolved. Sometimes it is difficult to tell whether we are talking to our clients or ourselves during particularly passionate speeches.

They asked a lot of us during graduate school, but one of the items they didn't press too hard about was why we were really there. Even if they did pressure us to be honest about our innermost intentions, I doubt we would have revealed the reasons that we barely admit to ourselves:

I've always been a busybody. I like to know kinky stuff about people's personal lives. I would love to have a license to ask people questions that they would not ordinarily answer.

I think it would be fun to be in a position of power and control over other people's lives, to have them hang in my every word. Nobody has ever listened to me much so I would like having the leverage to make them listen.

I don't think very highly of myself. Maybe if I am around people who are worse off than I am, I will feel better about myself.

I have suffered a lot in my life. It would be nice if I could make good use of these experiences to help others. Somehow, that makes everything I have lived through worth the pain.

This is, of course, a mere sampling of personal motives. What we missed by not having a clear idea as to why we wanted to be therapists is obvious in the personal pollution that could take place in our sessions. Since these motives were not given much attention we heard the message that regardless of your "stuff," if you learn the therapy craft you keep the rest under control. If only that was true.

Your Family Still Will Not Take You Seriously

It is utterly amazing how within the domain of your office people will pay you or your agency exorbitant fees for anything that comes out of your mouth, but a few hours later, your parents, siblings, or children don't pay any more attention to your opinions than they do anyone else's. Some misguided colleague, who knows far less than you do about a subject, may be quoted in the newspaper or television and his or her words are treated as gospel. You could try to set the record straight but you would only see their eyes roll up into their heads.

One nationally known expert in the area of child discipline complained:

My daughter calls me to tell me about the latest problems she is having with her son, my darling grandson who never gives me an ounce of difficulty. I calmly and succinctly tell her what the problem is and what she needs to do to fix it. People come from all over the place to solicit my expertise on these identical problems. Does she listen to me? Of course not! I'm just her father.

It is not that there is anything wrong that our families don't take us any more seriously than before we were therapists—it is just that this is so surprising. Nobody ever told us that after we went to all the trouble to become experts on human functioning that the people we are closest to wouldn't defer or deify us the way others do on the job.

To rub salt in the wound, we also didn't realize the extent to which other professionals would not respect us. Once part of this exclusive club, we imagined that we would be embraced as equals. Instead we have found that other practitioners who follow a different path to truth ridicule us and call us names. Even worse, those in other professions—doctors and lawyers and such, may make fun of what we do as well.

You Take Yourself Too Seriously

While it is true that learning to be a therapist is grim business, one notorious feature of graduate students is their loss of perspective on what is important in life. After fighting long and hard for admittance into the exclusive club of professionals, it is difficult not to take yourself awfully seriously. I don't mean that the work we do is not extremely serious, merely that we tend to exaggerate our significance. We are not nearly as important as we think we are.

One therapist who is reflecting on his life while struggling through the last weeks of terminal cancer settles on this one point as his final words of advice to his colleagues:

I took myself and my work too seriously. So much of what I thought was important in my life turned out not to matter very much. I wish I had spent more time deepening my relationships with those I love. I wish I had laughed and played more, worked less. The closeness that I felt with many of my clients, I wish I had created more of that with my friends.

This therapist died just a few weeks after he spoke these words, more convinced than ever that he had exaggerated his importance as a scholar, teacher, and clinician. While he had few regrets, he did wonder what his life would have been like if he had concentrated more on loving his family and friends rather than working so hard for immortality.

There Is Never Enough Time

It is a common complaint that we do not seem to find the same degree of quality time with our loved ones as we do with our clients. Rarely will we spend an uninterrupted hour with a friend or family member in which we give them our undivided attention, resist all distractions, and focus all our energy on responding to them at the deepest levels. Frankly, we are exhausted. We come home each night tired of being so damn patient and responsive all of the time.

As one therapist admits:

I get a little short-tempered with my kids. Maybe more than a little. But gee, I've spent all day doing just what everyone else wants to do. They want to talk about this or that, and I say, fine, whatever you want. The children want to play with puppets or draw pictures or play games and I tell them, sure, no problem. Then I come home and I want to be the one who gets to choose what we do. My kids don't understand that, and why should they?

There also is so little time to do the things we had promised we would do after we got out of school. We felt resentful of all the texts and articles that we were made to read under threat of being tested on the material. We fantasized about the freedom we would one day have to read whatever we like. We imagined the research studies we would undertake to confirm our favorite theories. We pictured how different things would be once we controlled our own time once again.

What time? Who has time to read a magazine, much less relax over the newspaper? There are forms to fill out, paperwork to process, journals to peruse for something useful. There is a stack of books waiting to be read that seems to be growing like a mutant creature out of control.

The Absurdity of What We Do

Part of taking our work seriously involves a reluctance to examine the underlying structure of what therapy is all about. On one level, it is ridiculous to consider the paradoxical nature of our work—that we attempt to build this relationship with a client that is supposed to be egalitarian but is really quite one-sided, that it is supposed to be open and honest yet is often quite manipulative, that is purported to be intimate and personal yet involves boundaries to keep things distant, and that we attempt to encourage independence by fostering a kind of dependency (Kottler et al., 1994).

As trainees, we dutifully learned the favorite theories of our mentors, all the while wondering how it could be possible that so many practitioners could operate in such different ways and yet produce comparable outcomes. We marveled at how it could be possible that one instructor could be so effective in her work by adopting a confrontational, directive style, while another could be just as helpful when he emphasized a softer, more empathic manner.

It is absurd to consider all the different ways that each of us works. Some of us help clients work through issues of the past, while others stay focused only on present concerns. Interpretation is the intervention of choice for some of us; reframing or externalizing symptoms or reflections of feeling or disputing beliefs is preferred by others. As if this doesn't seem absurd enough, consider that almost every year some new theory comes along that claims to render whatever we have been doing until that point absolutely obsolete.

As experienced practitioners, we can now shake our heads in wonderment. We know that therapy is indeed a mysterious process, one that defies adequate and complete description. As students, however, we were under the misconception that there really is a single right way to do this work, that it is possible to figure this out, and that everyone who doesn't operate the way that we do is incompetent.

Then there is the final absurdity that maybe we are all doing basically the same things in our sessions even though we think we are all so different. Maybe our specific techniques and theory of choice matter less than other factors that are more universal and personal.

Life Isn't a Multiple Choice Exam

If only our decisions were limited to four choices and we could be certain that one of them was correct. Imagine a new client coming in, and he was considerate enough to present us with four possible diagnoses (first item), four conceivable treatment plans (second item), and then four different ways of getting through to him so that he would be amenable to following our plan (third item). Furthermore, imagine that there was a way to determine that we had chosen the single correct path.

Even when professors didn't use multiple choice examinations, there was still a pervasive mood during training that there were right answers and wrong ones, and that it was possible to identify which were which. What a wonderful world it would be if things actually worked that way in reality!

A client comes in complaining of frequent and recurrent headaches. He is depressed about his predicament and feeling frustrated because he has yet to find out the causes of his problem. A physician has already ruled out any organic causes so it appears they are psychogenic in origin. Immediately, a few diagnoses come to mind: (a) chronic anxiety, (b) acute situational tension, (c) depressive syndrome, or (d) hypochondriasis.

After further investigation, it seems as if the symptoms are most typical of chronic anxiety. Indeed the man does lead a stressful single life, and although he appears calm on the outside, obviously he is metabolizing the pressure in unhealthy ways. Pleased with your assessment, you continue with your treatment plan.

You are quickly able to develop a solid working alliance and begin exploring some of his early associations with performing under pressure, his unresolved issues related to pleasing his parents as well as contemporary authority figures such as yourself. He is quite responsive and insightful, grateful as well for the new understanding of himself he has developed. Of course, his headaches are still a problem, maybe even a little worse, but you explain that is probably the result of the deep-level work that you are undertaking together. He seems patient enough to stay with the program.

Next you try a stress reduction program, exploring ways that he can make changes in his lifestyle, learning relaxation methods and cognitive self-talk. He is a highly motivated and able student, excited about his new life skills even though they don't seem to be having the desired effect on his painful symptoms.

You decide to switch gears, moving again to the level of narrative, but this time concentrating on his internal constructions of his life story, as well as his own perceptions of what his symptoms might mean within that context. Although his headaches persist, he seems much better able to cope with them and tolerate the discomfort. He has learned many things about himself. He has mastered several new skills that are useful to him both at home and at work. He may not have reached his primary goal of reducing the headaches but he leaves reasonably satisfied that he got his money's worth.

At times, your thoughts come back to him. You wonder what the symptoms were really all about. Did you handle the case correctly? What would others have done differently? Like most of your work, you never really know for sure what is going on with your clients nor do you have any definitive notion of what you did that made the greatest difference. It is fascinating, sometimes, to hear from clients months or years later what it was that you said or did that had the most lasting effect. Often it is something you don't even remember saying but it still worked its magic. Curious how the things you do that you think are most therapeutic turn out to be less important than the most mundane actions—the turn of a phrase, a spontaneous gesture of kindness, a remark made off the cuff, a supposed brilliant "technique" that was really a mistake.

Months go by and one day the client calls for another visit. You are curious and also a bit apprehensive. You didn't know what to do with his headaches last time; what makes you sure you will have any more success this time?

He very quickly lets you know that he has not returned for more therapy, merely to give you the courtesy of a follow-up report. Quite by accident it seems, he learned the origins of his problem and was able to banish the symptoms from his life forever. What did you miss, you wonder.

The client decided to sell his house and as part of the preparation to get things in order, he had a mandatory house inspection. Rather quickly it was discovered he had a leak in his furnace that had been sending toxic gas through his house for months. The headaches had been the result of being poisoned. So much for selecting the correct diagnosis and treatment.

This case is somewhat rare in that we do not often have the luxury of finding out the definitive answers to the questions we must regularly confront. Most of the time we are dealing with ambiguous situations, with clients who can't easily articulate what is wrong, and what they do say is not necessarily what is really bothering them. Furthermore, a half dozen different practitioners may very well come up with just as many preferred therapeutic options.

The Answers Aren't in the Books

During those times when we are most confused, at a loss for how to proceed with a given case, or with our careers, the answers we need are rarely found in books. There is a point in our development where reading, even attending lectures and workshops, do not produce the kinds of transformative experiences we need in order to work through personal and professional impasses. As students, we learned to look in books for answers; as veterans more and more we look both within and in the wider world.

Each time I (JK) have felt stuck, I do two things as a first line of attack. First, I go buy a book. It doesn't seem to be enough for me to borrow one from a friend or the library. I have to own the book in order to feel like the knowledge will be mine. That way I can underline things, write in the margins, savor its wisdom between my hands. I feel immediate comfort just looking at the books around me. They are symbols of what I must know and understand.

After that doesn't work, the second thing I try is to consult with trusted colleagues. There is no shortage of advice. Since they are just as frustrated as I am, having restrained themselves all these years from telling clients what to do with their lives, they can't wait to unleash their advice on me. Most of these opinions are actually quite brilliant. I feel humbled by their creativity, also more than a little chagrined that I wasn't smart enough to think of these things myself. Unfortunately, the relief that I feel is short-lived and by the time I am ready to put their advice into action, whether in my sessions, my classes, or my life, it just doesn't seem to fit anymore.

It is at this point that I remember to look within myself. I assume for a little while that I have the answers inside me if only I could locate them. I search my past experiences for clues. I reflect on what I know for sure and what has worked for me in the past. I ask myself what I am hiding from, as well as what I am afraid of. I revisit old themes that have gnawed at me from the beginning of my awareness—issues of approval seeking, of not being good enough, of being afraid of failure, of wanting to feel loved and accepted by everyone all of the time. I may recruit some help at this time from a friend or colleague to help me look deeper, but the emphasis throughout is to unearth what I already know even if I don't know that I know it.

Although looking inward has its draw, looking outward beyond the world of self, of books, of my parochial discipline, also has its benefits. Stop reading about something and start living it, I remind myself. If I read anything at all now, it is fiction or anthropology. Better yet, I start traveling. I travel literally by exploring other cultures, but I also travel by engaging people outside my work to find other layers of what I am capable of knowing. Mostly I travel with my clients and students to places in our minds that we have never gone before. If you have been practicing for awhile, this is quite a challenge since it often seems that we have seen and heard it all before. It takes a heck of a lot of energy to force ourselves to give up what has already worked for a long time in order to try something that we are not altogether familiar and comfortable with. When I balk at this prospect, I usually remind myself that I am asking no less of my clients.

Differences between Ethical Theory and Reality

Ethical dilemmas seemed so clearly demarcated in graduate school. Certain standards of behavior are expected; you meet them or pay the price. There are just certain things that you do, other things you don't do, and things you don't tolerate in others. Period.

Yet there are certain unethical behaviors that we all engage in and pretend we don't (Kottler, 1994). There are the little white lies we tell clients—for example, that we know we can help them when we are not even sure what is really going on, or that therapy is a safe place even though there are definite risks involved. There are the times we are experimenting with new methods that we have not adequately tested. There are the periods of self-indulgence when we pursue avenues of exploration that are less for the client's growth than they are for our own entertainment.

In graduate school, you learn about ethical behavior, about what to do and what not do, and what will happen to you if you get caught doing it anyway. You learn about legal statutes and precedents that dictate what is considered appropriate within various jurisdictions. You learn about consensual standards of care, supposedly what we all agree is a good way to act in various circumstances. You learn about appropriate professional conduct, that is, what will be expected of you in certain situations. You learn about what you are supposed to do when faced with predictable incidents, say a client who wants to know personal things about you, or a referral sources who wants to trade favors. Mostly, you learn about not what many professionals actually do but what they say they do.

In all arenas of ethical conduct, there is a great difference between what people claim they believe in versus how they actually act when faced with difficult conflicts. For example, among faculty and students in the profession, we could get almost universal agreement that bartering practices are clearly unethical; it even says so in the ethical codes. After all, such an arrangement could easily compromise the clear boundaries of the therapy as well as perpetuate conflicts of interest in a dual relationship. Indeed, there has been shameless exploitation of clients in which, in exchange for their sessions, they have paid their therapists with goods and services that far exceed the debt that is owed, or that involve them in activities that actually sabotage any therapeutic work that had been accomplished. In one case, for example, a client whose time was valued at $4.00 per hour was contracted to do odd jobs around the therapist's home, and those of his friends, in excess of a 1,000 hours to pay off his debt.

Clearly we need to be able to distinguish between subtle shades of unethical conduct in order to make choices based not only on what we were told by others but also by what we have reasoned through on our own. The world is simply not as black and white as we were led to believe, nor are ethical decisions a simple matter of blindly following the rules that were authored by others.

How to Be

What we learned in graduate school is what to do, not how to be. We learned behaviors, techniques, plans, interventions, actions. We collected alternatives that could be employed in various situations. We learned what to do when we were confronted with a particular case or dilemma. We learned where to go if we were stuck.

Raise your hand if you were prepared to be loving and caring. Au contraire, the culture of training is conducive to competition not cooperation, to achievement not serenity, to developing power not compassion.

Maybe it is not so much what we do with clients as who we are when we are with them that matters most. We are in love with our techniques. We can't wait to try out some new intervention that is supposedly guaranteed to cure people of their suffering. It is not that this new technology of helping works, it is that most everything seems to be helpful at some time or another.

There is increasing emphasis on outcome research, not only by empiricists within our ranks, but also by managed care organizations that wish to identify which therapies work most quickly with which diagnostic entities. Of course, what is left out of the picture is who the therapist is as a human being, who the client is as well, and how these two unique individuals interact together.

We didn't learn much about being loving during our training years. We didn't spend much time identifying which of our personal strengths might be harnessed to promote healing. We weren't given much opportunity to explore in depth the nature of our "dark side" that might sabotage our efforts to be helpful, nor did we spend a whole lot of time developing our personal characteristics of integrity, honor, courage, kindness, sincerity, and yes, love. The assumption was either that we already had these traits, or that we would somehow grow them on our own.

The place where most of us are right now is trying to do just that—to teach ourselves how to "be" with clients, as well as what to "do" with them. One of the ways that we can destroy the myth that we are able to walk on water is to accept our personal limitations and the contradictions they produce in our work. Consider just a few contradictions that have been highlighted in this chapter:

- We cannot know it all while hidden expectations tell us that we should.
- We seek perfection, but will never attain it.
- Failure must be accepted as a part of the therapy process, but we must not give into it.

- We are expected to be the healthy ones in a therapeutic relationship, even as we each have unhealthy aspects and times in our lives.
- Theory is vital for therapeutic consistency, but it never quite matches therapeutic realities.
- We must give full attention to major life problems of our clients, while also making adequate time and energy available to live our day-to-day existence in a healthy manner.

Three guidelines seem to be a good starting place for dealing with our limitations and contradictions. First, we must realize that as therapists we are entrusted with more power than our ability to reach perfection would dictate. Clients want to give us the power to cure them whether we have it or not. Simply getting them to agree that "they will set the agenda for therapy" does not make the power differential disappear. Our responsibility is to recognize and accept our potential influence in order to use it at only the most judicious times and places.

We must also face the fact that the better we do therapy, the more clients will see us as potential saviors and the more we will feel the accompanying pressure. The desire to meet their expectations will be great and our fear of failure will rise no matter how much logic, reason, or denial we use. The starting place is to share our personal feelings and reactions with other professionals as well as our professional opinions and conclusions. This is what we have intended to do throughout this book in order to help you compare your personal self to other professionals in the most realistic ways.

The third guideline is to maintain your therapeutic efforts as work that you do for part of your life and not the whole of your life. This can be very hard to accept as most of us find so much satisfaction and what Csikszentmihalyi (1990) calls a sense of "flow" in many of our client sessions. These are the times when all our skills are maximally put to use toward the accomplishment of a meaningful task when only a limited time period is available. It is when we are so fully involved that all our energies flow into the effort with no time left over for worry or distractions. It is a time of wonderful sensations; and when completed, we want more. There is the tendency, just as there is with drugs, to want nothing else but these very specific high points in our lives. We must learn to balance them with other aspects of our lives in which we can find meaning, joy, and flow. We must not give in to the temptation to make all the excitement and joy in our lives revolve around serving people and doing therapy to achieve them.

These basic guidelines support the idea of accepting realities and then broadening yourself in order to avoid the many expectation-related traps that await you. In later chapters, we will provide many of these personally and professionally broadening opportunities. The next chapter focuses attention in greater detail on both the myths and merits of our graduate school experience that are likely to continue directing our thoughts and actions as therapists. A better realization of the often unclear limits and merits of training should help in understanding therapist motivations and how to better distinguish between the theory and practice, fantasies and realities of being a therapist.

CHAPTER THREE

Limits and Merits of Professional Training

An intern had been working with a young woman in therapy throughout the semester, making substantial progress. The client wanted to return the following semester with her husband for some marital counseling as well. The student asked his supervisor a relatively simple question about the case: "Would it be all right to see them together if I've already established a relationship with the wife during our individual sessions?"

This seems to be a rather straightforward question that deserves a direct response. We suspect that you have formulated a clear opinion on this matter already, based on your experience, research, and a theoretical framework. Asking a similar question in a staff meeting, you would expect consideration of your opinion, specific guidance on the policies that your peers follow, an example of similar cases they had worked with in the past, and there would likely be general agreement reached about what to do. All of this, of course would need to take place in a matter of minutes since staff meeting time is precious, you are not the only therapist in the group with needs, and clients are waiting to be served. Efficiency, accuracy, practicality, and immediacy are the driving forces behind such a meeting, but they are not necessarily the most important factors in graduate school. An intern is likely to hear quite different feedback from that of the practitioner in the field.

The question of whether it is all right for the intern to see the couple after having seen one spouse remains so basic that surely experts would agree on how the case should be handled. Shock, however, sets in when the intern realizes how many different answers he might hear from a variety of supervisors, all of whom are experts in their fields. The different

49

opinions expressed by a number of faculty members and supervisors about
what the intern should do left him more confused than when he began.

*Clearly, you have already established a close alliance with the woman.
There is no way that you could ever be objective with the husband as
well. You must refer them both to someone else who can treat their
relationship.*

*Since you already know so much about her background, it gives you a
headstart on the case. The woman already trusts you. The husband is the
one who wishes to join her so he obviously doesn't see a problem. I would
say that it would be possible for you to work with both of them if you
guard against taking sides.*

*You can't switch back so easily from intrapsychic to systemic dynamics.
Once you have negotiated one sort of relationship, engaged in treatment
planning that addresses her individual issues, you can't just change gears to
start treating the couple. You will have to pass them along to someone else
who hasn't yet been distracted.*

*If you see them together there is the perception that you may already
be too closely aligned with the wife. First, you should schedule several
individual sessions with the husband so that you can establish a basis of
trust with him, then begin seeing them together.*

*Absolutely not! Are you kidding me? You should know that in marital
counseling the relationship is always the client, not the individuals. There
is no way that you could help them together right now, and you'd probably do some damage.*

*What I would suggest is that you do the following: (1) refer the hus-
band to another therapist within the clinic, (2) let them get acquainted and
do some preliminary work, (3) you continue seeing the wife, working
towards how she can get the most from marital counseling, and (4) schedule conjoint sessions with the husband and wife in which both you and the
other therapist can work together. Each of you will be able to bring a
different facet to the sessions, and each spouse will feel there is an advocate
in the room.*

This situation would seem ridiculous for someone outside our profession who sees us as experts working with agreed upon treatment policies and techniques. Most of us, on the other hand, will hardly be surprised by this lack of consensus, even about such an apparently simple dilemma. Conflicting feedback is not the exception, but rather the rule; this is particularly so in graduate school. Ask any group of faculty how they would handle a specific situation and you will see a certain pride in the fact that they have such different outlooks. Even more amazing is how certain instructors and supervisors believe themselves to be absolutely right and everyone else clearly wrong.

Is there any wonder that professionals recall how as students they felt confused, disillusioned, and overwhelmed with anxiety and frustration? The changeover from student to professional requires far more than learning to work with more clients more often. Each of us has had to come to grips with the tenuous nature of truth, the mythology surrounding what it means to be an expert, and the vast differences between what we learned in school versus what is required of a practicing professional.

DIFFERENT NEEDS AT DIFFERENT LEVELS

Why do the peer interactions with the therapist in our example lead to a practical conclusion while the student's interactions lead to more confusion? Why does the student's questioning lead to additional study and frustration while the therapist's question leads to timely relief? Why do those involved seek consensus for the therapist, but not for the student? The answers lie in the differing developmental needs of emerging professionals and the purposeful designs of university training programs.

Professional training is not designed, nor able, to equip individuals with everything they will need in the work place. There is simply too much to learn and the field of knowledge expands and changes too quickly. Instead, professional training provides a foundation of knowledge, attitudes, and skills that permit people to learn the rest of what they will need on their own. School cannot teach specific correct answers about what is the best solution to every possible case. However, it can teach professionals how to think for themselves and to formulate a defensible rationale for behavior that is supported by theory, research, and practice. At its best, professional training provides a solid foundation for the beginner, but it cannot create an expert.

Law schools are a good example of professional training programs that demonstrate pride in how impractical their education is when compared to what attorneys really do on the job. Medical schools require prospective applicants to spend years studying subjects that have no direct relevance to actually helping people. It is generalities of knowledge, skills, and behaviors related to being a professional that these programs seek to convey rather than the specific minute-to-minute bits of information and tasks that a vocational school might promote. Preparation of therapists, attorneys, doctors, or architects exists primarily to build the consistent ways of thinking and problem-solving needed by active professionals in ever-changing situations.

Distinct differences exist between the ways novice and expert clinicians function, especially with regard to cognitive activity. Whether in the practice of medicine, physics, chess, or therapy, experts are better able to encode information, organize memory, retrieve relevant knowledge, observe inconsistencies, connect disparate areas, discriminate judgments, track multiple tasks, explain rationales for action, correct mistakes, and develop novel responses (Ericsson & Smith, 1991; Etringer, Hillerbrand, & Claiborn, 1995). These qualitative changes require a base level of training, plus additional time, quality experiences, and information, that cannot be provided within the limitations of training programs.

The practice of group therapy provides an example of how experienced leaders process what is going on much more quickly, reach deeper levels of exploration, and exhibit greater flexibility in their interventions. By contrast, beginners rely more on conventional theory, are more cautious in their approach, and more regimented in their reasoning (Kottler, 1994). Obviously, the readiness and ability of a novice to learn is quite different from what is available to professionals at a latter stage of their development. Cognitive structures and processes continue to evolve as we gain experience, requiring us not only to learn new skills and strategies to match our developed capacities, but also to unlearn old ones that no longer fit.

Many appropriate styles and practices that served you well at earlier stages of training lost their viability as you progressed to greater expertise. Skills you once relied on have changed, from benign, active listening early in your career to more forceful, confrontive, strategic interventions as you gain ability, knowledge, understanding, and confidence. The complexity of how you conceptualize cases has also increased in direct proportion to your level of experience and expertise. Cases that at one time seemed hopelessly complicated now appear relatively straightforward, while at the same time you have come to appreciate intricacies that you would have missed earlier. The breadth of your knowledge base has expanded well beyond the parochial boundaries of your own discipline as defined by graduate school courses. Finally, the fluency and flexibility with which you can change direction depending on what you observe and sense is quite remarkable compared to the therapeutic ruts you found yourself in so consistently in the past.

Your developing expertise has clearly limited the present value of whatever training you once received in graduate school. That training was designed to get you started and keep you going, but it could never meet all your developing needs. The realization has probably hit, though we often try to ignore it, that we can't walk on water—in spite of what our clients believe. It is inevitable that you will make mistakes and reveal weaknesses, no matter how hard you try to stay current on the latest innovations. Graduate school could only give you a start because of its inherent limitations and your own overly high expectations.

DOING THE BEST THEY CAN

We have taken some solid shots at the limitations of graduate schools' ability to prepare therapists for the real world. This may sound extremely harsh in isolation, but we recognize that part of the problem lies in the unrealistic expectations nearly everyone has for the experience. The reality is that there are tremendous practical limits to what graduate school can offer, which must be recognized before we move on to examining the most valuable benefits of graduate training.

It's Impossible to Learn Everything

Therapists were once trained in a single year or less. Modeled after apprentice programs in many of the skilled trades, practitioners were supposed to learn much of what they needed on the job. Over the years, professional training has continued expanding to where even a three-year masters degree is often not considered sufficient. In some cases, newly minted doctoral graduates have spent more than a decade in school only to discover they must continue postdoctoral programs in order to make themselves marketable.

Most experienced practitioners recognize that no amount of time will ever be enough to fully prepare someone for the future challenges of therapy practice (Ellis, 1992); there is simply not enough time in a single life. Meanwhile, the myth continues that if only we added additional credit hours onto programs, extended the length of practica and internships, designed curricula to be more contemporary, conducted supervision and taught courses more effectively, somehow we would be able to provide therapists with everything they might need some day.

It's no wonder that the chair of a training program described her exasperation when asked what graduates felt the program needed: "They want more coursework in women's issues, men's issues, multicultural counseling, art and music therapy, and of course, more in-depth work in all their areas of interest. Then they insist all this needs to be done in a shorter time than the program takes now!"

The bottom line is that time in school must be limited and the time required to learn all you need to learn is unlimited. The two will never meet. Programs must therefore be selective in what they choose to provide for students. Most often schools choose basic information over specialization and thinking over action.

Thinking Comes Before Doing

A client coming to a clinical training center to get help with depression was told that his therapist would be a student. "No problem," he replied, "I don't need Freud, I just want someone who knows enough to help me. These people have studied for years, haven't they?"

Most clients want to be helped and they don't care much who does it. They do, however, have the reasonable expectation that whoever sees them will have enough knowledge to help and not hurt. Academic programs attend to this primary need by focusing on thinking and knowing before doing therapy. Information about people, how they think and behave, what drives them, and how these things relate to interactions with others are basic knowledge that professional helpers must have before they deal with their first person in pain. Even more ambitiously, they must also be considerably aware of their own strengths, weaknesses, beliefs, and idiosyncrasies so that they can function optimally. Add to these professional issues things like ethics, laws, assessment methods, diagnoses, and treatment planning, and there is enough to keep a student at an information-only learning stage for years.

There is so much thinking required of students that actually doing therapy takes a back seat for much of graduate school. One therapist reflected on his frustration with wanting more practical application in school, but now knowing how dangerous that would have been: "I thought the faculty were ivory towered jerks because they wouldn't let me see clients sooner. When I actually did get to see clients, it became oh-so-clear just how little I knew. I don't want to think about what I could have done to clients without the information that faculty forced down me first."

Just the information needed for a reasonable foundation for therapists is extensive. Specialization in society and our profession compounds those needs to enormous levels. Increasingly, programs are incorporating practical learning experiences into training, but they do so with the understanding that experience with insufficient information is dangerous. The reality is that thinking will continue to be the primary focus of early training. Clients need assurance that the words and actions of beginning therapists have been thought out, supported, organized, and broken down into their smallest understandable parts before a client is subjected to them.

Learning Is Divided into Arbitrary Pieces

Graduate training tends by its very nature to break concepts and behaviors down into their smallest, most recognizable parts. The idea is that while you may see the whole, you must study and practice the individual parts to understand and implement ideas effectively. The concept is accepted practice in most learning situations, but it clearly has its drawbacks.

The fragmented nature of training is not unique to therapists. High school track stars, for example, face much the same problem when they go on to a major college athletic program. A quality coach will break down the stride and body position to the smallest details for the budding star to study and practice. The result is that the young runner is likely to have slower running times as he concentrates on the details rather than the whole. Only after these details become second nature do his times begin to improve. It is much the same with therapist training where details are separated and studied to a point where the overall picture can be lost for a time while details are being integrated. It therefore becomes important that while learning information and behaviors piece by piece, some checks must be taken to see how well the pieces are fitting together.

Testing and Evaluation Override Everything

The amount and importance given to rigorous assessment of student progress in graduate school receives regular scorn from students and professionals alike.

I spent so much time worrying about tests that I never thought at all about what the information meant or why I was learning it.

If I was taking those kinds of tests and writing papers at work, I'd never get to see any clients.

It's just not realistic. Without all the grades, you could really get down to learning in grad school.

These graduates are right. Testing and assessment do become a major focus in graduate school, taking away time and energy from other more beneficial learning experiences. It creates enormous pressures that can get in the way of people doing their best. Every graduate student and faculty member has thought about the benefits of doing away with tests and grades, but it will never happen. The demand for rigorous assessment comes not from within programs, but from forces outside.

Like it or not, the responsibility given to a graduate program and its faculty is to determine whether students have an understanding and ability level sufficient to help and not harm clients. Granting a degree makes the statement that you are at least ready to begin work as a novice with a solid foundation. Certification and licensing boards routinely accept university judgments on students as primary factors in their credential granting decisions. This enormous faith placed in the assessment of students and professionals requires that those evaluations be made as thoroughly as possible, and that means testing. The continuous information and skill evaluations create a system where students selected must be those who can succeed under those pressures.

Students Are Selected on Academic, Not Personal Characteristics

A lot of interpersonally competent people will never become therapists simply because they do not possess the academic motivation and skills needed to enter and complete graduate training. The cognitive nature and evaluation emphasis in graduate school demands this, but it also makes for some strange conceptualizations about who we are seeking as new members of the helping professions.

A faculty member from an art department had this to say about his experiences with psychology students: "I expect our students to be strange. That's the way artists are. But psychologists who are going to work on my head? You got some weird people over there. Smart, but weird."

A client asking to have her therapist-in-training switched remarked to the supervisor, "He is very intelligent and I'm sure he is excellent. I would be proud of him if he were my son. But I think I would like someone who is nice and wants to listen to me."

The overwhelming student selection emphasis on grades, the Graduate Record Exam, and other cognitive measures make it clear who graduate schools will attract. Those with recorded intellectual prowess and academic success will be encouraged over those with emotional sensitivity, essential kindness, and interpersonal skills that are never formally assessed. Graduate schools select those who are especially well-suited to understanding things with their heads rather than their hearts. Reason and logic have been elevated as supreme standards of excellence, while the values of intuition, personal characteristics, and caring are relegated to "nice, but not essential."

We choose to believe that most clinician-training programs would like to de-emphasize academic criteria and increase the importance of other characteristics. Unfortunately, academic programs, like their universities, are not set up to assess and develop the emotional side of people in the thorough way they handle the intellectual side. Everyone agrees that there ought to be a better equity between the two, but for now that balance is not very practical.

Our legal and educational system has given extensive permission to evaluate and make decisions based on cognitive aptitudes and achievements. Written and observational assessments of personality or moral characteristics, on the other hand, are given much less credibility. We will remain in this intellectually driven selection model until there is greater acceptance of our ability to identify and evaluate nonacademic characteristics as critical to learning and therapy. It may not be the best of all training models, but there are reasons for it, and we will continue to tinker with it as long as it is the most defensible model available. In the mean time, there are still many positive things each of us did take away from graduate school.

WHAT YOU DID GET FROM GRADUATE SCHOOL

Graduate training clearly has limitations, but that training also promoted your professional growth in many ways. Our intent here is to include some balance in the presentation, since so far we have been rather critical, lamenting what wasn't covered that you so desperately need.

The reality is that graduate training programs, and even continuing education in the form of seminars, workshops, and graduate courses, provide a great deal of lasting impact. Those influences are sometimes tied to specific course titles, content, lectures, exams, or papers as might be expected. More often, though, lasting effects are tied to a variety of experiential learning opportunities that surround formal training where students personalize their exploration of ideas, behaviors, and techniques (Chapman, 1992). Relationships with faculty, students, supervisors, clients, and the demands of being continually evaluated on performance in a wide variety of pressure-packed situations each offers its own set of valuable experiences that create our professional selves.

The Scientist-Practitioner Model

The scientist-practitioner model for therapists has become the norm in our profession. Students are taught to learn what there is to know on a subject, develop hypotheses, and test results. They are shown how to use the process in both academic pursuits and in therapy. The model has been effective in solidifying and standardizing the practices of our profession, which in turn has encouraged the public to have greater confidence in our work.

The scientist-practitioner model makes sense when you consider the potential pressures involved in clinical practice. A judge in a civil case will be favorably impressed with your ability to demonstrate that your work with a client was based on previously published research. Not only is the legal system pleased with the scientist-practitioner model, but therapists themselves can also raise their objective confidence level through its use. Take, for example, the comments of one therapist on his growing recognition of how the scientist-practitioner model has helped him:

It felt like everything I had to do in graduate school was focused on judging, evaluating, and studying. It all seemed to push me away from the client relationships I wanted.

Now that I've been in practice for a few years I get to do the relating the way I wanted to, and I love it. I know that I'm much better now than before or during grad school. Sometimes it's hard to admit what they did for me, but one of the best things I got is this habit of evaluating everyone and everything. I don't make nearly as many stupid mistakes mostly because I never take for granted the words, actions, and information that people, including myself, convey.

Validity and reliability are the critical issues in judging therapist knowledge accuracy, observations, appraisal activities, and outcome measures just as they are in basic psychological research (Tosi Hosmand, 1991). The scientist-practitioner model emphasizes a well-reasoned approach to collecting information, applying it in an objective manner, and evaluating outcomes before going on to a next set of actions. This information collection, implementation, and evaluation process is what most follows students into their professional practice, rather than the specifics that were memorized and recalled for tests, papers, and projects.

The particular statistics, research models, and assessment tools that are thrown at you in training have relatively little long-term transference to professional practice. Let's not kid ourselves, most of us will spend little time using formulas for MANOVAs, regression analysis, or even simple standard deviations in our practice. Of the hundreds of appraisal instruments studied at one time or another, you will use only a handful on a regular basis, and half of those you learned on your own, not in school. It is processes learned rather than the instruments, formulas, and details of evaluation that good therapists take most directly from training. Below, several practitioners describe how their implementation of the process makes the difference between being successful at therapy and just being a good listener and talker.

I evaluate my work on every client. In my notes I try to see whether what I know about the client matches what I feel, and whether both of them match what the client is projecting.

I look for behavioral change over time. Is this client doing different things or is there no behavior change? I focus my efforts in the next session based on my assessment.

I don't do much with notes, but I try to ask myself, is their thinking different? That's what I try to look for, because once it changes then I know I can work with other aspects of their life. If they are in the same old thought patterns, then I work on those patterns.

The rules say I should evaluate on the basis of DSM criteria change so I do that on paper. But what I work with most often are the changes in how the client and I are relating together. When that relationship works, it usually translates into improvement on DSM criteria.

The therapists above are successful with their work in the eyes of their colleagues and themselves, yet they have very different methods of interviewing and evaluating clients. Their approaches range from cognitive to behavioral and to more humanistic emphases—although you would get a major argument from each if you tried to pin them down. All their differences do not stop them from maintaining a common commitment to the scientist-practitioner model with their clients as a basic element in deciding what to do next. It is exactly this commitment to a knowledge-based approach, followed by objective evaluation, that is increasingly required in health care systems (Belar, 1995). For all its weaknesses, this model continues to prove itself valuable in the development and maintenance of consistency within our profession.

A Common Professional Heritage

The scientist-practitioner model has evolved along with the growth of our profession, and both will continue to evolve as the world changes and professional leaders expand the boundaries of knowledge. Understanding, using, and being ready to implement these changes requires a knowledge of the patterns of development that have shaped our profession. Learning about our common professional heritage helps students begin placing themselves in a historical family context in much the same way that stories told by parents and grandparents cement personal family ties for children.

Historical figures can become something like relatives that people use to explain who they are and why they believe the things they do. Freud, for example, becomes a quirky great uncle of sorts in our family of therapists. His place in history is confirmed by the initiation of a great professional movement and the continuing use of key concepts even today. He becomes more real as we look at his drinking and smoking habits, publicly childish interactions with peers who dared disagree with him, and the sexist nature of his ideas. These serve not so much to detract from his significance as they do to open his human side for better story telling.

Jung's collective unconscious, Erikson's developmental stages, Adler's inferiority feelings, Rogers' core conditions, Horney's basic anxiety, Maslow's needs hierarchy, Skinner's reinforcement, and Bandura's modeling are some of the building blocks that have added bits and pieces to modern day therapy. What were once all-or-nothing theories for their originators have now become pieces of a larger whole. Professionals blend these and other ideas into a set of beliefs, techniques, and styles that promote their own personal therapeutic model. Part of that choice is made based on understanding created by the study of the people and stories at the heart of those theories.

Graduate school emphasis on history also provides a picture that places our status as a profession in a realistic perspective. Problems like the need to strengthen licensure laws and press for prescription privileges, the struggle over increasing regulations, and the dearth of minority therapists can create a picture of a profession in a dark time. Although the professional issues we deal with today are troubling, an understanding of our profession's historical development more clearly identifies these problems as advanced steps in a long progression of past challenges overcome. The last 50 years alone have seen therapists gain legal recognition in every state. Our work is sought out by doctors, insurance companies, and businesses that at one time or another have fought our practice tooth and nail. New professional organizations struggling to survive have become established professional and political entities that influence both the further development of the profession and society.

The mental health professions have even come to fighting among themselves now that many external challenges have been overcome. This is similar to the infighting of close families where members seek confirmation of old roles or changes to new ones. Arguments over the similarities and differences between clinical psychologist, counseling psychologist, professional counselor, rehabilitation counselor, psychiatrist, clinical social worker, and family therapist have taken over a significant portion of our verbal and written professional discussions.

The profession's inability to come up with commonly agreed upon answers is influenced both by internal power struggles and the fact that every professional gain we make creates a new set of problems. We are a new profession compared to medicine or law and even they can be seen continuously struggling with new challenges brought on by the advances they make. A simple addition of a new licensing standard, for example, creates the need for new training, record keeping, ethical guidelines, and enforcement policies. The picture of those historical developments acquired in graduate school is what makes you less likely to make the same mistakes twice, to know better what it takes to successfully overcome current hurdles, and to recognize the newest set of complex choices likely to emerge at the next professional development step.

Preparation for Complex Choices

Modern therapist training programs have moved away from the old idea of training all students in only one theoretical orientation, one diagnostic model, or one assessment package. Programs are still forced to attend to whatever current "hot model" captures everyone's attention for a period of time, because the employment of graduates depends on their ability to do what is currently leading the field. The fact that programs continue to promote the study of a variety of models in the face of these pressures points to the critical long-term value of examining multiple viewpoints to promote solid decision-making.

The education of therapists focuses on decision-making about client diagnoses, the therapist's own personal/professional belief system, technique appropriateness, assessment tool use, interpretation, and termination of treatment. Students are pressed to examine everything they study from various viewpoints, match them against their personal beliefs, abilities, and actions, and then create workable models they can employ effectively. The process promotes a wide variety of alternatives, forces choices among the alternatives, and then demands that those choices be questioned.

The emphasis on this approach is to increase productive individual decision-making on an ongoing basis. Acquiring new information demands that revisions be made to previously appropriate decisions. The process drives students to distraction as they attempt to get the one right answer, but it also promotes a pattern of good decision-making behaviors that insure their continued development in the future. A new therapist who had been struggling with a more diverse clientele than she had ever seen in graduate school commented on how her experiences helped her learn to deal with these problem issues:

One particular professor frustrated the hell out of me. When I wanted the ONE best theory, the ONE best assessment tool, the ONE right diagnosis, the ONE best technique, he would force me to look at all aspects of everything. Then when I would do everything he asked and decide on the best ONE, he challenged me to look again and again.

That never-ending search he put me through drove me crazy, but it was that same model that has made me into a good multicultural therapist. It taught me to keep searching for different viewpoints, new ideas, and somewhere along the line it convinced me that I should never be satisfied with just what I currently believe about people. It saved me from just counting some people out as losers.

Education may be limited in its practical applications, but it can work to ingrain a set of reactions and a belief system that should foster further development. It is this set of reactions and beliefs that stopped the therapist above from discounting her new client population as simply inappropriate. She hated it when her instructor would never accept anything as fully right just as she hated it when nothing she tried matched her new clients. Her instructor pushed her to never be satisfied with looking at things from only her own viewpoint. The repeated exchanges with students and faculty to explain herself also taught her about articulating these decisions to others.

Articulation of Ideas

A quality graduate program forces students to define their views and find ways to express those positions to faculty, peers, and supervisors. It is a hard lesson for students who have spent fifteen or more years learning to either say only what someone else has said, or to just give their own unsupported opinion. Providing a logically connected argument that combines the ideas of others along with your own ideas represents a new level of writing and oral presentation skill for most graduate students.

Old preprofessional reasoning statements like "You said . . ." or "The book said . . ." get little credibility from the clients, colleagues, supervisors, employers, insurance companies, and legal professionals who you deal with on a regular basis. You are expected to make arguments that use all available knowledge plus a full range of presentation, listening, and writing skills. The correct answers provided on a test might have been appreciated as an undergraduate, but those behaviors continually decrease in value to the emerging professional. In the words of one graduate student coming to understand what would be needed as a professional:

At the beginning of the program, faculty were on my back continually about interacting more and writing better. It wasn't until internship that it really became clear how much I needed better ways to stand up for myself and my ideas. I was going nowhere as a professional if I didn't get better.

Challenging student opinions in class, forcing presentations, and requiring paper after paper have an impact that is broader than simply learning information. These are designed to move the quietly receptive student into a professional who communicates effectively and persuasively.

Training for Future Disappointments

All of us recall the times in training when someone withheld the respect or admiration we so obviously deserved. Sometimes that was because the presenter or participants were out of touch or jealous or needed to raise their own self-concept by lowering ours. At other times, it was because we simply were not as good as we thought. These experiences added up to considerable practice at eating humble pie. It might not be the most pleasant lesson in the world, but learning to deal with these situations was good training for the professional world where more of the same can be expected.

Egos exist in the professional world just like they do in the academic world. None of us are loved and appreciated in all the ways we expect and by all the people who should recognize our accomplishments. We have learned to live with that fact, not run away from it or pretend it does not exist. Graduate school offers a number of unplanned firsts to provide training for these future professional disappointments. The first poor grade, a lack of appreciation of our best work, and the experience of being professionally ignored are not joyful events; but they are better experienced in the safety of a forgiving academic environment where opportunities to practice dealing with this disappointment are available.

Therapists hate getting their feelings hurt in a staff meeting as much as students do when they receive a poor reaction to a long-planned presentation. A male therapist gave his own example:

I had hardly started presenting a female client in a staff meeting when on the first mention that there was some history of abuse, a female staff member jumped in to say I was undervaluing this issue because I was a man. Before I knew it, I felt like no one wanted to hear what I had to say. It was that insignificant-student feeling all over again so I did the same things that proved effective in grad school. I swallowed my pride and waited for them to get their biased opinions out of their system just like I did when my advisor wanted to talk more than listen. When they were done, I gave them more credit than they deserved to soothe their egos, and then I worked the conversation back to my client and my ideas.

There is no way to get around the pain that goes with not being shown appropriate recognition for the things you feel most proud. Graduate school taught you how to recognize the problem situation and the hurt feelings and then gave you practice in getting through them productively. Ways of working through the hurt without dropping out of professional relationships or losing even more respect in the eyes of colleagues are possible now because they were practiced before in graduate school. Learning to deal with the loss of face, embarrassment, and disrespect that sometimes come in the best of professional relationships also teaches another positive lesson about how to gain recognition when it is not easily given.

The Means for Securing Professional Recognition

A therapist recalled her most cynical professor offering the following model for becoming a professional: "We set up hoops for you to jump through. You jump through them. If we like the way you do it, we let you into the club. Then when you go to work, you set up the hoops for the next generation."

This cynical advice should grate on all of us. It ignores the quality activities, information, challenges, successes, and conceptualizations that are supposed to emerge in graduate school and carry over into our professional work. It makes training and the process of mentoring new professionals sound like games rather than the human development processes they are intended to be. It conveys a feeling that often comes out in these words spoken by a student in a hurry to get on with his professional life: "I have skills and I know stuff, so why not just let me get on with my life? Why make me jump through these irrelevant hoops?"

"Hoops" is a pretty accurate description of the steps, requirements, and formalities that need to be accomplished to gain recognition in graduate school or in a professional career. However, these hoops only reflect the necessary assessment of easily quantifiable accomplishments and not their content or implications. Clinicians and students alike need to demonstrate success to the satisfaction of others in order to win desired approval. The public demands that we police ourselves by purging potentially inadequate or harmful professionals. We judge our ranks by arranging these hoops as formal assessment points where necessary reflection, debriefing, and feedback can be at least minimally assured (Lewis & Williams, 1994).

Graduate school taught us a great deal about how to obtain recognition as well as how to accept living with less than we want. Everyone has at one time or another gotten a paper back that did not receive the approval we wanted in the instructor's eyes. Students learning their lessons about gaining recognition went back to the professor, other students, and books to find out why. Success came with incorporating these new dimensions in the next paper, and more in the next, until the work actually did receive the instructor's approval. Those not learning these lessons simply put the paper away, accepted their lesser recognition, and probably doomed themselves to the same status on the next assignment. These two different directions are likely to follow the two students into the professional world where one continues the work of gaining approval and the other concedes a lesser status.

This student/faculty/paper approval process is virtually the same as the practitioner/editor/journal article approval process. We have never met a professional writer, no matter what their level of success, who did not feel slapped in the face whenever they got a review back with negative comments. There is no new trick in how to win approval of a case study, a proposal for a new agency program, a grant, or a manuscript for publication. You just find out what the supervisor, editor, reviewer did not like, identify what they do want, and then rework your ideas to fit their requirements. You may not agree with their opinions and you have the right to write them off just like you had the right to ignore a professor's comments—if you're willing to suffer the consequences. You don't need to seek approval, but if you want it, the steps to achieving it are complex in practice but clear and simple in theory:

1. Learn what it is about yourself or your work that the other person does not like.
2. Don't do those things.
3. Figure out what the other person is looking for in order to give approval.
4. Find the means to meet the other person's expectations in ways they require.

Secure in these basic competencies, you will recall other times when putting your ego on the back burner as you sought a better understanding of a situation paid major dividends. Using your interpersonal skills within these general guidelines to gain a clear perspective on what another needs requires the blending of leader and follower behaviors that are often seen as entirely separate.

The Importance of Blending Leader and Follower Behaviors

It is sometimes easier for the successful therapist to follow the lead of their clients than to follow the lead of their peers or supervisors. Theories and techniques courses provide extensive information on why and how to deal with the complex task of being both leader and follower in client sessions. Client comments, goals, needs, and conditions are emphasized while you are encouraged to maintain professional control of sessions and treatment plans. No such similar lessons on how to deal with professional colleagues appear in the catalog descriptions of classes, even though the issues can be even more complex. Whereas therapist/client boundaries are generally clear, relationships between colleagues come in an infinite variety and produce a similar range of problems.

One therapist recalls an aspect of graduate school that he hated at the time, but which has served him well since then:

I avoided group projects with other students at all cost. People in those groups never agreed on how to do things and you never got credit for what you did yourself. Some jerk would talk big and do nothing, which always meant a lower grade and put more responsibility and work on everyone else's shoulders. Then there was always someone else who had to be the leader no matter what. Everything had to be done her way no matter what anyone else wanted. The groups never worked as well as if you did the work yourself.

As much as I hated those projects, I can say now that they taught me more about dealing with other professionals, and even clients, than anything I read in books. I learned that the blowhard would need to say his stuff no matter what, but if I waited him out, I could go on. I learned to get quiet people involved so that I didn't wind up doing their work later on. I learned that sometimes I had to push and other times I had to sit back and wait (the part I hated most). I learned that if I have to work with someone who MUST be the leader, then I should just go ahead and make him the formal leader, and then work around him.

We have all trained hard to become leaders. We lead clients out of trouble. We lead the public in understanding our worth so they will keep returning for our help. Some of us lead professional organizations so that they represent our needs effectively. We lead families and friends in productive relationships. But being leaders often makes it difficult to accept the fact that following is part of what good leading is all about.

Group projects, presentations, student support groups, practice presentations, social gatherings, and the often awkward relationships with faculty and peers were the graduate school mechanisms that taught about leading and following. These often frustrating activities helped us develop the combination of leading and following behaviors that are now needed in both professional and client relationships.

Balancing leader and follower roles sounds much easier than its actual implementation. Therapists put this past practice to good use with clients and their work with colleagues, supervisors, and supervisees. You have learned that quick and easy solutions are not expected, but you know how to experiment with potential words and actions and to be patient with professional relationships when under pressure.

Skills for Maintaining Self-Discipline and Self-Confidence

Every experienced therapist we ever met can relate to a time when, if only for a moment, he or she wanted nothing more than to escape the pressures of a particular client or a difficult situation with a colleague, supervisor, or supervisee. Just the fact that many therapists become "experienced" means that they have found ways to overcome these urges, since such pressures are a normal part of the therapist's work. Becoming successful requires self-discipline under pressure, which is often a developed characteristic encouraged both directly and indirectly in graduate school experiences.

It comes as a big shock to many students when they find that the excellent test scores they achieved as undergraduates will not be sufficient to get them through graduate school. The most quiet students will be pushed to get involved in class, expand on ideas in discussions, and challenge themselves to be more direct in relationships. Extroverts are asked to test themselves by doing more quiet listening, reflecting, thinking, and less speaking. Students are commonly challenged to confront personal conflicts in ideas, thoughts, and behaviors rather than avoid pressured situations in which conflicts arise.

Developing the self-discipline needed to face difficult situations in productive ways is no easy task for students, faculty, or practitioners. How well professionals model the behaviors they ask of students has been called into question in the literature (Kottler, 1992) and recognized by students as well:

Faculty avoided confrontations just like we did. You could always see when they were ducking an argument or someone's strong emotion. The big difference is that they had to make choices in front of everyone during these situations. We got to sit back and be quiet unless we were in the middle of it. The worst times were when you were in the middle and you worried for days afterward how you did. Usually you did all right, but if you didn't then mostly you could find ways to do something that would show yourself in a better light later on.

Professionals must acquire the self-discipline to make themselves respond in difficult situations even when their self-confidence is low. We sometimes have to fake that self-confidence just as we learned to fake it in graduate school. Vague circumstances often demand confrontive and definitive responses that go beyond the information available. Couching definitive responses in a context that also accepts the vagueness of the situation is a difficult lesson to learn and to remember in stressful situations.

It takes tremendous self-discipline to work effectively under pressure when clients want answers, colleagues expect answers, HMOs require information, the police have "just a couple of questions," and a supervisor asks, "What exactly are you doing with this woman?" You cannot just go quietly off to your room, pull out the *Book of Solutions*, find the right answer, and then go calmly back to the problem situation with solutions in hand. Acquiring the self-discipline to do hard work during difficult times is a major characteristic for therapists often instilled as a part of the graduate school experience.

I never realized how many hours in a row I could stay up to study for just one test.

I would have given anything to get out of that first presentation. I never did get over the stuttering until the very end. Thank God I got better over time.

That thesis was all I did for weeks at a time. My confidence would go up and then come crashing down. First I thought I had the idea, and then the words looked like garbage. It was a roller coaster ride of emotions and ideas that I had never experienced before. But I chose to keep working on it until I finally got the damn thing done.

We have all dreamed of running away from our most difficult professional and personal tasks. Maybe you even did it in certain circumstances, like leaving jobs to avoid difficulties, referring a client too early, or telling a client that it seemed like he was much better in order to speed the ending of a difficult relationship. But you cannot get away with too many avoidance tactics and maintain a sense of professionalism for long. Difficult situations come up so consistently that one would have to be in a constant state of avoidance, which would destroy both ability and credibility. The self-discipline to work under difficult circumstances with no clear end in sight is the characteristic that now keeps you in the profession and fighting through the difficulties. The outcome of those battles is the opportunity to enjoy the beauty and creativity in your work.

Indulgence of Your Creative Potential

We have clients who hurt and work that is never-ending. We are threatened, confused, overworked, and frustrated. So why exactly do we enjoy our work so much? Part of that answer lies in the opportunity it provides to play with ideas in our imagination and in reality. Thinking, brainstorming, creating useful analogies, and trying to translate ideas so others can understand them are all part of our daily work that makes it as much art as science (McClure, Merrill, & Russo, 1994). Sure it is work, but it is also fun and some of the most exciting and enjoyable occasions of mind play were in graduate school.

The grind of seeing people hour after hour, day after day makes it easy to fall into the trap of seeing therapy as simply spending time, implementing steps, and moving people through a process. No therapy ever works that directly because originality is needed to adapt a process to each unique individual and set of circumstances (Lett, 1987).

Creating, sorting, organizing, and testing ideas is our daily fare. We had to pay monetarily and personally to practice manipulating ideas in graduate school so that now we get others to pay us for doing the same thing. It is a good deal if you like mixing the scientific and intuitive domains (McClure et al., 1994). There is not nearly enough information available to answer even a fraction of our questions, so playing with ideas can sometimes become more important than relying on facts. Thinking and acting creatively is required simply because there is no alternative.

Every aspect of the human condition is open to our consideration and examination. A more accurate diagnostic category, a more viable technique, a more enlightening theory, a revolutionary conceptualization of reasons behind behaviors, or even a clearer picture of all we as individuals might become: This is the potential we are paid to explore. We can do it with differing levels of intellectual, emotional, and physical abilities. We can explore different questions and issues based on who we are rather than having to act and think like everyone else. We get to be artists of the mind rather than slaves of tools and techniques.

Graduate school forced us to sacrifice money, relationships, time, and security for the chance to be something different. The end product was a professional degree, but what we paid for was time—time to put reality on hold for awhile as we explored the world of ideas. It is an unlimited world that requires concentrated attention periods just to touch on an understanding of its potential. Your hectic and pressure-filled professional life requires that you take this world of ideas in smaller doses. It was graduate school where you had more time to find the joy, excitement, and wonder that this world of ideas can produce.

Moments of Wonder

The experience of therapy provides moments of wonder for clients and therapists alike that are among the most personal reasons we enter the profession. Just when it seems like a session will drag on forever, a burst of insight occurs that radically changes the way participants see themselves and the world. The flash of sudden illumination turns the therapy session from detail work to a bold search for new and exciting possibilities. We live for these moments of wonder.

I was counseling a role-playing colleague when it hit me that we weren't role-playing at all any more. We were talking about real issues and I was using all my new skills and knowledge in a natural way for the first time. It was such a high I could hardly talk about it, but at the same time I wanted to scream about it to everyone.

We were in an experiential group as part of our training when it all came together for me. All at once I realized how clear my perceptions had become of the group members. The stages of group seemed so clearly observable. The connections between my emotions and knowledge made sense for the first time. I knew exactly what to do. It felt so good I never wanted the group to end.

Maslow (1987) gave major attention to such peak experiences and continued emphasizing their importance throughout his career. Others have noted them in all ages from children (Hoffman, 1992) to the latter stages of life (Chinen, 1991). These life-changing moments are rarely found by searching for them in books. They are more often found in intense relationships with others, with ourselves, or with nature – where you come to see yourself and the world in an entirely new way.

Think about a recent time in which you felt giddy with excitement, relief, or moved to tears of joy and exaltation. There is a good possibility that one or more of those times will be part of your graduate school experience. This is a time in your life of extraordinary potential, demands, frustrations, self-examinations, victories, failures, and new growth. It is the very nature of these potential highs and lows that prepares you for the similar wonders of clinical practice where the ample safety nets of graduate school are not there to catch your mistakes.

Graduate school prepares people for the many troubling realities of professional practice, but it also highlights the most inspiring parts of our work, as described in the words of one therapist:

As many years as I have practiced, there is still nothing that gets to me as much as the light in a client's eyes when he or she sees the way out of what seemed like a dark hopeless corner. Our words only confirm what we realize is the truth: The world is a better place. I float home after those sessions. I'm not as dumbfounded as I was the first time I saw it as a graduate student, 25 years ago, but it still gets to me just the same.

THERE'S MORE TO TRAINING THAN MEETS THE EYE

No graduate school program can teach all there is to learn in a profession where "unlimited" defines the knowledge base. Some programs focus on research, psychological detail, and assessment as the cornerstones of work with clients. Others demand the development of relationship-building skills above everything else. Still others want to ingrain students with knowledge of how society, family, and culture impact every aspect of work. No matter which program one attends, or the focus it promotes, each one fosters habits that make us better professionals.

We came to graduate school looking for the information and skills necessary for christening as entry level professionals. Those were provided, but to our surprise, we also expanded our abilities as thinkers, doers, fighters, learners, innovators, speakers, leaders, and followers. These are not talked about in the textbooks or journal articles. They are not meant to be memorized and restated, but instead internalized and implemented. They are as necessary to our continuing professional health as the clinical information we possess. These developments are not the answers we desire, but they do form the foundation upon which we build and maintain our searches for the answers.

Continually seeking answers that are never fully available is a burdensome undertaking. The task can appear insurmountable when we realize that so many answers we have unsuccessfully sought for years are now becoming irrelevant because of new directions in the profession. Even those concepts and techniques that seemed to have substantial credibility and long-time stability are under question. Graduate school taught us ways and means for adapting that remain critical in a rapidly changing future.

The next chapter discusses some of these new ways of conceptualizing old phenomena as well as some new pressures in the evolving modern professional world. It may seem like a daunting task to reconfigure the way we look at our world; however, the habits and characteristics we developed in graduate school will be those factors that help us successfully navigate into our new worlds.

CHAPTER FOUR

Organized Confusion

A QUIZ!

What is the relationship that determines the progression of the following set of numbers?

$$8 \quad 5 \quad 1 \quad 7 \quad 2 \quad 0$$

WHEN CONFUSION REIGNS

A very few of you may have quickly gotten the answer to the quiz above, but most will be considering what to do about not recognizing the pattern. Ignoring the question is one way to handle it; hunting through the chapter for the answer is another. Each of you will soothe your curiosity or frustration with a personalized approach that has worked in other situations where basic knowledge and skills just don't seem to apply. Take for example the awkward situation described by the therapist below:

I was not surprised to see a Japanese woman enter my office, as there was a small but significant Japanese population in town. She said, "Hello, my name is Dokwan," and I introduced myself. It became quickly obvious that those were the only English words she could speak and I could speak no Japanese at all.

Dokwan began crying and talking in Japanese. I couldn't leave her in obvious distress, but I also couldn't understand a word she was saying. Nothing I ever learned prepared me for this, but we were there together and I had to do something. So I was attentive, offered tissues and tea, maintained good eye contact, made motions to confirm that I couldn't understand her words, accepted her motioned acknowledgment of our communication problems, and held her hand when she reached out for mine.

When confusion reigns, we seek structures for ideas and behaviors that have served us best in the widest variety of past situations. This therapist fell back on essential nonverbal behaviors and the recognition that even these small steps can help one get through a problem situation in a productive way. Everyone, whether novice therapist or graduate student, has to fall back on something when confronted with confusion. One student described his panic reaction to an unexpected situation and his fall-back position that sought any human help available for support:

It was my second client, a guy, and he started sobbing almost right away. I just knew this had to be bad, so I told him to excuse me while I went to get my supervisor who I thought was in the next room. When the supervisor wasn't there, I asked another student if he would come in with me. I figured two people not knowing what the hell they were doing was somehow better than one.

No one can control all the conditions surrounding the therapy process. The examples above demonstrate extreme cases where all the details you learned about being a therapist seem worthless, yet you still have to act. Every therapy session has times when deciding what to say or do with a client is at best unclear. It is these times that highlight the need for some fundamental structure to guide your thoughts, interpretations, and actions. These structures, referred to as theories, frameworks, or paradigms, are the means we use to organize situations even when confusion does prevail.

Graduate school was the place that most of us were first introduced to the notion that there were vastly different ways to conceptualize people's problems and the best ways to help. Faculty and books explained "theories" as the ways we systematically organize knowledge and make it applicable in a wide variety of circumstances. These systems provided assumptions, accepted principles, and rules of procedure to assist us in analyzing, predicting, and otherwise explaining what was happening with our clients and in therapeutic relationships. It was less clear to us why there were so many different theories and associated assumptions, principles, and rules.

The more we looked at theories, the more confused we became. It reached the point where there seemed to be voices competing for attention in our heads. The voices, which verged on being hallucinations at times, each spoke a different language:

The unconscious desires of people will lead you to the root of their problems.

Behaviors and their reinforcement are real. Everything else emanates from them.

People want to do good and with the proper relationship, they will make themselves whole.

We all suffer from inferiority and overcoming it is the goal that drives our actions.

Irrational human beliefs are what take people away from a reasonable approach to life.

All the various theories, concepts, and terms began to run together into a junk pile of pieces from different conceptual puzzle boxes. We sorted the fragments out as best we could in order to choose the correct answers for class exams and licensing tests, but the puzzle pieces never quite fit together, so we promptly forgot the details until the next test came along.

Faculty and textbook authors also seemed to become confused with the plethora of theoretical details. Their solution was to systematize the similarities and differences between the theories into what they called "frameworks." These broad families of ideas placed theorists like Freud, Jung, Adler, and Sullivan into a common psychodynamic framework. Existential/humanistic approaches highlighted by the work of Frankl, Rogers, and Perls were grouped together as individuals speaking essentially the same language, but in different dialects. Skinner, Bandura, Krumboltz, Ellis, and Meichenbaum provide examples of a behavioral evolution to a modern cognitive-behavioral framework. Likewise, other frameworks have been described as systemic, constructivist, and problem-solving to help organize theoretical concepts. Each of these attempts at organizing confusion made things a little easier—as factor analysis is designed to do—by reducing the number of variables to their essential common components.

The movement from theories to frameworks made the job of categorizing theoretical information easier, but it has not significantly changed the way we view people and therapy. The profession continues to search for a new vision rather than a simple reorganization of old information. Attempts at finding this new vision are beginning to emerge under the heading of "paradigm shifts."

The "new paradigms" terminology has become a byword for change in the 90s. The local representative of an HMO tells us we will have to make a shift to "new paradigms" or go out of business. Consultants, looking for a phrase to explain why they exist, refer to the critical "new paradigms" that they can help us confront effectively. Ivory tower theorists needing to display their intellectual superiority must let us know how the "new paradigms" that they have conceptualized for us will change our lives. And of course, any self-respecting therapist who is confronted with these challenges must provide the obligatory positive nod of the head to demonstrate understanding and agreement with the power of THE phrase.

Paradigms, for all the significance heaped on them, serve much the same organizing purpose as theories and frameworks. They provide examples that serve as patterns or models on which we base thinking and actions. These are the internal belief systems that add necessary efficiency to our lives by eliminating the need to think through, evaluate, judge, and only then act on every aspect of our world in every moment of our existence. Without these systems, we couldn't begin a therapy session for want of continuous consideration of all potential alternative behaviors and their implications. Paradigms allow us to efficiently begin sessions simply because "we always do it that way since that's how you do it, and it seems to work."

The paradigm concept is a broad concept, but not entirely separate from other common conceptualizing words used in our profession. This can add to the confusion. A theory is a form of "systematic organization of knowledge and application" that helps us direct our lives and our practice. Theories and paradigms have lots in common by definition, but our evolving use of the words appears to be differentiating them more than would their formal definitions alone. Theories are increasingly being portrayed as "old," "rigid," and "limited," regardless of which vision is being discussed. Paradigms are being conceptualized as "new," "evolving," and "all-encompassing" ways of looking at people. The word *paradigm* has, in recent years, become the way to speak of positive change and the future, while *theories* are being increasingly criticized as the models of the past.

Perhaps disparaging an old word (theory) and picking a new one (paradigm) operates somehow like leaving one partner (divorce) in order to acquire the freedom desired to develop a different relationship. Entirely putting aside the past and starting with something brand new is often seen as easier to do than the more difficult task of changing those things that have been entrenched for years. We still need examples, systemization, and models, but by relieving ourselves of old wording and dogma we may be able to identify new conceptualizations with less interference from old ideas.

The quiz at the beginning of this chapter serves as one example requiring you to make a paradigm shift in order to get the correct answer. The standard model for evaluating numbers that has gotten us by for our whole lives must be put aside in order to find a new way to answer the question. The relationship that determines the order of the numbers in this instance is the fact that they are listed in *alphabetical* order. The numbers have no numerical relationship whatsoever. You have to drop a traditional paradigm of looking for numerical relationships between numbers and find a new way of looking at numbers in order to visualize the true answer.

We ask clients to make such paradigm shifts all the time and wonder why they find it so difficult. Clients have developed their own unique ways of looking at the world and the choices available to them. Whether and how much they can improve on that world is therefore limited, as the client below would attest:

My world is over now that George died. We did everything together, we were our only real friends. There is nothing that can be done about it. There is just nothing for me to live for anymore.

The phenomenological world in which this woman lived has disappeared with her husband's death, so its not surprising that she has given up hope. Repairing her old world will not work. The therapist will need to help her conceptualize a new world for herself in order to make a paradigm shift away from the model she has successfully lived with for years.

Similar paradigm shifts are being debated within our profession as we are increasingly asked and sometimes required to view clients, people, society, therapy, and our manner of practice in ways that differ radically from previous models. These shifts signify the potential revocation of previous paradigms rather than making changes within those models we have come to know and understand. It is no easier for us to envision such radically new therapeutic worlds than it is for clients to envision potentially new and more effective ways of dealing with their worlds.

Even if you wanted to make a radical change right this minute, the problem is that there is no clear best way to go. Internally you will face the paradox of both wanting the consistency and security of your current paradigms while also desiring new and better ways of visualizing your practice. These are the same forces that drive our need for perfection while knowing we cannot achieve it. Several practical paradigm shifts impacting our profession seem to emanate from more external forces.

EXTERNALLY DRIVEN PARADIGM SHIFTS

Therapists as a whole are a caring and highly motivated lot. Earlier chapters described how badly we want to do right by clients, heal their hurts, and prepare the next generation for a better life. We would give almost anything for the formula that allowed us to achieve anything close to these goals. No such perfect formula, theory, framework, or paradigm yet exists, but we continue searching because we want to find better ways to do more.

The persistent internal pressure to do more and better things for clients is compounded by external demands as well. People experiencing greater change, more problems, and additional pressures are asking for faster and more thorough relief. Individuals, companies, and governments paying for increased therapeutic demands look for all possible ways to keep costs down. We have little choice but to seek new ways to increase services, improve therapy outcomes, shorten the process, and do it all while attending to the financial requirements of insurance companies, the government, and our own personal needs. Whatever the final solution may be, it is clear now that some old paradigms for interacting within the therapeutic world are being suggested for replacement by relatively untested paradigms with new responsibilities for clients and therapists.

SHIFTING RESPONSIBILITIES

One old paradigm envisioned therapists working with clients to help them change their lives through a process where change was fully within the client's control. This paradigm that placed clients fully in control is no longer the norm of the profession where biological influences have taken a primary place in understanding causation and healing factors. Unfortunately, the strength of the belief that biological and cultural influences impact human development and therapy is more extensive than our current understanding of how to utilize them.

After World War II, the medical profession and insurance companies began recognizing that 60–90% of client visits were not related to physical problems. These statistics are remarkably similar to more current statistics, which show that 60–80% of doctor visits are stress-related (Shapiro, 1991). It became clear then, as it is now, that one's physical health was heavily influenced by outside stressors and that there ought to be cheaper ways to get these needs met than through a medical doctor. In fact, it was this recognition that gave the early development of professional therapy a major boost. Health plan providers realized that sending someone to several visits with a therapist was cheaper than sending them to the medical doctor for the same visits (Sweet, Rozensky, & Tovian, 1991). Therapists became a less expensive treatment of choice even though insurance companies were not clear on what exactly was being treated. Some of those same questions about why progress occurs in therapy remain today along with who or what is responsible for the progress.

Therapists provided new ways to help people with their problems, usually in dyad relationships, where clients learned about themselves and how to make better decisions. The issues and solutions in this paradigm were seen as being contained *within* the individual. Much of this internal locus of control emphasis has maintained itself in current practice, but the influences of biological advances and cultural theory on the treatment of individuals has provided a view that can lessen the responsibility people take for their own problems and solutions.

The biological treatments and mood altering medications discussed in a previous chapter have revised expectations between clients and therapists. The head of quality control for a health maintenance organization recently confirmed that the single largest mental health cost factor for her organization was doctors writing prescriptions for Prozac. People do not need a therapist's sensitivity and knowledge in order to take a pill; they just need to get someone to prescribe it for them. The only true responsibility people have in this model is to take the medication when told.

Breggin (1994) echoes many of these concerns in his searing condemnation of the "new psychiatry." He makes a strong case for the abuses of medicine as authoritarian measures that may cause long-term brain damage by altering brain functioning as quick antidotes for psychological disorders. These sought-after solutions, requiring only passive client involvement, lead to an ever-increasing model of dependence on drugs and avoidance of personal responsibility on the part of therapist and client.

The questions become, "What are the responsibilities for clients and therapists regarding who sets goals, treatment techniques, decision-making, and the commitment to the hard work of getting through life's problems? Who decides whether and how to work on productive growth rather than simple comfort?" Old theories don't deal well with these questions and the increasing emphasis on specialization over a generalist approach to people is complicating it further.

GROWING SPECIALIZATION

A thoughtful young man pondering a career as a therapist sought the advice of an experienced professional regarding his choice of a graduate program:

I wonder if this program will have all the courses I need to become a therapist working on posttraumatic stress disorder (PTSD) with Vietnam veterans who are confined to VA hospitals. I don't want to waste my time learning about lots of other stuff and I just want to concentrate on the things that will make me an expert in this area. If they don't have lots of courses and expertise in this area or if I have to take a bunch of general stuff, then I think I should try another school.

Experienced therapists quickly recognize the folly in the naive idea that one can discard a general foundation of knowledge and skills in order to focus on one small specialization. Learning how to deal with the commonalties of human beings is a prerequisite to understanding and treating their uniqueness. People suffering from schizophrenia, PTSD, dysthymia, panic disorder, or simple anxiety all have far more human characteristics in common than they have unique differences. Specialization needs to evolve out of a solid grounding in generalities, but this direction does not necessarily match the model of today's society where details and specializations are the focus of attention.

You are expected to be able to treat only those clients for whom you have training and experience. A lawyer emphasized this point for a therapist on the witness stand in court, "I know you have worked with the depressed before, Doctor, but I don't think you have ever worked with a depressed person with all the characteristics of this one. Is that true?"

Of course it's true! No two clients will ever be completely alike. Therapists see surprises of one type or another in every client. Our profession is advancing in ways that teach us more new things every day. We would become completely stagnant if we only did what we had experienced previously, did not explore new aspects of clients, and stopped treatment every time something confusing came up. We must be generalists even as we are being pushed by outside influences toward increasingly minute specializations.

This movement toward diagnostic details, medical diagnosis, and clinical specialization makes presumptions similar to those used in attempts to develop artificial intelligence. Simon's (1973) study in artificial intelligence identified several problematic assumptions, including the beliefs that all difficulties can be overcome based on unambiguous information, clearly defined goals, and readily apparent treatment paths. Nothing close to this degree of clarity exists in real-life problems that would allow us to operate upon these assumptions (Etringer et al., 1995). Perhaps that is why we are never fully successful and generally cannot even agree on what success is.

Problems often seem to have simplistic solutions, but they rarely work out that way. Rather than consider the most professionally complex situations therapists face, consider what seems on the surface to be a remarkably simple human problem. We know that the solution for 99% of those people who want to lose weight is simply to eat less and exercise more. Billions of dollars are spent by overweight people on doctors, therapists, weight loss programs, and books that mostly produce no lasting weight loss and often result in reactionary weight gain. The apparent simplicity of this problem and its solution are obviously dwarfed by factors we cannot understand and over which we command little consistent control.

Logical, clear, detailed, and objective language is the chosen model to explain and solve problems in modern society. We presume the use of this language will lead us to straightforward solutions. Unfortunately, language is based on an assumed foundation of truths about life that we do not currently possess (Elkind, 1995). The result is that our attempts at verbalizing decision-making processes are communicated through language that must be considered as ambiguous as its vague foundations. We are becoming more and more reliable in our language, diagnosis, and specializations, but the question of how valid these descriptions are in the real world remains unanswered. People are rarely stopped, however, by questions of whether their words or actions have true validity. When our theoretical model for how to act is questionable, we must act anyway, and we do.

JUST GET IT DONE!

Therapists make their living by identifying and implementing specific techniques of therapy on a daily basis. The pressures of helping people in immediate need, the human desire for quick solutions, waiting lists of clients, and insurance company pressures to get people in and out of therapy as fast as possible demand extra attention to techniques and allow less time for consideration of overall theory. One therapist put it this way after a particularly full day of clients:

If I just listed all the things I did and everything I said with each client today, you'd probably question how they form any consistent whole. I'd probably question it too right now. But on those rare occasions when I have time to really think about my work, I have been able to connect what I do into a reasonably coherent theory. There is not time to do that often though. You just have to have faith from client to client and day to day that the things you do really do make theoretical sense, or at least they get results.

It is the practitioner rather than the theorist or scientist in each of us that demands immediate techniques over contemplation of theories. Even our professional organizations focus more on practical techniques than theoretical possibilities (Cummings, 1995).

In the past, professional conferences produced a bulk of programs offering explanations of theories, new developments, conceptualizations that would help in understanding them, theories related to specific kinds of clients, and sometimes implementation would be the focus. Gestalt, psychoanalysis, person-centered, Adlerian, existential, and rational emotive were always theory names that one could seek out in program titles and thus plan a whole two days' worth of programs to attend. Professionals came to these conferences with a theoretical direction, ready to develop their personalized theories and perhaps explore other theoretical orientations to people and clients.

Today's professional conferences provide few clues for us as to how you would pursue your own theoretical development. Theory names have disappeared from most program titles and references to theorists play little part in program descriptions. A myriad of programs on specific techniques for dealing with selected client problems in the fastest way possible have taken their place. Now people pick their workshop agendas on the basis of looking for words in the title that speak to their most immediate client problems, legal and ethical issues, or how to do things faster. Experienced program planners have come to realize that a program with the words "theory" or "analysis" can be placed in the smallest of rooms. The large rooms must be set aside for programs emphasizing specific techniques, building a practice, clinical issues, or any word that suggests "brief" or "immediate" in the title. Consider this sample of titles from a recent national conference:

Managed Care: Making the Most of Your Practice Group
Creating Change through Solution-Focused Brief Therapy
Family Therapy Applications with At-Risk Youth

Impact Therapy: A Creative Approach with Immediate Effects
The Critical First 15 Minutes: Doing More with Less Time

These conference program titles speak directly to the demands of clients in a hurry, insurance company rules, cost-cutting supervisors' dictates, and your own personal pressure to do the best possible job. You want to return from the conference with learning that will allow you to do your work better tomorrow rather than with a general increase in your understanding of theory.

These pressures and therapists' reactions to them create a new picture of what we are to be as therapists, our goals, and our means of reaching those goals. Clearly, we are being influenced by appropriately attending to societal patterns in order to be responsive to the cultures of our clients. The question is: How much should we reflect societal pressures and how much should we use our knowledge and experience to direct societal and therapeutic change? An important factor in this mix is that the development of theory and practice in the past has originated from a highly Eurocentric culture which does not match the changing cultural influences in our modern world. The recognizable influence of culture on therapy increases at a rate that demands our consideration of culture as a rapidly changing paradigm.

The preceding examples of changing professional models identify the kinds of paradigm shifts that have altered the ways we look at the profession and the world. Two of the most broadly accepted paradigms, chaos theory and postmodern philosophy, are given particular attention in the following section.

Both of these ideas hold great potential for being the all-encompassing paradigms that could draw many other models together. The extensive attention they have received from so many different disciplines makes them unique in the study of new paradigms. We have chosen to present them in some depth not only because they appear important for the future, but because they are representative of models that have been developed since most of us finished graduate school.

Journals and books about changes in the arts, sciences, mathematics, philosophy, and therapy all utilize these new paradigms to consider professional futures. Their influence includes extensive attempts by a range of professions to redesign old terms, concepts, origins, and outcomes based on analogies borrowed from these new models. Many other paradigm shifts are used as descriptions of pressures to change, but the chaos and postmodern paradigms are instead used to develop the necessary comprehensive pictures for understanding and visualizing the evolution of a rapidly changing world. In many ways, they make much of what we learned in graduate school obsolete.

CHAOS AS ORGANIZATION

Chaos theory sounds like an oxymoron. The definition of chaos, "a condition or place of great disorder or confusion," would seem to be the opposite of the definition of theory, "systematically organized knowledge." Perhaps it is this strange combination of terms that most directly identifies the significant nature of this paradigm shift and the difficulty people have in rearranging their thinking to fit it. The chaos paradigm asks us to consider a systematic organization of the knowledge surrounding those things that will continue to be disordered and confusing. This is not Western society's normal pattern of thinking, learning, and living.

Virtually all the information and skills we began learning as early as grammar school presumed that order in the world was based on a linear relationship between cause and effect. ("See how A causes B to occur, and then how they combine to produce C.") Before the influence of chaos theory, major scientific paradigms allowed us to reject the unexpected, the unwanted, and the incomprehensible as extraneous variables (Gelatt, 1995). We could run our lives and work with clients in ways that assumed the information available would lead us to logical, controllable outcomes. Chaos theory now pushes us to accept the idea that although we can envision connections between ideas and behaviors based on a theory, we are, and always will be, ignorant of most of the connections within that theory (Michael, 1983).

Chaos theory began its attack on traditional theoretical views within the world of mathematics, but it quickly spread to physics, meteorology, ecology, and other science-related fields where it is now well-established (Gleick, 1987). The social sciences expanded use of the theory by quickly moving to evaluate its potential impact in many human circumstances (Gregersen & Sailer, 1993). Psychology has more recently become interested in chaos theory from a variety of angles, including applications to humanistic theory (Krippner, 1994), systems theory (Stevens, 1991), alcoholism (Ehlers, 1992), psychotherapeutic process (Butz, 1993), psychological assessment (Haynes, 1995), therapist training (Wilbur, Kulikowich, Roberts-Wilbur, & Torres-Rivera, 1995), and even the debate over whether psychologists should be allowed to obtain prescription privileges (Butz, 1994). All this attention has not made chaos the prevailing model for work in any of these areas, probably because old ideas and ways of doing things die hard. Its most impressive effect has been to give a variety of professionals, including therapists, a new way to visualize the discontinuities between theory and practice.

We see examples of the chaos model on a regular basis in our clients where the unexpected can either make or break their progress. A recent example is a middle-aged woman who was suffering from an incapacitating depression brought on by her husband's suddenly leaving her for a younger woman. The life she had accepted as being totally devoted to being a dutiful wife was now crumbling around her. Two months into therapy the woman had acquired a more positive perspective of herself, taken actions to explore new careers, and created situations where she was developing enjoyable new male and female relationships. It was an orderly progression from the depths of despair to logical actions and thinking that would produce an exciting new future. However, the best-laid plans of the therapist were unexpectedly reversed in an instant when the client called to cancel their next session.

I know you'll think this is crazy and maybe I do too, but I've decided to work on getting my husband back. I'm going to fix up the interior of the house, do some landscaping outside, and keep myself available for him to come back.

I saw him with his girlfriend in the store yesterday and I think they weren't that happy. I think he'll be getting tired of that little apartment and start thinking about home. Fixing up the house will show him what he is missing even more. I'm not coming to therapy anymore, but thanks, you've been very nice.

A chance encounter stirred the client's imagination to run down a path of thinking that weeks of therapy had replaced with other ideas and actions. Chaos theory calls attention to how small influences that are unknown to us ("sensitive dependence") can change physical as well as cognitive patterns. A small stick breaks off from a limb, frightening a fish to move closer to shore, where a bear jumps in after it and creates a major wake. Downstream, the now small wake moves the last stone that had held a giant boulder in place for the last 40 years. A fisherman is astounded to see a ten-foot-high boulder begin moving in the middle of a placid stream for no apparent reason. Both the client and the boulder examples demonstrate one of several key chaos principles that tell us we can never trust the patterns we see to provide full understanding of what will occur next.

We may not be able to recognize what is causing many of the changes in the patterns of our clients' lives, but we can study the patterns ("strange attractors"). The longer and more thoroughly we observe, the more consistencies in the details of patterns we see, even though the pattern's sources remain unclear. A surprisingly positive or negative reaction by one client looks like an anomaly to a novice therapist, but can be seen as the continuation of the general pattern ("iteration") by an experienced therapist. Neither novice nor expert may know what actually caused the reaction, but the experienced therapist can use recognition of the pattern for understanding and planning future actions.

The chaos paradigm tells us that all the small specific events in a therapist's experience, health, and training, added to the vast array of client life events, provide unpredictable influences on the movement of therapy and its outcomes. This is a far cry from the theoretical models that would allow people to understand and control their lives with a quantifiable set of limited principles.

Agoraphobic clients who refuse to leave the house have taken control of their security very effectively, even if in a limited way. By staying in the house, they create the illusion of being able to avoid all potential dangers that others who venture outside must face. They succeed in retaining strict control over many factors at the expense of the more fascinating and growth-producing aspects of life. Most therapists seek to help agoraphobics expand their environment beyond the stringent confines of the house. We want these clients to see the creative life-confirming possibilities available to them even in the face of increased anxiety over problems. Chaos theory provides a similar paradox whereby individuals must give in to the ideas of chaos and inconsistency in order to recognize the new and creative potentials that can then be used to gain additional control of their lives.

Therapists who use all the skills and information acquired during years of training will have consistent success with many clients. They will also have numerous failures, in part because they do not look beyond their linear application of information and in part because of the chaos experienced by both client and therapist. Chaos theory asks you to look beyond the linear models, which assume you will know what to expect and how to deal with each client and his or her progress.

Chaos theory is perhaps best seen as a way of thinking and acting in a world that is inherently ambiguous and more complex than our ability to organize it. Trying to apply these ideas in the face of increasing demands to give definitive answers and concrete solutions is a major challenge. Meeting this challenge may not be in our immediate future, but chaos also teaches us about the need to live with ambiguity and complexity, and to teach others how to better deal with that situation. This was a lesson we did not learn very well in graduate school, where "truth" and "right answers" were often emphasized.

An even broader philosophical position that has influenced our world for decades is the belief that a modern world is one where science reigns. However, a postmodern philosophy is challenging the notion that science is the all-powerful model for moving humanity forward. This postmodern philosophy incorporates many of the concepts attached to chaos theory, but goes beyond it in determining a broader view of life and human nature.

MODERN TO POSTMODERN PHILOSOPHIES

Modern-era art, music, religion, science, education, and the practice of healing all evolved from feudal times. This evolution stressed the rationality of Descartes, the freedom of Rousseau, the predictability of natural phenomena a la Newton, the universal laws of Einstein, the democratic beliefs of Jefferson, the global theories of Darwin, and the transformative social changes of Marx.

Blind spots and flaws also evolved in modern thinking and have led to exclusionary policies against minority peoples, weapons of mass destruction, and the glorification of the individual over family and culture. Elkind (1995) describes how postmodernism began to provide a model that rejects many of these influences. Some of the differences that we can easily recognize in the latest innovations within our own field is a shift from:

individuality	to	diversity
rational thought	to	language-based reasoning
objective truth	to	subjective perceptions
linear progress	to	historical and social contexts
universal principles	to	culturally specific issues
regularity	to	irregular exceptions
nuclear family	to	kinship bonds
parochial views	to	global world views

The new heroes are linguists like Wittgenstein and Chomsky, philosophers like Foucault and Nietzsche, semanticists like Korzybski, sociologists like Mannheim and Goffman, psychologists like George Kelly and Kenneth

Gergen, biologists like Humberto Maturana, family therapists like Karl
Tomm and Paul Watzlawick, and narrative therapists like Michael White
and David Epston. Perhaps the best example of the differences between
modern and postmodern thinking is illustrated by Anderson (1990, p. 75)
in a parable about three baseball umpires:

*They are sitting around over a beer, and one says, "There's balls and there's
strikes, and I call 'em the way they are." Another says, "There's balls and
there's strikes, and I call 'em the way I see 'em." The third says, "There's
balls and there's strikes, and they ain't nothin' until I call 'em."*

   The objective modernist is represented in the first umpire who knows
how "they are." The second is a mainstream constructionist who knows
what he sees. The third umpire is a postmodern radical who believes there
are no such things as balls and strikes until he places them in context.
Perhaps, like the postmodern umpire, we are headed where everything
becomes relative to our individual perceptions. Even in the so-called "hard"
sciences, there is less certainty about the most obvious premises. For example, the basic unit of "organism" is arbitrarily decided. Is it a plant, an
animal, a colony, or even a planet? Cellular biologist Lewis Thomas (1979)
muses about such things as whether a colony of ants, with its organized
behavior, might not be a single organism, or whether the planet Earth is
actually the single cell of a larger creature and we are all just pieces of
mitochondria floating around in the cytoplasm we call home. The mass of
confusion surrounding this latest trend is almost comical.
   During one convention program on the subject of a postmodern philosophy, the participants sat around offering their own definitions of their
self-identified labels. The amazing thing was that these values sometimes
represented polar opposites. To some people, postmodernism signified the
ultimate in flexibility, while to others it represented a higher degree of
strict rigor.

*One avid constructionist uses postmodern values as the engine to drive her
greater flexibility: "To me, it is kind of like humanism in that it helps me
to let go of preconceptions and to be with clients as they are, respectful of
their background and feelings. Yet it is much more than that since this
approach looks at the individual within a larger social context. What this
means, practically speaking, is that I spend more time learning not only
about the client's world, but also about the family, culture, and historical
narratives."*

One *"old timer"* chimed in: *"I get so sick of every generation of therapists discovering the same thing all over again. You can pretend you have discovered something new and wonderful but what it sounds suspiciously like to me is phenomenology or Piaget or even Buddhism, just with different dressing."*

Another disagreed: *"I have a colleague who calls himself a social constructionist, a true fanatic in every sense of the word, and yet he is the most rigid, dogmatic, judgmental person I have ever met. If you don't think like him, you just don't 'have standards.' His message comes across loud and clear that you are just plain wrong, if not downright incompetent. If that is what postmodernism teaches or empowers in its practitioners, I want no part of it."*

There seem to be an infinite number of constructions of constructionism, some of which resemble the most flexible of ideologies, and others that border on fascism in their commitment to imposing a particular reality on others. Even multiculturalism, feminism, and other "isms" that seek justice for the disadvantaged can be used as the power base to advocate a different kind of oppression.

Constructionism certainly has its critics as well. Minuchin (1991) takes issue with the claim that reality is unknowable, or that language is far more important than actual behavior, or that the therapist should not present herself as an expert who is intent on using power to influence people in particular ways: "What keeps the therapist humble is not the realization that truth is necessarily unknowable, but that it is always partial." He goes on to say that each part of the story—from the client and every other person in his life—contributes to something that certainly resembles reality: "If we want therapy to count, to make any difference, we'd better play it for real" (p. 50).

Even if you are not a full-fledged postmodernist, social constructivist, or constructionist (the differences sometimes elude us), you can nevertheless feel the dramatic impact of their influence on your thinking and style of working. The family therapy movement and emphasis on multiculturalism are consistent with postmodern ideals. When you take into consideration the cultural origins and gender role indoctrination of clients, you are then attending to the social constructions of their beliefs. Separating "real" truth in client stories from perceptions of events is a way of applying the same principles. The increasing attention we are giving to narratives and how a client's stories may be reframed in a different light are direct outgrowths as well. Finally, techniques like externalization (White & Epston, 1990) have revolutionized the ways some practitioners are operating. Rather than following the traditional line of helping clients to accept responsibility for their plight, they are doing exactly the opposite! They are actually encouraging clients to disown their symptoms in an attempt to avoid the cycle of blame.

Talk about a disorienting change in mission, the whole role of therapist in this paradigm changes from that of healer to editor. Rather than being experts, we are skilled consultants who help clients to rewrite their life stories in language that sets them free from plots written by others (television, movies, myths, legends, family) without their consent or active participation. Exactly what lies ahead for us in this grand picture is not clear, but many therapists are developing their own paradigm shifts that may or may not fit the models being found extensively in the literature.

THERAPIST PARADIGM SHIFTS

Dealing with the confusion of a changing modern world is the challenge. You search through journals and books like this one to find the theories and new paradigms that might help you make the necessary transitions. Conferences and workshops with enlightening titles pull you away from the office in hopes of finding the best five-step model to success. You learn more from some sources and less from others, while none satisfies your need for a holistic model. Eventually, a number of recognized puzzle pieces come together, not as the whole picture, but at least into something recognizable. This is the point of discovering a new personal paradigm that allows you to look at life and work in uniquely different ways.

Personal paradigm shifts are those times of enlightenment when a new belief system or adaptation of an old one enters your consciousness as a guide for thought and action. New structures for your thinking make past experiences more sensible, current problems more manageable, and the future more meaningful. Confidence soars at these times as you feel more in tune with the world around you.

This section uses the voices of therapists to recognize those personal paradigm shifts that have made significant differences in their work. The shifts are not meant to be evaluated according to traditional scientific criteria. Instead, their value should be judged on the significance they hold for the individuals who experienced them. Perhaps one or more of these personal enlightenment examples might also be the spark that guides you to a more productive paradigm by pulling together pieces from your own studies and experiences.

Valuing Confusion

It always had seemed clear to Ann that the true causes of problems for clients, herself, and the world in general were confusion and uncertainty. Eliminate them and control, order, and reason would work everything out. Of course she was always frustrated because whenever it seemed like control, order, and reason came together, the effects were never quite what she expected. Her attendance at a particularly poor workshop on treating clients with AIDS really helped her look at things differently.

I was so frustrated with the lack of direction that I began writing the presenter an angry letter rather than listening. My letter began by explaining what I had wanted to get and how that would have helped me in my work. Putting that down on paper got me thinking even more about the needs of these and other clients, so I wrote about that too. I became even more angry and driven as I realized from my own words that there were specific actions that therapists should be taking that the presenter was never going to consider. I wrote down all those things too. This letter was really going to show him what he needed to be doing.

Only later in the day did I realize that this was the best thinking I had done in weeks, maybe years. Some of the ideas didn't work at all, while others were major insights for me. I had created my own new directions, ones that I guess were hidden somewhere in me all the time. It was all because of the confusion and frustration created in me by this dud of a presenter. His incompetence directed my thinking and allowed me to work my ideas out. I could hardly believe it; I was starting to feel grateful to this jerk.

That experience got me thinking about all kinds of things, including therapy, in a whole new light. Confusion and disorder are needed to stir the pot. People need dissonance in order to see the need for change and improvement. Systems have to cause dissatisfaction or we would never move to create better ones. We like to organize ideas, issues, behaviors, and systems and the only way we can do it is if they don't work in the orderly way we want.

It is clear to me now that creating and recognizing confusion is as important in therapy, marriage, career development, and world politics as putting them in order. Now I encourage clients to seek the confusing aspects of their lives and create somewhere necessary as a mechanism for progress.

Spiritual Awakenings

Jim had worked with a wide variety of clients in his 15 years as a therapist. He had helped severely emotionally disturbed clients to develop ways to get by from day to day, unemployed people to seek new career paths, and wealthy professionals to find new meaning in their lives. It was, however, some volunteer work in a hospice for the terminally ill that caused him to look at life and therapy from a very different angle.

I had always operated on the belief that a therapist's work was helping people create the most viable physical existence possible. It worked well enough to get me lots of positive feedback, but never enough to let me say "this is really it." The people at the hospice changed that for me. They were all in pain, had virtually no time left to alter their lives, and many had no support system outside the hospice. My practical view was first to medicate them for the pain and then provide whatever other support I could muster. They appreciated my efforts, but that only seemed to re-move a degree of physical pain from their lives rather than add anything to a rather hopeless situation.

One evening I recognized the reaction of one particularly troubling person to a minister making his rounds. She had no religious background, but still her eyes opened wide, she smiled, and she didn't complain for the first time all day. I came to realize that for this woman and for many others, including myself, it is hope and a recognition of one's place in a larger picture that provides the extra dimension I had been missing.

I don't have this "paradigm" all figured out yet and I don't know if I ever will. It's not about church, the Koran, or the Bible, although I have found things in each of these that bring me closer to a feeling of connectedness. It's the realization that the demands, agonies, and problems of everyday life are not the whole picture, and that somehow this realization gives my clients and myself more power to deal with each day as it comes. I now seek ways to clarify and maintain that perspective in my clients and myself, but it's not easy. The day-to-day pressures hit you in a physical way, but the spiritual ones need to be sought. I try to encourage that search.

Joining with Nature

Emerging under the term "ecopsychology" is a new-old way of looking at people, the physical world, and the spiritual world. Little agreement currently exists on definitions, methods, or even purpose related to this area, but there is a common foundation of belief: Echopsychology views humanity as interdependent with all other life forms, including earth itself. This is a far cry from current models which emphasize humankind's independence from, and superiority over, all other life forms.

Spurred on by concerns of an ecological crisis, a variety of therapists and nontherapists are seeking additional information about connections between people and all other nonhuman forms of existence. The term echopsychology is new, but the most frequently examined manifestations are ancient. Wisdom passed down in the form of stories, legends, myths, and spiritual teachings are given equal attention in this paradigm along with the more commonly accepted scientific sources of information. Ecopsychologists are seeking to restore credibility to these ancient information sources so that some of their historical benefits and wisdom can be recaptured for the modern world.

The information on ecological issues that has only recently found its way into our professional literature is primarily exploratory and focused on potential directions for the profession, but it has much older historical roots in other fields (Howard, 1993). Rachel Carson's (1962) classic *Silent Spring* first made most of us aware of how human beings are changing biochemical systems far beyond what had previously been considered. More recently, Al Gore's (1992) *Earth in the Balance* focused our attention on the critical nature of ecological problems facing our world as we approach the twenty-first century. Consideration of all these issues separately causes anxiety as you realize there are innumerable great issues needing more of your attention than it is possible for you to give. Part of the lure of echopsychology may be that it suggests a mechanism for finding common principles on which to base efforts in all areas, as one therapist has come to believe:

As a Native American, I felt pressed to be a "scientist" while working in town, but a "spiritualist" when I was on the reservation. I've been looking for ways to integrate what I know about people from the academic world with those things that drive my life and my soul when I come home. I see so much practical value in both sides that I just have to believe there are major connections between them that will eventually be found.

The connections this therapist sees, or more likely feels, are the core for all of the new paradigms we are called upon to master. We realized long ago that living with ambiguity and confusion come with the territory of our work. Each of us is driven to make sense of what we experience in our offices each day, to organize that confusion into concepts, models, theories, and yes, paradigms, that help us to understand better what is going on with our clients and within ourselves.

We first learned in graduate school about the fickle nature of knowledge in our field, ever-changing and evolving as quickly as we can grasp existing ideas. While this conceptual development is exciting to be part of, there is also something very faddish about the supposedly revolutionary trends we are faced with every few years. There are times when we even want to scream out: Enough is enough!

CHAPTER FIVE

Enough is Enough!

What is it with these paradigm shifts? Why must we reinvent the same aspects of our confusion over and over? Just when we get a handle on the current state of practice, professional standards, a conceptual model, and the most current interventions, we are served notice that the rules have changed again. What we once came to think, believe, and do is out and the new paradigms are now the only ways that will allow us to call ourselves professionals. When is enough, enough?

One practitioner unloads his frustration in a burst of anger:

Damn! I just wish they'd call a moratorium on new stuff for a year or two. Just until I can catch my breath. Maybe I'm out of the loop or something; but by the time I figure out what is hot, manage to read the right articles and attend the right workshops, then practice it for a while, I'm told I'm already behind the times.

*I remember in the seventies, neurolinguistic programming was supposed to be **the answer**. I was skeptical. It seemed to me those guys were more marketing experts than they were genuine therapist trainers. I resisted as long as I could. After all, I was pretty pleased with rational emotive therapy at the time. I had invested a heck of a lot of time and energy into learning that system. Got pretty good at it too. Then I'm told by my buddies that unless I learn NLP, I will always be living in the stone age. So I gave in, bought the required books, and attended the mandatory workshops.*

I'll never forget this. I paid several hundred dollars to attend the sanctioned training sessions of Bander or Grander, or whoever they were. Just a few weeks before I was to make my pilgrimage, I read somewhere that NLP was already obsolete! Couldn't believe it. So I canceled out. Why bother? They never returned my money but I was still relieved that I hadn't joined the new religion.

So now it's EMDR, eye movement desensitization and reprocessing. Everyone is now telling me that I gotta learn this stuff. Right. Here we go again.

This kind of frustration and cynicism are all too familiar to most of us. On one level, we do feel grateful and excited about innovations in theory, or new research that spawns better ways of understanding and helping people. On another level, our initial reaction is one of annoyance: "Just leave me alone! I've got enough to deal with already."

Look back at the past several decades and you will see a clear series of mixed messages superseding and contradicting each other. First we heard: "You must delve into the past in order to unearth the unconscious." Then: "Get with it, the past is out. Attend only to the here and now." This was followed with: "Ignore the feelings, focus on the thinking." Simultaneously, we heard from another corner: "It's observable behavior that counts most. We've got to see the results." Then, moving in a different direction altogether: "Working with the individual will never get it done. It's the whole family system that really matters." This was followed up with: "Family systems is a good idea, but really you have to look at the whole cultural context." Then, finally, we were told to forget the culture and explore instead the client's perceptions.

The list goes on and on with new directions continually adding to, revising, or replacing old ones. There just isn't enough time to get really good at anything new. Which great new way do we follow and which ones do we ignore? "STOP the train, I want to get off! Put me back on some solid ground where I can get back to basics for a while."

BACK TO BASICS

How many of these changes are essential? Are these new paradigms asking us to drop everything we know and start over again? How necessary is it to continuously unlearn all our old patterns and replace them with new, improved ones? We accept that change happens and that we had better prepare for it or become lost and inadequate. We also recognize fundamentals that have stabilized our relationships with clients throughout all our changes.

All these new paradigms and innovative models provide alternative perspectives for viewing our day-to-day work and lives. They don't so much change our lives, as offer new language systems and conceptual maps to see and deal with life more effectively. The earliest inhabitants of our planet explained emotions and events with gods of the sun, moon, stars, and earth. People listened to the explanations, believed, and acted in ways that proved useful. Perhaps whatever model we choose to believe in today provides its greatest value in the faith and follow-through with which we practice the model.

Lest we scoff at these notions, believing we have moved far beyond such primitive conceptions of reality, recall how quickly "truth" has changed in our lifetimes. For any of us beyond age 35, we can recall being told by our parents as children, *with utter certainty*, that going into a swimming pool immediately after eating will condemn us to an excruciating death by stomach cramps. There was some precise, but unpublished, chart that moms of the world swore by as their guide.

Picture a hot summer day. You're dying to get in the water. But you just had lunch. You ask your mother or father when you can swim.

"Well, what did you eat?"

"Un, just a few fries and a coke."

"Okay. Fifteen minutes."

"Thanks, Mom."

"Wait a minute! Did you have ketchup with those fries? And didn't you finish your sister's sandwich?"

"Kind of."

"Make that 35 minutes, and not a minute less!"

I (JK) will never forget when I first took SCUBA diving lessons and the instructor gave us last minute advice before we showed up for our first open-water dive. "Remember," he said soberly, "eat a big breakfast before you go in the water or you will get hypothermia. Your body needs nourishment to maintain its body temperature."

"Uh, excuse me?" I quickly interjected. "What about the danger of stomach cramps?"

He laughed uproariously. "Oh yes, I bet your mother told you that one."

"Soooo?" I responded a little defensively. I started thinking about all those summer days I spent sitting on the sides of swimming pools, dangling my feet in the water, impatiently waiting to be allowed in the water, asking my parents every few minutes: "Is it time yet?"

The interesting question is now to consider which unassailable "truths" we accept as readily as we did the myth about drowning from stomach cramps. Not too many years ago, people in our profession were attempting to cure emotional problems through applications of "animal magnetism."

Common Denominators

We would submit that almost all systems of helping, whether traditional ideologies or contemporary innovations, subscribe to some fairly basic principles that are part of all effective therapy. A number of authors have attempted to identify these essences that drive all successful therapies (see, for example: Frank, 1973; Kottler, 1991; Mahrer, 1989; Norcross & Glencavage, 1989; Omer, 1987; Prochaska & DiClemente, 1984). These underlying ingredients are part of the ways that all good therapists think, process, and behave no matter what they *say* they do. Keeping their significance in focus is the stabilizing force that allows us to continue experimenting with new professional innovations. Amidst our continuing struggle to find "the best way," the stories that bind therapists together continually reflect the basic factors described below.

The Human Connection

A common denominator among clients is their disconnection from some-thing exceedingly important in their lives. Sometimes that disconnection is attached to factors such as a death of a loved one, loss of a job, relocation away from friends, a marriage breakup, or one's children leaving the home. Other times the break will be more psychological as a close relationship degenerates, a perceived loss of respect is brought on by some inadequate action, or the feeling that arises when no one appears to perceive the joys and sorrows of one's world. The heart of our therapeutic work is to help those clients build bridges to reconnect themselves with old sources of support or create connections to new support systems. Whatever tech-niques you use in building these bridges, it is the human connection between yourself and the client that provides the foundation for change.

Useful human connections go beyond love and friendship. The abused wife who returns again and again to her husband depends so completely on that human connection that she continues to select it, seeing nothing to put in its place. Enemies develop relationships when they have no one else for support in times of trouble. Clients are so desperate for close human connection that they will put up with therapist blunders, incessant ques-tioning, exposure of their greatest weaknesses, and continual pushing and prodding to take difficult actions. The obvious impact of this connection is a continuous reminder of its importance to the work of therapy, as one practitioner describes:

Why am I regularly surprised when clients say how much I mean to them? Often I've done little other than be there with them. They live in apartment complexes with hundreds of people within shouting distance. They come from stable families. They work in human service offices. Yet they still don't feel connected. Somehow that's a critical gift I provide.

People do not necessarily feel part of a society, a neighborhood, a family, or even a therapeutic relationship just because they are in the presence of other people. We are in the vicinity of other people all the time while we often benefit little from this physical closeness. The ability to encourage and maintain that human connection is a critical healing factor that is promoted as much by your ability to communicate who you are as a person as by the therapeutic model you use.

The Person of the Therapist

The most direct reason clients come to therapy is to make their pain and suffering go away. They want their problems fixed and if they could find a therapist who could do that quickly and directly, that's who they would prefer. Unfortunately, even the best-trained therapists don't have the ability to advertise, "Results guaranteed in two sessions or your money back!" Clients might desire a results-only focus for selecting a therapist, but even they know that's not really likely. Their second priority will rarely be related to the therapist's theoretical approach but instead to the characteristics of the therapist. Typical of what clients often think are the following:

I know it's his job, but I still want someone who really cares about me, because no one else does. Without that I might just as well read a book on what to do.

I know she'll be with me when I'm smart, grateful, and do the right things. What I really appreciate is loyalty; someone who will be with me when I'm stupid, lazy, irrational, and angry.

I want a rock! I know I'll be up and down and all over the place. I want stability I can always depend on.

None of my friends will tell me what I need to hear so I don't trust them. I need the truth, even if it hurts. And I need to trust the person or I won't believe it's the truth.

Clients want to get better, but they select and appreciate therapists more for who they are rather than the theoretical approach they take. Most effective clinicians have characteristics in common that clients need. Clients believe in the potential for a close partnership in their struggles when the therapist's sincerity and compassion for their situations are visible. Awareness of the internal battles between demanding and fearing therapist honesty, makes clients realize that only a therapist with great sensitivity and integrity can give the necessary attention to both sides. It is the person of the counselor that the client seeks and that effective therapists provide. The professional tools you use are the vehicles designed to bring those qualities out in ways that will increase your ability to influence clients in positive directions.

The Capacity to Influence

The laws of physics demand that stationary objects stay that way until moved, and that objects moving in one direction will not move in an opposite direction of their own accord. A person's behaviors, feelings, and thinking patterns that have solidified over time are no less amenable to change. The enormity of the changes we ask clients to make in their lives cannot be overstated. Whatever different methods we use, a common thread among effective therapists is our ability to influence clients toward change.

I saw a former client in a department store chatting with two other women and flashed back to those many agonizing sessions and her unwillingness to leave the house or talk to anyone but me. The idea that I was an integral part of that change still floors me every time I recognize it.

Somewhere along the line I began seeing how I was changing people's lives and it scared me. That was more power than I ever expected to have over other people.

I'm not exactly sure what makes me successful. I just know that I've always had the ability to influence people's thinking and acting. As I've become better at it, I sometimes worry about how much it is like brain-

washing. There is a lot of potential abuse in this ability that I feel a keen need to respect.

It is a major responsibility that comes with our ability to influence change in people. We can use it too much or not enough, at the right times or the wrong ones, and in the most or the least effective ways. We can use it for good reasons or bad, as the numerous ethical problems within the profession will attest. Personal characteristics and useful knowledge give your influence with clients meaningful direction. It is clear that none of us know all we'd like to know or need to know, but the knowledge we do have proves again and again to be enormously helpful.

The Imparting of Knowledge

We do know some things that will benefit most people. Some of this consists of things we learned in professional training, some from professional experience, and some from life. What is particularly valuable to our clients is that we know when and how to use that information. Clients may not get the answer to all of life's questions from us, but we can give them pieces of information that have practical value.

A teacher referred a student to me for behavioral and social problems. I almost fell out of my chair when I saw and smelled him. He was dirty and clearly didn't bathe. Eventually I found the right time to mention this to him and how it turned people off. He was honestly surprised, cleaned himself up, and it did a great deal for his self-image and his relationships. The teacher thought I was some kind of magical therapist.

So often I see a clients' eyes open wide when I say, "You know, what you are experiencing is not unusual at all," and then go on to give a simple description of how their situation is similar to others and what can be done about it. What I think is basic information, many people have no awareness of whatsoever.

I think of this guy who had lost a leg in Vietnam and had attempted suicide on his way home to the States. He was sure his life would be confined to sitting indoors until I told him of an artificial leg and physical therapy that was available to him. I knew of another guy with the same type of leg that loved the outdoors so I put them in contact. Knowing the possibilities and that other guy was the most therapeutic thing I did for him.

What appear to be brilliant informational tidbits to clients are often taken for granted by therapists. After years of study with intelligent peers, more knowledgeable faculty, and then continuing contact with other professionals, we begin to assume that our knowledge is not very special. It may be relatively common among other professionals, but it is extensive and exceedingly important in the eyes of clients. Like all knowledge, it serves little purpose when remembered or offered in isolation, but it becomes memorable and essential when we can provide it at the right time in the development of a client's life story.

Storytelling

One purpose of telling stories is to give clarity to the structure of one's life. We use the patterns of those stories to organize thoughts, learn from the past, operate in the present, and plan for the future. When people begin confusing that story or forgetting key parts while magnifying the importance of others, the process of learning, acting, and planning begins to break down. Therapists know how to help clients reconstruct their stories to include the parts that have been altered or eliminated.

We listen, reflect, envision the progress of a client's story, and express the specifics of our confusion when the story line is breaking down. Clients are regularly surprised to find out that they left out critical aspects of the story.

I had forgotten about how my mother helped me get back on my feet after I screwed up royally. All I've been able to imagine is her disappointment when she finds out I'm pregnant.

Why would I have left my brother out when I was telling you about the family? I don't know. Maybe I resent him more than I'm willing to admit because of what he did.

Sometimes your simple reflection of the story as told by a client is enough to put it in a different perspective. Hearing the same story come out of the therapist's mouth can provide confirmation or a shock that they could have been one's own words.

Clarifying the stories related to people, events, actions, emotions, and thought processes is the process by which people begin to reconstruct the reality of their situation. Therapists who can demonstrate understanding, reflect, and take a positive role in those stories become invested in the clients' past, present, and future. This role allows for the joint creation of outlines for future life story chapters and provides direction for the thera-peutic tasks that can make those outlines become realities.

Using Therapeutic Tasks

It is not just the behaviorists among us who believe clients need practice once they leave our office. All therapists recognize that we provide a safe environment to devise new ways of thinking and behaving, but that the real test comes with their implementation in the real world. Each of us has devised favorite methods to get people to apply new ideas to their lives.

Clients forget what they have done that is productive or nonproductive over the week so they don't get a clear picture of progress. I ask them to write briefly each night in a journal the one or two things that they did that day related to what we are working on. We start the next session by recalling what they did and then go from there.

I try to make any task much smaller than the client wants to try. I find that they tend to work at proving me wrong by easily doing more and taking more pride in their accomplishments.

I just state it right up front. We must decide on homework assignments, and if you're not going to do them, then you need to work with someone else. It sets a good structure for a productive working relationship.

We provide clients with an environment that is very different from what they are used to. The safe and healthy atmosphere focused directly on their most pressing needs is in stark contrast to a day-to-day existence where others do not effectively listen, human connections are not readily made, people keep to themselves, and where each individual's personal story is fighting for attention. Our understanding of this situation, ability to sort through it, and then provide the most productive mechanisms to translate therapy-session gains into real life changes are critical keys to our professional success.

SKILLS AND KNOWLEDGE FOR THE FUTURE

The practical, theoretical, and philosophical worlds are changing so quickly that keeping up on everything has become impossible. Some among us may retreat from this confusion by changing professions or isolating our-selves from anything new and challenging. Others will hold onto the most valued basics of the past, while adding to them after carefully testing new ideas and altering them in ways to suit their clients and personal style.

But where does that process begin? What are the new skills, perceptions, and areas of content that will insure a productive future? These are questions for those of us committed to continuing improvement.

The combining of theoretical models with shifting paradigms and changing practical demands will require new skills, new knowledge bases, better models for learning, a greater emphasis on teaching, and more productive ways of using our basic skills. These developments will take us even further beyond the boundaries of our graduate school education than in the past.

The remainder of this book is designed to provide the practical direction and tools you will need to make this journey without the graduate school faculty and peers who gave you so much comfort and support. The first of these practical discussions gives attention to one area rarely mentioned in graduate school. So many therapists are interested in private practice, either as a full-time career or part-time source of additional experience and income. Yet this was one of many areas we are forced to educate ourselves through trial and error.

SECTION II

Moving Forward

CHAPTER SIX

Maintaining a Private Practice

There are two main reasons why therapists choose to go into private practice, both of them based on unrealistic expectations. The first is the fantasy of unbridled freedom, of working as a self-employed professional, responsible only to yourself and your clients. Just think of the possibilities—setting your own hours, working as little or as much as you like.

You will, of course, want to see your clients when they are able to come in, which means working evenings until 10:00 p.m., Saturdays, lunch hours. Some days you may have an appointment at 7:00 a.m. and another one as late as 9:00 p.m., with a few others scattered in between.

The second motivation is based on illusions of generous financial rewards, if not enormous wealth. Ah, the possibilities are endless. $100 or more per hour. That's, what, almost $2 per minute for your time! Just consider it: If you see 8 clients per day, 5 days per week, that's $4,000 per week, $200,000 per year! When you've been a starving student, that *is* rich.

Naturally, it is sheer fantasy to think that you will ever see 40 clients per week on a regular basis. If you should manage to fill up your schedule, it will be with the majority of clients paying reduced fees—$75, $50, even $20. Fine, you think. Even if you average $50 per hour, that's still a lot of money.

Of course, you haven't deducted your overhead.

Huh?

Office rent, payments on your furniture, computer equipment upgrades, billing service, accounting service, legal fees, collection service, phone, secretaries and support staff, advertising, marketing, entertainment budget, professional dues, and office supplies. Then there are the taxes—personal income, business, FICA, personal property – and insurance – malpractice, health, accident, income protection, workers compensation, life, and disability. Oh yeah, there are also retirement contributions if you have anything left over.

HAVING CHOICES

Lest we sound overly cynical and negative about the benefits of private practice, you do have more freedom in some areas and less in others. Compared to the bureaucracies and political maneuverings contained within most community agency settings, private practices are downright staid. That is not to say that all human conflicts are eliminated, but they are significantly reduced, if for no other reason that people are not really required to work together very much. Furthermore, you do have the option of setting your own hours, if you are prepared to live with the consequences. One therapist explains:

I'm not in this for the money. In some ways, I was better off before when my employer was putting away retirement for me and paying my health insurance. I can't seem to save anything and we are always short of cash.

One rule I've had, and stuck with no matter what, is that I won't work evenings past 6:00 p.m. I won't work Fridays and weekends. Has that hurt me in terms of income and referrals? Of course! I could be making twice as much if I was more flexible but my time is worth more to me than anything else.

This therapist has amazing restraint, even courage, in resisting the temptation to accommodate her schedule to whatever her clients require. In her opinion, this would be no different from what she experienced before, working for a company.

If freedom means having choices, having the power to control what you do and how you do it, then private practice truly provides more opportunities than any other setting. It is ironic, however, that although private practitioners *can* have more freedom than colleagues who work in organizations, often they don't as a practical matter. They may, in fact end up working longer hours for less compensation.

It is another part of what we were not prepared to handle in graduate school – the self-control and wise lifestyle choices that permit us to balance work in appropriate doses. Contrast, for example, two therapists who work in the same office. Kenneth sees an average of 16–20 clients per week, just enough to pay his bills and live comfortably. He has no problem turning down referrals once his allocated time slots are filled. When it comes to choosing between earning more money in exchange for less time writing poetry, reading fiction, or being with his family and friends, he turns down new clients happily.

Trina, on the other hand, vowed since childhood she would escape the poverty to which she had become accustomed. In her mind, she couldn't make enough money to continually improve her wardrobe, car, and home. Whatever discretionary time she has during occasional cancellations is spent ordering clothes through catalogues. Seeing 45 clients per week, plus the accompanying paperwork, scheduled over 6 full days, leaves her little time for anything else. She is making more money than she ever dreamed of but has little time to enjoy it.

These case examples make it readily apparent that private practice can promote a lifestyle filled with freedom or constriction, depending on the choices that are made and how actively time is constructed.

DO YOU HAVE THE RIGHT STUFF?

Not everyone is right for independent practice. It takes a certain disposition, a particular mindset, a set of attitudes, maybe even certain personality characteristics, to be successful. Some of the most satisfied, and also the most miserable, therapists we know are operating in this setting. For some, there is a perfect match between the requirements of the job and the things they love to do. For others, illusions are quickly dispelled by the realities of what is involved on a daily basis, tasks that often have little to do with what you were originally prepared for.

Salameh (1990) lists several of the most prominent qualities that are necessary to flourish in this setting:

- Are you flexible? Can you adapt easily to the ever-changing circumstances of the marketplace and your own domain?
- Can you live with uncertainty? Very little is guaranteed when you are out on your own. Your income will fluctuate wildly from week to week, season to season.
- Can you save money? Without an employer that is deducting retirement contributions on a regular basis, it is very difficult to exert the discipline needed to save on your own.

- Are you prepared to take risks? If you crave stability, stay with a regular job. The lifestyle of independent practice is a roller coaster, one day flying high, the next in the depths of self-doubt.
- Can you make sound business decisions? These must be based not on your dreams and preferences but on the realities of what is taking place.
- Are you diplomatic? You are a therapist, so of course you have diplomatic skills. However, are you willing to do what it takes to "sweet talk" and develop relationships with potential referral sources? Even more than being willing to do so, will you enjoy it?
- Are you self-reliant? Can you make things happen on your own?

Many of the qualities can be learned over time, if you have the right training and supervision. The problem is that most of this stuff you didn't learn in graduate school but must teach yourself on your own.

THINGS YOUR TEACHERS NEVER TAUGHT YOU

Among the things you never learned in graduate school were some skills unique to successful private practice. In fact, one of the favorite occupations of practitioners during canceled appointments is to sit around and laugh about all the specialized strategies they had to learn since they graduated. The following are some of these methods.

The Hook

The object of the first session is to get the client to come back for a second one. In the parlance of sales experts, if you can't close the deal in the first contact, you lose the customer.

Therapists working in the public sector are used to dealing with long waiting lists of clients who want their help. They have the luxury of adopting a very different attitude than private practitioners whose very livelihood depends on being able to convince clients to return.

I (JK) will never forget the time I was sitting in my office waiting for a new client. I had been in business for a few months and was so proud of my beautifully appointed office. Referrals, however, were not materializing the way my contacts had promised.

I had endless bills to pay and very little income. I had burned bridges behind me so there was no turning back. I had three clients. One dropped out. Now I was down to only two. But I had hope! After all, a new prospect was due any moment. This new client would double my current income.

I paced restlessly until I heard the outside door close softly. I peeked into the waiting room and, sure enough, there she was. I rubbed my hands together in glee, I really did. Just as I had been schooled in the outpatient clinic where I had completed my internship, I greeted her politely and gave her an intake questionnaire to fill out—you know, the usual stuff: billing information, presenting complaints, history of medical problems, medications she is taking, and so on. I told her I'd return after she was done. She nodded nervously as she scrutinized the pages.

I went back to my office, already calculating that if she could afford my full fee, maybe I could pay my phone bill on time. Maybe she would even need to come twice per week, I fantasized.

After what I estimated was plenty of time, I returned to the waiting room, only to find it empty. Primly perched on the chair where she had been sitting was the clipboard, but the client was nowhere to be seen. I giggled hysterically with an instant image of a space ship that had sucked her out through the ceiling. How had she snuck out without my hearing a sound? I mumbled to myself in shock. Scrawled across the front page of the form was written: "Sorry. I couldn't go through with this."

I was crushed. Devastated. I wanted to cry.

I vowed in that moment I would never let a client escape my grasp again, at least not as a result of my not having had the chance to sell my services first. The lesson I learned was one I could never have imagined from graduate school, or even after years working in public agencies: If I wanted to survive I had to become an expert at convincing people to return for more therapy.

Indeed, as the story illustrates, there is an altogether different mentality in the approach taken by a private practitioner. Whereas the therapist in an agency might communicate: "Look, this is what I do and how I do it. If this fits for you, great! If not, go elsewhere because there are plenty of others who want this time slot." Under such circumstances, you feel grateful when certain clients don't return. Not so with private practice where a different sort of message comes across: "What is it that you want? Whatever it is, I can probably do that. If not, I learn very quickly."

How to Run a Business

The actual task of doing therapy with clients represents less than half the work involved in being a private practitioner. That means that graduate school prepared you to do very little that is actually involved in the daily work.

What a shock to find yourself completely ignorant of what is involved in negotiating a lease, selecting a billing system, managing an office, or planning a marketing campaign. Who would have thought that your primary professional identify would change from that of healer to entrepreneur?

A number of manuals and guidebooks have been written for newcomers to the private practice scene, instructing them on the intricacies of office design and management, marketing strategies, billing procedures, managed care policies and such (see, for example: Beigel & Earle, 1990; Levin, 1983; Margenau, 1990; Schreter, Sharfstein, & Schreter, 1994; Syme, 1994). All of them hope to make up for holes in the education of most practitioners.

Beigel and Earle (1990) unabashedly admit their job in writing a book on successfully building a private practice involves teaching practitioners to think like business people. If this involves the art of self-promotion, market analysis, public relations, and running a profitable enterprise, so be it. Indeed, according to the authors, it is difficult to reconcile the values associated with being a helper versus an entrepreneur—being altruistic, receptive, process oriented, and ethical rather than materialist, aggressive, and product-directed.

You have to like the tasks associated with marketing and generating referrals. In an article on the new identity of private practitioners (Wylie, 1995), one clinician proudly proclaims that he loves "making contacts when he takes his kids to softball league games, or calls old graduate school chums, or picks the brains of his providers for corporate acquaintances, or culls names from business publications, or . . . " (p. 24). In other words, to succeed you have to enjoy the challenges of generating new business.

Every week will challenge you to make decisions, *informed* decisions, about how to spend your advertising budget, which referral sources are most likely to pan out, whether to incorporate yourself or remain as a solely owned business, how to handle a conflict between staff members. Once you are on your own, you must also deal with things that come up on a regular basis, either as challenges to be faced or opportunities to be exploited. You've never served as an expert witness before but now you are being asked to do so. You are called to court to testify on behalf of an ex-client. You are approached about putting together a program for a large company. Each of these invitations can be exciting or anxiety provoking, depending on the support system you build around you.

The Reality of Unpaid Vacations

During those dreams of financial prosperity and unrivaled freedom, you were never told what price would be paid. Ah, just think: You can take time off whenever you want to without having to ask anyone's permission. No limits on the number of vacation days you can take. In theory, this is perfectly correct; in practice, quite another situation prevails.

Imagine, for example, you are billing $4,000 per week with expenses of $1,000 per week to keep your office running. After working hard all year long, you feel entitled to reward yourself with two weeks on a secluded island. It's been awhile since you've had more than a long weekend away from work so you decided to splurge. The trip itself costs about $3,000, a hefty amount, but heck, you're worth it! Then you remember that while you are gone, you will still owe $2,000 in expenses. Although it would be a nice gesture on the part of your clients, you doubt very much that they will offer to subsidize your vacation by paying for sessions that you won't be attending. When you add the lost income to everything else, it occurs to you that this little adventure will really cost you $13,000. Then you think about the consequences of being away from your clients for two weeks. If past experience is any guide, several of them will decide while you are gone that they are doing just fine without you and don't really need therapy any more; your caseload is likely to drop while you are gone and any new referrals who call may decide to call someone else if you are not immediately available. Add another $5,000 in lost future income to the cost of your trip.

Maybe you could just stack all of your clients on Monday and Tuesday, put in 12-hour days, and then escape for the rest of the week. It is not a pleasant thought, but neither is the prospect of major financial loss.

On a smaller scale, a similar phenomenon occurs every time a friend asks you to lunch. You calculate what it costs for you to give up two prime appointment hours, add that to the price of lunch, and most of the time you find yourself wolfing down a sandwich between sessions.

While these examples paint a bleak picture, there are indeed private practitioners who plan carefully so that they can take 4–6 weeks vacation per year. As one therapist explains, however, this takes considerable self-discipline:

When I sort out my priorities I realize that family comes first, then travel, then work. I love my work, I really do, but other things are even more important to me. At the beginning of the year, I know that I'm going to take 6 weeks off during the summer so I can travel with my wife and children. I put away money all year long so I have a cushion to live on. My clients know what to expect as well. Sure, I lose a few referrals, and some clients don't return in the fall. But I think of this as simply the price I pay for being in business.

I know many colleagues who refuse to take off much time. In my opinion, many of them are burned out. I think the reason I still love what I do after two decades is that I feel so refreshed when I return in September.

The Reasoning of the Private Practice Mind

It is a strange feeling to have clients tell you they've gotten what they need and are ready to quit. The assortment of reactions that your mind goes through in that moment of revelation is staggering: "Well, good for you!" you think initially. "I'm so proud of you and what you've accomplished. I'm pretty proud of me too. I did a good job here."

Then, a creeping voice whispers indignantly: "What do you mean you're quitting?" We just got started. We haven't even made a dent yet in all the issues you've got to resolve. Running away from your problems isn't going to help."

You wonder, though, about the source of your irritation. "Now what am I going to do with that time slot? Losing this client means a reduction of $400 per month in my income. That's $5,000 per year! Gee, the least you could do is give me notice, or even refer a friend to fill the spot." Now you realize you are being a bit unreasonable, if not altogether self-centered.

You feel guilty about thinking about your own problems instead of feeling elated for the client. "Have I lost perspective or what? I feel terrible thinking about money at a time like this. I can't sort out if I am urging him to stay longer for his sake or mine. What's the difference, though? If we both profit, so much the better."

So goes the reasoning of the private practice mind.

SO ALONE

Most of us were attracted to the practice of therapy because of a love for people. We enjoy being part of a profession where we spend our days involved in intimate conversations and interpersonal connections. We have been highly trained to do just that—to relate to others effectively, to listen compassionately, to articulate complex ideas, to create memorable encounters. Furthermore, we enjoy the camaraderie of being part of a larger professional family, one whose members have similar values. We like swapping stories of victory or defeat, of trading gossip and exchanging ideas. We are intrigued by intellectual debate and drawn to emotional conflict. Above all else, we are people-oriented in the ways we perceive the world. We are nourished by our interactions with others.

In graduate school, we enjoyed a feeling of belonging to a special club, even if we didn't get all that we needed in the way of content and skills. It felt good to be under fire in the company of like-minded compatriots who shared our dreams and watched our backs.

Graduate school prepared us to be team players. Over and over we got the message that this inexact science of helping requires continual consultation and reality checks. Bouncing ideas off others, testing hypotheses, and challenging assumptions are the lifeblood of our work. Supervision and cooperative case management are imperative in a field where personal biases and distortions can so easily lead us astray. In addition, the emotional toll this work takes on our psyche is brutal. Continually, we are bombarded by assaults on our ego. In almost every session we must confront the most frightening human issues—of death and meaninglessness and loss of control and infidelity and a thousand others. By definition, our job is to listen to stories that no one else will hear and wrestle with themes that are so terrifying they threaten to eat people alive. Throughout all these challenges the one thing we can count on most is the support of our peers.

What a shock it is for the private practitioner to adjust to the isolation of such a private activity. Whereas clients definitely prefer the perfect solitude and protection of their privacy, for the clinician such seclusion can be suffocating. There are therapists whose whole days are spent only in the company of their clients. Besides a few quick notes to officemates and a few phone conversations into the outside world, virtually every minute is spent ensconced in the psychic bunkers of clients' lives.

Even those in group practices often find themselves famished for human companionship. Whereas in community agencies, staff members are required to attend meetings, inservice workshops, case conferences, independent therapists participate mostly on a voluntary basis. There is also a "foxhole mentality" to most clinicians in the public sector, a feeling of being unappreciated and underpaid for working with the most needy clientele. It becomes a major priority to spend time together over breaks, in the hallways, after work, bolstering one another's spirits. In private practice, there is the same need but less opportunity (or at least less motivation) to get together in similar ways.

"I keep saying I will meet with a few colleagues on a regular basis," one therapist admits sheepishly, "but something always seems to come up. It amazes me how my friends in university counseling centers and mental health centers actually get paid for sitting in meetings. For me, the meter is only running when I've got a customer who is talking."

The isolation is your greatest challenge in private practice, perhaps even more so than the pressure to stabilize your income. It is so easy to neglect your need for social nourishment. It is so easy to forget to take care of yourself.

With this potential for burnout and isolation clearly in mind, we suggest the following proactive means designed to encourage social contact:

- Schedule breaks in your day in which you spend time with people. This could involve meeting a friend for coffee or lunch, lounging at a health club or bookstore, setting up routines where you spend time walking or talking with colleagues.
- Become active in your local professional association. This is not only good for networking and referrals but also to help you feel a part of a larger community.
- Organize a support group. Meet on a regular basis (at least twice per month) with several trusted colleagues. Establish and agree on certain rules that are conducive to intimate contact rather than case or business meetings.
- Go to workshops, and when you are there, force yourself to reach out to others. Long after the content of the session has faded, you will still have friends you can rely on.
- Join a book club. Talk to people about ideas unrelated to your work.
- Get a life outside the office. Diversify your interests. Make friends with people who aren't in the same profession. Better yet, spend time with people who can't help you get referrals.
- Choose your officemates with the same care you would use to choose roommates. You have to live with these people for a significant part of your day. Make sure you are surrounded by those you can go to for a hug or a word of encouragement when you really need it.
- Add other professional activities to your day. Teach a course. Do a workshop. Consult with an organization. Do something that gets you out of your secluded chambers on a regular basis.
- Face the reality that in spite of how appealing these ideas sound, you will probably not do them. If you don't believe us, go talk to some veterans and ask them how often they take time out from schedules to nourish themselves. It is true that some therapists do, but not nearly enough. Scare yourself with the consequences of not reaching out to others—that you will become a burned out shell of a person who feels isolated from the rest of the world.

THE CLIMATE OF MANAGED CARE

You wondered when we would get to this. We saved the best part for last.

The peculiar phenomenon is that most of us went into independent practice because we yearned for freedom and autonomy. We were willing to trade the security of a regular paycheck and pension plan for the freedom of working the way we prefer. Now our professional judgments are no longer sacrosanct. The public is stuck seeing whoever is on their plan, no longer able to choose the practitioner who was recommended as most qualified to help them.

Karon (1995) summarizes the strategies of managed care organizations as:

- Spend no money on prevention of problems.
- Ignore high-risk populations.
- Employ less expensive personnel to do the work.
- Set quotas and limits on services provided.
- Make it difficult for consumers to get more service than has been allocated for them.

The absurdity of this reasoning, Karon argues, is that these companies are not interested in saving money in the long run but only over a period of 12 months. After that, the client will be on someone else's plan, thus *their* problem.

In one expose of the system, described in *Newsweek* (Beck, 1994), therapists speak of being blackmailed into compromising their standards and beliefs to conform to an immoral system. How much more intrusive can things get, one therapist asks, when he is queried by a managed care representative as to how *many* times his client was raped, was she *really* that bad, and couldn't AA work just as well as therapy? It is enough to chase people out of practice, and indeed it is doing just that.

"I've had enough!" one therapist sighs in exasperation. "It's time to move on. This just isn't fun anymore. If I wanted to be a technician and paper pusher, I would have gone to air conditioning repair school."

Bennett (1994) asks whether the prospect of making therapists compete with one another is really in the best interests of the public. Certainly in any market economy costs would be driven down. Unfortunately, you get what you pay for. He also wonders about the values implicit in a system that forces professionals to outbid one another for contracts rather than cooperating and collaborating together.

There are also consequences to compromising the therapeutic relationship by disclosing any information to a third party (Alperin, 1994). The clinician's trustworthiness is diminished. The client is made to feel even more uncertain and anxious about the future. Therapeutic ingredients like the placebo effect are reduced since the practitioner's own confidence is diminished by the continual doubts expressed by managed care reviewers: "Are you certain that you can help this person?" "Wouldn't it be better to try an alternative plan?" "We don't think this person is a good candidate for what you do." "We have decided you can't see this person any longer because we don't think you can help him."

Both client and therapist never forget that someone is watching every step they take, critically evaluating whether another one should be allowed. If that doesn't pollute the alliance and stir up unaccounted factors that could sabotage progress, we don't know what could.

ON THE OTHER HAND

Not everyone is lamenting the end of an era. Harris (1995) describes his mostly positive experiences with managed care. He has found case managers to be reasonable and open to his recommendations. When brief therapy is not indicated, he will not use it: "I don't believe in one-minute neurosurgery either."

In spite of the gripes and complaints, an overhaul of the mental health system was critical with costs spiraling out of control. Abuses by a minority of clinicians became a problem for everyone. Seeing clients far longer than necessary is a common example emphasized by cases involving celebrities such as director Woody Allen and musician Brian Wilson. They solidified public opinion that reform was necessary. In the latter instance, the former Beach Boy's therapist actually moved in with him, charging him for 6–10 hours of therapy per day!

Managed care was intended to help curb costs; in the process, it has made us more accountable for what we do. Other consequences of the new system are supposed to include greater access to our services by a larger segment of the population, and greater consistency among a variety of clinicians as to what we do with various presenting complaints. It would appear as if, in many ways, the managed care system is accomplishing its goals.

"At what price?" we can hear the chorus rising. Confidentiality is all but gone in the therapeutic relationship. If clients had any idea how easy it was for almost anyone with a little patience and skill to access their computer records, they would never open their mouths.

Many utilization and review managers seem to care less about client welfare than saving their company money. Treatment decisions are often based on expediency rather than on sound clinical judgment. There is a bias among reviewers in favor of problem-solving models that can specify goals and measure symptom alleviation. Clients who need a different sort of help are left out in the cold.

Once upon a time, many of us gravitated to this field because we enjoyed helping people grow, learn about themselves, find meaning in their existence, improve the quality of their lives, reduce conflicts in their relationships. Now we are told that this work is only possible for the very wealthy who can afford the services out of pocket. The rest of us folks are only permitted the luxury of a therapist if we have some specific, identifiable mental disorder that is amenable to treatment in a month or two. Chronic mentally ill? Too bad. Marital problems? Unfortunate, but no help available. Personality disorder? Tough luck. General malaise and unhappiness? Sorry.

In its best form, managed care should really be about accountability and external reviews of our work during an era when cost effectiveness has become paramount (Goodman, Brown, & Deitz, 1992). This, in itself, could be quite a lovely thing *if*: (1) the people reviewing our work are qualified, and (2) their intent is to provide better quality services to clients. Ah, if only that were so.

In reality, the credentials of external reviewers are woefully suspect, if not altogether inappropriate. In many cases, nurses, physicians, and managers without extensive training in therapy are the ones evaluating treatment plans. Nevertheless, even under these conditions, one consequence of managed care is that it is forcing us to wrestle with some difficult questions:

- Is the client a good candidate for what we do?
- Is my approach consistent with usual standards of care practiced by others?
- What outcomes are reasonably expected within what time parameters?
- Are the treatment goals and plan we've established appropriate and realistic?
- What am I missing?
- Is the approach we are using the most efficient means to help this client?

Questions such as these help us think more critically about the work we are doing. Even though we may resent the intrusion of answering to some external source, such accountability does help us to refine our methods.

DECISIONS, DECISIONS

In this presentation of the good, the bad, and the ugly aspects of private practice, you feel yourself being drawn to this type of setting or away from it, depending on where you are developmentally in your career. Should you be interested in pursuing this lifestyle, there are a number of issues for you to consider in the kind of practice you would create.

For example, would you operate as a part-time or full-time private practitioner? These two kinds are *so* different. The former is a hobby, a way to earn extra income, or balance other aspects of professional life. The latter clinician operates without a net.

It is quite common for those who wish to build a practice to begin slowly, while keeping their "day job." Once you have a sufficient referral base and case load, then you can make the transition. Others prefer to jump right in with both feet, an option that works well only if you have sufficient savings to carry you through the first year.

In addition to this decision, there are quite a few others for you to consider:

- to work alone or as part of a group practice
- to work in a home office or an outside office
- to design your office space economically or lavishly
- to hire a billing service or do it yourself
- to hire a supervisor/psychiatrist for ongoing consultations with caseload or on a case-needed basis
- to use a secretary/receptionist or an answering machine or service
- to invest in state-of-the-art computer equipment or keep things basic
- to specialize in one area (mediation, sexual abuse, etc.) or run a general practice
- to locate in an upscale market or a working class area
- to set your fees high, medium, or low
- to use a marketing and advertising budget or rely on word of mouth and personal contacts
- to generate your own referrals or have someone else do it
- to go after managed care contracts or private pay clientele

- to use a brief therapy model primarily or conduct medium-term relationships
- to incorporate as a business or operate as a simplified proprietorship
- to schedule limited hours or extensive availability

This is but a sampling of the decisions you must consider. Based on the ways you answer these questions, you set the tone for your practice. Will you operate in a formal manner? If so, you will have written contracts with your clients clearly spelling out the rules and boundaries. If there are last-minute cancellations, you will collect fees just as agreed in the terms. There are so many other questions to consider: How you will handle collections when clients don't pay their bills? How will you deal with holes in your schedule? What support will you build for yourself to counteract potential burnout? The essence of successful practice is related to the integration of work and play (Beigel & Earle, 1990). It is not a job or a career, but a lifestyle in which all parts of your life contribute to other segments.

In the next chapter, we consider another area that was all but ignored in graduate school, yet one that is also a critical part of successful practice. Preparing and delivering public presentations, whether as a means to generate new referrals or as a way to discuss current research efforts at a professional conference, will be our next topic.

CHAPTER SEVEN

Upgrading Your Presentations

Sooner or later success will bring offers to translate your knowledge into meaningful presentations to trainees, luncheons for business people, parent groups, or workshops for other therapists. Stepping out of your clinical world and into this presentation mode is never as easy as it might seem. First attempts at holding listener attention, communicating useful information, and making a positive impact will not work nearly as smoothly as your work with clients. These early frustrations will either lead you to become a better communicator of what you know or to quit and give all your attention to your clients.

Doing quality therapy takes a high level of communication skills and knowledge that we expect will transfer into all aspects of our lives. It never turns out to be that simple. Therapists get into inappropriate arguments, make enemies, and get divorces just like everyone else and a prime culprit is communication problems. Some of the very best therapists can also make the worst public speakers and teach the worst courses. The sad fact is that the communication skills we have fine-tuned with clients do not automatically transfer to other audiences.

IT'S HARDER THAN IT SEEMS

What we learned in graduate school about giving presentations was a mixed blessing. We witnessed the best and worst of this craft—professors who were so tedious, boring, arrogant, or disorganized that they made our teeth grate and others who were magical in their ability to captivate a classroom.

It is one thing, however, to have a captive audience of students who are required to attend each week, regardless of how bad the presentations are, and quite another to speak to volunteers who may, at any moment of their choosing, walk out of the room. In addition, professors are spoiled because they have the leverage to force students to pay attention, to take notes, to pretend interest they may not feel—after all, they will be tested on the material later.

Public speaking was another of the crucial skills that we didn't learn in graduate school, except for our own critical observations of our teachers. Even the opportunities for class presentations or acting as a teaching assistant may have provided relevant experience but often not much systematic feedback or supervision. Whereas most of us received intensive supervision talking to a client, and even guiding family and group interactions, speaking to larger audiences in lecture, workshop, or professional presentation formats was not covered in our education. Like so many other areas in which we identify deficiencies, we have been largely left to develop speaking skills on our own.

Just as most university faculty receive virtually no systematic instruction in the art of teaching—the assumption being that expertise alone is what matters most—so too are practicing therapists required to learn such methods through trial and error. Again, it is assumed that because we are good talkers during therapy sessions, it is a small matter to generalize those skills to a larger audience. Although it is true that public speaking does require abilities that therapists certainly have in abundance (fluency, flexibility, spontaneity, confidence), there are also many other qualities that may not be part of our repertoire.

At an international conference attended by representatives from two dozen countries, the schedule was packed with offerings by therapists—research papers and theoretical models, as well as more practical sessions. The presenters were brimming with confidence. Many of them were university faculty; others were seasoned veterans and supervisors. All of them were articulate, verbal, and like most therapists, used to speaking persuasively.

With such expertise and experience, you would expect that the quality of the presentations would be at a very high level. Most of the programs, however, were disorganized. Others, rich in content, were difficult to follow because the presenter's style was tedious. Even more amazing for a group of professionals who are supposed to be experts at helping people learn, they violated most of what is known about the rudimentary assumptions of educational psychology. Furthermore, the quality of the programs at this conference was not much different from those offered elsewhere.

The fact is that therapists have received very little training in the art and mechanics of presenting themselves effectively to large audiences, nor have they received systematic supervision that might improve their skills. When is the last time, for example, that you sat down with a group of colleagues who gave you specific, constructive, and useful feedback on a presentation to a large group?

Interestingly, all of us are expert critics of other people's work. We sit in the audience muttering to ourselves about how boring a speech is. We whisper to friends about how superficial the ideas are, or about some irritating mannerism of the speaker that interferes with our attention. While watching others in action, we seem to have little trouble identifying all the things they are doing wrong, all the things we would do differently if we were in their place. So why don't we?

The answer is that we might recognize a lousy presentation when we see one but that doesn't mean we can construct our own that is informative, engaging, and influential. After all, clients come to us in the first place because they can't see things in themselves that we recognize with little trouble. The same holds true with our own work before large audiences: We may be making some serious miscalculations and errors in judgment, but who will tell us if we don't ask?

WHY SUBJECT OURSELVES TO OTHERS' SCRUTINY?

Being sought out on a daily basis by people in need of our therapeutic services produces feelings of competence and acceptance that strengthen us for the more difficult times. Seeing clients get better from our efforts is rewarding and gives unquestionable purpose to our work. It is frustrating, however, during those times when we say such insightful things, pleased with our streak of brilliance or eloquence, and then recognize that our client never even heard us! We look around, waiting for applause, or at least some acknowledgment that our witticism or offering was heard, and we see the client staring off into space. At least when we are talking to a larger group, there is a greater likelihood that *someone* will understand what we are saying.

Indeed, speaking to a larger audience provides many of the same rewarding feelings you get from doing therapy, only on a larger scale. Here is a whole room full of people who find value in your knowledge and ability to communicate. It is such a kick to stand there before twenty or a hundred people or more and *know* that you have them in the palm of your hand. They are with you. They are laughing at your jokes. You can see by their faces they are understanding what you are saying. Even better, they are finding the ideas useful. Some people are looking thoughtful: You can practically hear the gears turning in their brains as they personalize some concept you have just introduced. Others are so animated, practically levitating with excitement and energy that you helped generate. A few others are looking puzzled, disturbed, or even upset, and that's okay too because it means that you have provoked something within them.

In addition to the personal satisfaction that comes from public speaking, you are also able to create wider recognition and acceptance of your practice, ideas, and abilities. These conditions bode well for a greater sense of success, which is good for your mental frame of mind as well as your economic status. Better business, greater therapeutic success, and a massaged ego: That's a pretty good deal for doing a little presenting, and we haven't even discussed being paid.

All good presenters work for no fee at times when communicating a message is the overriding goal. On the other hand, some therapists manage to turn presentations into a major dimension of their professional career. The most obvious example is the university instructor who gets paid for teaching students as a part of the job. The other highly visible example is the relatively small number of "hot" presenters who give up most or all of their clinical work to do speeches, workshops, and usually also write books. The vast majority of paid presenters, however, treat this part of their career only as a productive aside to their primary work. These therapists don't become millionaires by making presentations, but they choose to enjoy the variety of professional benefits including a few extra spending dollars for their efforts.

WHAT MAKES A PRESENTATION MEMORABLE?

Good presenters are asked to speak again and again because they gain a reputation for communicating meaningful information that others can incorporate into their daily lives. If you think about the best presentations you have attended, it is likely they had certain elements in common. What made this experience so fine was hardly that it was chock full of things you didn't know, nor that it was meticulously organized and impeccably delivered. Certainly these are laudable qualities of a good lecture, ones that we should all strive for; we would contend, however, that what most often makes a presentation memorable is that it touched you in a profound way. It may have reached your head, your heart, or even your soul, but on some level you walked out of the room a bit different.

So, how do we do that? How do we speak, or present ourselves, in such a way that we can impact a large audience with the same power and influence with which we reach our clients?

Reading the Audience

It is amazing how often professionals who are supposed to be experts at initiating learning seem to forget the most important principles when they are outside their offices. During the past few decades, for example, increasing attention has been moved away from the presenter to how the learner is reflecting on the information and process of the presentation (Houle, 1980; Schon, 1983). Good presenters are thus intimately connected to their audience: They know what they are thinking.

This is, of course, no different than our work with clients. The problem is that whereas when we are working with clients we suspend a formalized lesson plan in lieu of responding to "teachable moments" as they arise, when we are speaking we often become overinvested in our agenda so that we fail to make necessary adjustments according to how people are responding to what we are doing.

Seeing the Bigger Picture

The next step toward understanding your audience is realizing that professionals do not consider presentations their primary learning tool. A therapist confronted with a new client problem doesn't look first for a workshop or course to solve the problem. The first stop is a look through office bookshelves to see what might be available close at hand. The technologically adept therapist will likely also do a library search from the office computer. One study of male professionals clearly showed that this self-directed approach to vocation-related problems is consistently chosen as the preferred learning model (Matthias, 1991). Good presenters recognize that they only have a small, although significant, role in a professional's development.

The self-planned learning style preferred by one group of professionals (physicians) tends to be evenly split between more sedentary, cognitive approaches and active, experiential techniques (Fox, Maxmanian, & Putnam, 1989). Reading, thinking, and reflecting are the primary cognitive tools used when problems don't require immediate action. More intense situations, demanding immediate action, make learners more likely to revert to a limited number of tried and true sources of short, quick answers like manuals or consultation with peers or supervisors.

Speakers must realize that the presentation of numerous facts, no matter how eloquent or important, will never completely fulfill either of these preferred learning models. Instead, it is the ability to tap into an audience's energy and resources, and to use them effectively, that creates audience involvement and learning.

Harnessing Audience Energy and Resources

Social factors also help determine a presenter's impact on an audience. Therapists may plan their own learning, but they don't make choices in isolation. Learned pieces of information are mentally and then realistically tested in social and professional environments to see how well they really work (Boud & Griffen, 1987) and how credible and memorable that information will ultimately be (Baskett & Marsick, 1992). Presenters who recognize and tap into those environments are the ones that audiences see as asking the right questions and developing viable answers.

Just as when we are working with families or groups, we capitalize on certain dynamics that predictably arise as a result of human interaction, so too do large audiences play off one another's reactions. We see people whispering to one another, making eye contact, writing notes back and forth. We watch body language and facial cues that tell us whether what we are offering is useful or provocative. Good presenters use all of this information constantly. They not only read their audience, but also use what they sense going on in order to reach them at a deeper level.

Creating a Context

Progress in understanding how to train professionals has not overcome the reality that research continues to produce mixed results on exactly what works best for who and under what conditions. What may at first glance appear to be simple training concepts have proven to be much more complex in application. Attempting to identify and control all potential variables connected with directing and changing the thinking and actions of professionals remains a nearly impossible task (Fox et al., 1989). We may know many of the factors that influence learners, but the holistic picture of what would make a successful presentation is not yet in sight.

This complexity is even more of an issue working with the mature professional learner than the young student. Adults have a wealth of real-life experience and a need to know that new information directly relates to their experiences. In comparison, elementary, high school, and college students have less real-life experiences into which new information can be integrated. This is reflected in the learning tools that work better for youth than for adults. Rote memorization, for example, makes more sense as a childhood tool where there is little real-life context to give the information meaning and value. Adults, on the other hand, choose what they want to learn based on who they have been and what they want to be, making rote memorization increasingly less useful and more distasteful than information in context.

This view of adult learning that calls for the integration of past and present experiences with new knowledge and skills is referred to as a *modern constructivisim* (Smith & McCormick, 1992), an approach we spoke of in the earlier chapter on new paradigms that are impacting the field. As you may recall, this is an emerging postmodern philosophy driven by a variety of relativistic and relationship factors that focus attention on the infusion of information into the realities of an individual's existence. No beautifully said phrases, cute memorization schemes, hilarious jokes, or brilliant research findings will make up the learning gap left by a presenter who cannot connect information to the evolving real world of their audience.

The heart of this constructivist philosophy may well be the emerging study of *reflective practice* as a teaching/learning model. Reflective practice, like many familiar theories, emphasizes that selecting the best ways to think, feel, and act in the future requires first bringing related past events into consciousness (Jackson & Caffarella, 1994). People use past experiences to find the recognizable details, processes, and outcomes necessary to comprehend and internalize newly presented information. Such an integration of old and new information provides for maximum motivation to learn and demonstrates the practical implications of learning that audiences find most valuable.

A modern view of training adults, and particularly professionals, focuses on the importance of presenting information in a context clearly related to a particular audience's past experiences, current situation, and future plans. It encourages the use of the planning, observation, listening, and attending skills that all good therapists already understand and employ with clients, but often have difficulty transferring to their presentations.

Intellectual Stimulation

One of the misguided expectations that inhibits therapists in their speaking efforts is the belief that their job is to tell people things they don't already know (this is also true for those who feel blocked in their writing). Indeed, people do buy books and attend lectures and workshops because they think the expert will tell them something new. Disappointment sets in once it is realized that what is being heard (or read) is not that novel or is just another variation of a familiar theme.

Actually, in most situations, the job of a presenter (or writer) is not so much to supply some amazing new insight or content, as much as it is to stimulate constructive thinking and reflection in the audience. As one veteran attender of hundreds of workshops remarked:

I've been in this field a long time, so long in fact, I am no longer surprised that what I hear is something I once heard before in a slightly different form. No, what I'm looking for is someone to get me to think in new ways, someone to stimulate my brain and heart.

How does someone do that? Gee, I'm not really sure or I'd be doing that myself.

After further dialogue with this therapist, it is apparent that she does know how to stimulate growth—she does it every day in a different context. So do you.

HERE'S THE PLAN

Having just attended one morning convention presentation and another all afternoon, the exhausted therapist expressed her disappointment with the presenters in no uncertain terms:

The woman in the morning told jokes and stories that led nowhere that I could figure out. The guy in the afternoon started explaining an interesting idea in a way that was dull as mud. My mind started wandering and I lost all track of what he was talking about. Maybe together they might have made a decent team.

Entertainment, interest, details, big ideas, examples, and logical connections each have a special place in a quality presentation. Many presenters are better at some of these, often to the exclusion of others, which makes their presentations unbalanced and leaves audiences bored and confused. The trick is to recognize that the relationship between presenter and audience, much like any relationship, goes through stages requiring different considerations and interaction styles as things evolve. In the beginning, people may want to laugh and be entertained; they want to feel connected to the speaker. In the middle, they want handouts, they want "stuff"—they want to feel like they got something for their money. Next, they want the opportunity to apply the concepts to their own situations and lives. By this time, they are tired of sitting passively and need more active involvement. Finally, they may crave some sort of motivational speech that will insure that the effects will be enduring.

Professional Preparation

The overriding emphasis at the preparation stage is to know yourself, the issues, the audience, and the methods that will fit the particular combination best. Having a clear grasp of the strengths and limitations of yourself, your audience, and your presentation topic is the starting place.

Presenters gain respect and attention when audience members believe in the speaker's knowledge and ability to convey it. The most sought-after presenters have been through similar presentations so often that both they and their audience know beforehand how the presentation will go and how the audience is likely to react. These initially high expectations can often make even a weak presentation seem effective. No one starts out with such a reputation, but the time and energy used in preparation and self-examination will provide some degree of the same benefits.

The following questions will help you prepare for a presentation; the content and accuracy of your answers will go a long way in determining its relative success.

- What is the essential message for your presentation that all other objectives, content, and techniques will support?
- What do you know and how do you present best? How does it fit this particular situation and audience?
- How will you recognize and emphasize your strengths while identifying and limiting the negative impact of your weaknesses?
- How will you construct your presentation? Primarily for the purpose of informing, persuading, inspiring, or entertaining?
- Are there essential things you must or must not say or do?
- How will your audience benefit from your program? How will you assure that they recognize and value those benefits?
- When imagining yourself in the audience's position, what is their physical, emotional, and cognitive reactions to the content, process, and style of your presentation?
- How will you evaluate and react as your relationship with the audience changes?

- How well do your plans match audience expectations of topic, purpose, style, and length of presentation?

A Fast Start

You need to quickly engage the audience by creating a personalized and focused working relationship. The beginning is no time for thoughtful analysis and lists of important details. Making immediate connections is the key, just as it is in a therapy session. There is an unlimited variety of ways to begin, but jokes, storytelling, and questioning are among the most often used methods.

Humor, for example, can form a quick bond between people and situations that gives direct attention to similarities, joys, and hardships. Ineffective humor can be insulting and drive the audience and speaker apart. Humor that is not well-connected to the audience or topic may get people to smile, but leave them wondering about the value of the presentation. The safest bet is to focus any humor on your own situation as the speaker and your relationship to the audience and topic. Listeners will not be as insulted if the humor is on you and the transition from humor to topic gains credibility when they are related from the beginning.

We (RH & JK) don't use jokes, finding them contrived and artificial. We prefer instead to tell some story that reveals us in an authentic, vulnerable light in much the same way we have done throughout this book. That style may not work well for you at all, but we have found that modeling a kind of openness and sincerity, by sharing our fears aloud, makes it much easier for participants to take similar risks later.

It probably is advisable to avoid using one-line jokes as a connector to the audience. Listening and storytelling are the heart of therapy and each of us can recall innumerable touching moments, both poignant and lighthearted. The trick is to pick those stories that can briefly present meaningful points of emotional and experiential connection between audience, speaker, and topic and then present them in the most personal way possible.

Just as in therapy sessions, the most personal and effective stories are those with the most immediacy. What happened ten years ago to you will mean little unless its immediate impact on this particular audience is made obvious. A story that is happening as one speaks is best and the older a story gets the more attention needs to be paid to demonstrating connections to the present. Talking with organizers, leaders, and people in the audience beforehand will often provide current examples that can be used to connect your stories to the ones most recently recognized by participants.

I (RH) also like to start off every presentation by attending to those things being sought by the audience. You can do this in small groups by simply asking directly for comments as you begin. The largest groups require mingling with participants beforehand to get a sample of their experiences and what hopes they bring to the presentation. Most, if not all audience expectations, can generally be accommodated with a little flexibility on your part, since you and the audience should be coming together with similar assumptions. Even on those rare occasions where there is a major gap in presumptions, you are better off knowing of it beforehand. An openly admitted adjustment of your presentation and limiting of audience expectations is always better than plowing through a preplanned presentation that will disappoint everyone.

One Clear Message

We all know what it's like to be presented with tons of great-sounding information, only to end up feeling like we don't know how it all goes together. It's frustrating and makes remembering any individual point nearly impossible. Good presentations begin by providing a key message in the form of a simple sentence or an example that can be used throughout to hold all the pieces of the presentation together. This message is NOT the subject of the presentation, which might be brief therapy, clients with AIDS, communicating empathy, love in relationships, or a million other interesting topics. The message would be something different that encapsulates a meaningful set of actions, such as: "Empathy has no value to the client until you communicate it effectively" or "You can't avoid the insurance companies so develop the best possible relationships with them."

This one clear message model is not unique to making good presentations to professionals. The most memorable speeches, songs, theater productions, movies, and books have one main message repeated throughout to bring the audience back time and again to the main theme. Martin Luther King let everyone know in one of his most inspirational speeches that there was hope in a multitude of dimensions that he and everyone can view together because of his continuously emphasized experience, "I have a dream!"

Dr. King's speaking greatness was related, in part, to always presenting a simple but strong message that held a speech together. Each speech placed primary attention on one individual message throughout. Nonviolence, hope, strength of commitment, the unacceptability of bigotry, or equality for every human being, would each get their turn in the spotlight for a given speech on a given day. Audiences could recognize all the concepts, but only one example and one message would be repeated throughout to pull everything together. The audience left knowing the one message so thoroughly that all the other pieces could eventually be learned through its context.

A Handful of Ancillary Points

Solid preparation will always leave you with more information to present than people can effectively remember at one time. It has been known for some time there are limits to how many things people can remember reliably, usually not more than a handful. Think of treating these ancillary points, which are part of your main message, as you would with any client. When a major insight occurs during therapy, you stop exploration and focus instead on stabilizing immediate gains. You highlight the insights, examine them in detail, review them, and send the client home to experience them in order to solidify the gains.

Giving time and emphasis to a few key client insights per session is the same principle as keeping key presentation points to a manageable number. Highlight them in the introduction, use vivid examples for emphasis, lay them out in an organized way in the body of the presentation, and summarize them during the conclusion. Give ample time to flesh out the logical and experiential connections between points. Answer questions in ways that show relationships between examples, the message, and key points. Make the relationships between points as memorable as the message itself. This will send the audience home with memories and definitive feelings about the importance of your points rather than a head spinning with details immediately to be forgotten.

What do you do with all the extra useful information that goes beyond the ancillary points? Put it in handouts that people can use later and tell them how to get additional resources. The best single purpose of handouts and related materials is to provide an audience with the means to expand on the enlightenment they get from a presentation. It is the memorable message and key points you communicate that will encourage, remind, and direct the reader to learn more from other sources.

One More Time with Feeling

"Tell them what you'll say, say it, and tell them what you said with emphasis." This simple basic rule is often ignored when it gets to ending presentations. You got them excited, laid out your goals and plans, and followed through with an interesting body of information. Unfortunately, many conclusions are lost to poor time management that has people ready to leave before you've finished. At other times, speakers can feel so relieved that things have gone well that ending, not summarizing, becomes the primary aim.

Conscientiously following a plan that provides for a meaningful summary of critical issues is essential for a successful presentation. This is the time when the audience can confirm what they have been thinking, fill in any missing gaps, and place the overall presentation in context once more before they leave. They should be nodding their heads in agreement at this point in that "Yes, I really do have it!" pattern that tells you the message has been received as planned.

Uses of Technology

The worlds of teaching and pedagogy are influenced as much by recent innovations in technology as every other mode of communication. Evolutions in computer hardware and software, developments in video, audio, and presentation equipment are now revolutionizing the ways we present ourselves to audiences. By comparison, the meager overhead projector as a teaching aid seems primitive.

Certainly becoming familiar with, if not a master of, computer technology can enhance your presentations. It is so much easier to bring multimedia—music, films, slides, charts, graphs, illustrations—into the room with a minimum of fuss. Unfortunately, too often technology gets in the way of good presentations. Equipment sometimes doesn't work properly. Transitions between segments appear abrupt and disorienting. Most important of all, presenters forget that their best tool is not their computer or fancy transparencies, but the connection they develop with the audience.

We thus urge you to explore the creative use of technology in your presentations but to do so cautiously and judiciously. Remember that the medium IS the message, but the medium is YOU.

A Challenging Send-Off

A message that has value needs to be acted upon as well as understood; before an audience leaves, challenge them to take action. Sending your audience out with thoughts, emotions, and the will to implement what they learned is the same as providing meaningful homework assignments for clients. Your ideas become energizing rather than merely interesting: That is exactly the type of presentation that keeps people coming back for more.

Selecting meaningful challenges for your audience is dependent on their situations, the information presented, and the style in which you work best. The combinations of these circumstances creates an unlimited number of potential challenges, but a few samples of how to lead in to them may be helpful for starters. Any steps made toward commitment to action at this time will greatly increase the likelihood of concept application later.

- Ask participants *how* they will apply the information and *when* they will do it.
- Develop contracts for participants to complete before they leave.
- Have participants verbally commit to action to someone sitting nearby or the group as a whole if it is small.
- Provide options for greater and lesser commitment, emphasizing that either is better than no commitment.
- Model what you want participants to do by declaring commitments that you intend to complete.

A presentation plan begins with an opening that gets everyone excited about your issues. A smooth transition into the body of the presentation uses the excitement to explore the key points and details. Continuity of issues and a building of ideas, one to the other, leads the audience to a summary where a realization of their learning and enjoyment is confirmed. You then provide the challenge which only now are they ready to accept. An enlightened and aroused group then goes out to make great changes in the world!

That is the way it would work on paper every time. Plans on paper and in theory are great, but of course they never work out as smoothly in real life where interpersonal relationships must be taken into account. Just as teacher and student interactions are critical to the eventual success or failure of learning (Hazler & Carney, 1993), presentation success depends on the relationship between presenter and audience. No plan can assure that the personal dimensions of relationship building will be implemented effectively or how they will be received. Our experiences have convinced us that the following relationship factors can make a major difference in your success or failure as a presenter.

THERAPEUTIC TECHNIQUES IN TEACHING

A graduate student walked into the office, shut the door, and immediately began to sob. When she got herself together, she looked up and said:

I just don't get it. Dr. Jones was the most caring, reasonable, attentive, person I ever met when he was my therapist just last year. Now as an

*instructor he degrades people in the class, belittles my comments, has no
sense of humor, and shows no respect for any of us. How could he have
changed so much?*

Dr. Jones had not changed at all in this regard in the last fifteen years.
He was exciting, caring, attentive, observant, and thoughtful as a therapist.
Put him in front of an audience or a group of supervisees and he becomes
dull, arrogant, defensive, and derisive. He was never able to incorporate
into his presentation model the human relations skills he so professionally
practiced in the clinic. Dr. Jones may be the extreme case, but most
therapists suffer from milder diagnoses of the same problem: the inability
to integrate appropriate therapeutic skills into presentation behaviors.

We have mentioned several times how doing presentations and doing
therapy involve both the same and different skills. Clinicians know how
vital the skills of attentiveness, observing, and listening are to clinical
practice. Paying close attention and summarizing client thoughts lay the
foundation for using all our clinical knowledge and intervention techniques. "You must meet the client in their world first" is the starting place
for therapy and it holds a similarly high position for the best presenters.

It is amazing how much you can learn about audience members just by
watching them as you do clients. Their faces alone tell the stories of how
much they know, what their mood is, whether they are with you or
attending to some other world. Anger, joy, frustration, satisfaction, disappointment, exhilaration, boredom, and enlightenment are as equally available to your senses in the classroom as in the office. Effective attending to
them allows for evaluation of the situation, appropriate choice of reactions,
and provides the mechanism to form the most productive relationship
with an audience. Unfortunately, the different pressures that come with
presenting often cause therapists to overlook, disregard, or misinterpret
this information when it comes from an audience.

The differences between situational pressures that influence therapists
and presenters are real, but the size of these differences is often overesti-
mated. Clinical roles make it clear that we are to listen first and speak
second, while presenter roles might seem to suggest the opposite. The
reality is that we must also know the audience and we have every right,
obligation, and ability to directly seek more information about them. We
immediately invest clients in their work by asking why they have come
and then using all we know to facilitate their growth from that point. The
process works the same with an audience by allowing speakers to mold a

presentation around a solid understanding of unique audience characteristics.

Therapists and presenters both have expectations placed on them to be right all the time; we have a small margin for error. Inner struggles have taught us how to fight these expectations off as therapists, but the battle is often harder for therapist-presenters. First of all, we don't spend nearly as much time making presentations as we spend in clinical work. There is simply much less practice time available to develop our presentation skills. Then there is the fact that the tens, hundreds, or even thousands of people in an audience multiply the effects of those expectations of perfection far beyond the single individual we see in therapy. You can judge quickly how to react to one client sitting three feet away, but when there are multitudes at varying distances it becomes impossible to gauge each one individually.

The pressure to be brilliant, wise, and right is greater on the presenter in many ways, but the way out is the same: You personally reject the idea of your perfection, let the listener know, and then prove it by admitting when you are guessing, when you are confident, and how you are arriving at your decisions. This model promotes your integrity; it allows the validity of your ideas to be seen while maintaining your most human characteristics and foibles.

ATTENDING TO AUDIENCE NEEDS

We begin working with clients based on where they are when we first see them. A client arriving in a highly emotional state is allowed time to calm down before beginning complex cognitive work. We follow rather than direct the client who begins immediately talking about his problems. A hot drink is the ticket for a person shivering from the cold. Each decision about how to proceed is based on our assessment of the client's immediate needs as well as long-term goals. The same should hold true for presentations in that we must evaluate and attend to immediate audience needs as well the information we are to present.

Maslow's (1968) hierarchy, for example, offers a structure for making a quick determination of immediate audience needs. Is the room too hot or cold? Do participants need breaks to empty their bladders or replenish nourishment? Are they feeling socially comfortable around other people here? To what extent are fears of failure inhibiting their courage? How much direct challenge can they handle?

Poor presenters often presume the audience is operating at the self-actualization level, seeking nothing more than their self-directed individual growth. It does not take brilliance to quickly recognize that people who are hungry, cold, hot, sleepy, worried about the bee flying overhead, or thinking about getting home through the storm outside will be attending to those needs more than the presentation. Physical signs like squirming in seats, looking out windows, checking watches, or a far-off look are easily recognizable signs. We know this sounds so obvious, especially for experienced therapists. We are amazed, however, how professionals who really should know better don't, in fact, notice these fairly basic cues.

BE WHAT YOU WANT OTHERS TO BE

The best learning and the most enjoyment for an audience comes when the information presented matches what is actually happening during the presentation. Outstanding presenters who are excited about their topics will be demonstrating both the sensations and the use of the information, as well as conveying the pieces of information through words. Combining visual and verbal cues in your presentation to convey the cognitive and emotional elements of a topic produces a more holistic learning experience that is far preferable to what information alone can offer.

Many presenters find success in presenting the verbal and visual aspects of their ideas by speaking about the cognitive factors and using exercises or visual aids to demonstrate the more emotional ones. The audience benefits from the two dimensions, although care must be taken to assure that the two presentation modes effectively match. The problem is that the discussion of a topic comes from your point of view and knowledge base, while a video or group exercise comes from someone else's phenomenological arena. Taking time to switch presentation modes is also time-consuming as each move requires an introduction, body, and conclusion for maximum value.

The most effective way to coordinate the verbal and nonverbal elements of a presentation is to do them yourself. Audience members have great appreciation for this model because it is not seen that often. They may not recognize exactly what is happening during such a presentation, but they certainly see the benefits.

I could see what he was saying would work because he was doing it right there in front of me.

She was a walking advertisement for her ideas.

I was worried that I wouldn't get it because the ideas were so complex. It was seeing her perform the ideas while she was speaking that simplified them and made them recognizable.

The more you can integrate the behavioral and emotional aspects of the concepts into your personal presentation, the more strength and meaning they will convey. For example, a logical, cognitive, and challenging style better fits a cognitively oriented presentation, while conveying more empathy, listening, and caring would be in tune with a discussion of more experiential approaches. A sad subject should have a slow pace with a quiet presentation, just as an upbeat and exciting issue should be accompanied by heightened voice level, a faster pace, and more demonstrative body movements. Maintaining congruence in all aspects of your personal presentation provides for continuity and can also be used to call the audience's attention to what is happening for reinforcement of the concepts.

GROWTH AS A PRESENTER

The concept of growth as a presenter has two sides: consolidation and expansion. Consolidation refers to a desire to do a better job with those things we cognitively understand but have a hard time practicing in our presentations. This consolidation of abilities and knowledge often fights with a desire to expand our work into new audiences, new skills, and new abilities. We must recognize that these competing desires require different proportions of our energies and time, depending on where we are in the growth process.

Consolidation is needed when we have more good ideas about presenting than we can presently implement to our satisfaction. Practice is an obvious need; however, it will not succeed on its own if you are not practicing the appropriate behaviors. The starting place for this form of growth is evaluation of your work by others. Formal assessments from your audiences and giving attention to the more informal verbal and nonverbal audience expressions provide separate means for examining your work. Asking an experienced colleague to attend a presentation for the specific purpose of evaluating your work provides another form of assessment. Without the need to learn from your presentation, this outside evaluator can take more time to judge both the generalities and details of your work. Evaluations that identify where and how we are not implementing what we already know are essential to establishing the things we most need to practice.

Growth can also be viewed as exploring those areas we do not currently know exist. You may have read some of the material here and said, "I knew that," thereby consolidating what you already knew. There should also be ideas that struck you in a different way, "I never thought of that!" These are ideas you needed to seek in a new resource such as a book, article, lecture, life experience, or even a new relationship. The most essential element in developing exploratory growth is to put yourself in new situations with new resources for information and feedback.

Exploratory growth promises more excitement than consolidation, but it also carries the baggage of more anxiety. Striking out to speak about new topics, to larger audiences, or the same audiences in significantly different ways, will bring you into conflict with the need for security of the known over the unknown. All the highlights associated with overcoming major obstacles and conquering new worlds are available if you can find the energy and psychological strength to go beyond your present work and overcome a nagging fear of failure.

You may make giant strides or only small steps in your presentation future. There will be choices to make about going forward or enjoying your present status. The quality of your decisions will not be based on which direction you choose, but instead on the satisfaction you and your audiences feel about the image you offer and the viability of the information you communicate.

CHAPTER 8

Publishing for Profit and Pleasure

You work days, evenings, and when you can't get out of it, weekends as well. There is never enough time for it all: helping clients in distress, tending to emergencies, learning new therapeutic methods, consulting, supervising, teaching, expanding your client base, and trying to earn a living. If you are lucky, you may even squeeze in a little leisure time. So why would any overloaded therapist consider taking on the additional work needed to write and publish original ideas?

Therapists publish for a number of personal, professional, and economic reasons:

Recognition. There are few kicks in life more pleasurable than seeing your name in print. Likewise, there is tremendous satisfaction in showing your latest publication to your parents or children, your partner, colleagues, and friends. It feels wonderful to be recognized for a job well done, to have a part of you that is now in black and white.

It is often so frustrating that we say such wonderful things to our clients who may or may not even be listening. We create such interesting ideas that nobody ever hears about outside of our immediate circle of peers. To be able to circulate our ideas to a wider audience, and have others respond to what we've written, is sometimes more than any of us could expect. It is even more fulfilling to see something we've written cited in another publication, telling you that you have had an impact on someone else, you have made a contribution to the professional literature.

Fame. Whereas recognition is a modest but attainable dream, fame is an unrealistic fantasy for all but a few people every generation. Like the striving for riches, the pot of gold at the end of the journey is not as

141

important as the fun we have with the image of ourselves having really made it to the top.

Fame, or actually a kind of reputation of expertise, translates into increased credibility. There are two ways for a therapist to attain this recognition: first, through word of mouth from hundreds of clients you've helped over a period of decades; second, through the dissemination of your ideas through a widely read publication.

Immortality. One thing that is true for writers is that our words live long beyond our own physical occupancy of this planet. It is exciting to consider that in libraries, or even people's homes, there will rest on shelves an obscure copy of something you wrote long ago. Decades, even centuries from now, some therapist in the future can look back and read something that you once described.

Opening doors. There is no doubt that publishing leads to a number of options that would not be available otherwise. For those in academia, publishing is a necessary part of job survival. However, even practitioners find that publishing leads to opportunities for consulting and collaboration.

With the increased popularity of electronic media via the Internet, more and more therapists are also "publishing" their ideas through various interest networks. While such writing efforts are not subjected to the same sort of rigorous editing and peer review that is common for traditional publishing, this medium does give the author a similar experience of what it feels like to send ideas out into the world and have them responded to, even circulated to others. These communications often lead to networking and other interesting opportunities.

One therapist in New Zealand sent out a request for help with a case to a contact in North America. She wanted information on dealing with multiple personality disorders. Her contact passed the message along to another colleague who was experienced in this area. She then sent the New Zealander a host of valuable information on the subject that was then circulated to others in the country. This lead to an invitation for the author to come across the Pacific to do a workshop on the subject.

Any number of other opportunities for travel, interaction, consultation, and collaboration are possible, but only if other people in the world are aware of your ideas. This is only possible if you arrange to publish what you create.

Fortune. Well, not exactly fortune; more like a few extra dollars for spending money. In spite of myths to the contrary, very few writers ever make enough money to even compensate them for their time. 90% of books that are published don't sell enough copies to break even, much less shower the author with wealth. Still, it is a motivation for some therapists to write with the hope that they will be paid a fair wage for their creative efforts. Certainly, it is a pleasant surprise to receive even a modest check in the mail for a magazine article or book that you have written. Although financial rewards for writing are rarely realized to the extent that the author hopes, this fantasy does act as an incentive for some to continue their efforts.

Personal satisfaction. This reason is the most crucial of all. Since the life of a writer is filled with rejection letters, critical reviewers, and endless drafts, it has got to be a labor of love, one you undertake because you enjoy the process of creation as well as the end result.

Altruism also plays a role in the motive of a writer. For the same reason that we see clients in order to make a difference, publishing our contributions helps us to reach a wider audience. This has less to do with self-promotion than it does fostering a spirit of scientific and artistic innovation. We all wish to make a productive contribution to our profession and our community. It is unfortunate that so many practitioners with wonderful ideas inhibit themselves from taking risks just like their clients.

PROCRASTINATION AND INHIBITION

Therapists are professional communicators. We use language to inform and influence our clients. We have been trained to speak persuasively and poetically, in such a way that people will listen to our messages, even when they would rather not. We convince them to do things they don't want to do. We tell stories that are designed to teach lessons about life. We describe things in such a way that people see nuances that were previously hidden from view. In other words, we are very good talkers—articulate, cogent, and convincing.

Why, then, do so many therapists inhibit themselves when it comes to expressing their ideas in written form?

Each of us (RH & JK) edits journals and columns in a professional newsletter, as well as a series of books. In addition, we read hundreds of papers written by student counselors each year. During the inevitable discussions that take place over these written pieces, whether in face-to-face interactions or by letter, fax, phone, or e-mail, we are struck by a consistent theme—the pervasive feelings of inadequacy and low confidence that very polished speakers experience when they try to write down their ideas.

Certainly there is a more rigorous set of rules related to writing then there is to speaking. Some of the apprehension is related to a lack of skill and practice. However, most of the inhibition comes not so much from a lack of aptitude as it does a fear of criticism. Editors do indeed go through each line you write with a magnifying glass. The prospect of this once-over is enough to strike panic in the hearts of many clinicians who would very much like to invest more time in writing but don't want to subject themselves to such intensive scrutiny. Inertia and procrastination result.

People spend more time thinking about writing and talking about writing than they ever do actually sitting down and doing it. Certainly such reflection and engagement with others about ideas is useful, even necessary, in order to attain some degree of excellence in what you create. There is a difference, though, between systematic preparation, research, hypothesis testing, critical thinking, and flat-out procrastination.

Often a manuscript arrives at our doorstep that contains some serious contributions. We make several suggestions for revision, edit the prose lightly, and then promptly return the piece for a bit more work. Often the reworking of the article can't take more than a few hours additional work—on a bad day. Yet weeks go by, sometimes even months, before we hear from the author again.

At first, we wondered whether it was the person's prerogative not to make the changes we wanted. We figured they sent the article elsewhere or maybe even decided not to publish it until they could refine their ideas further. Only through follow-up have we learned that most often the authors just sit on the manuscript. They say they are too busy. They say they meant to get back to it but just got distracted by other things. They say they are still thinking about how they want to revise it. The real reason for the inertia, we have discovered, is not for any of these stated excuses but rather something far more familiar to us.

After all, so many of the clients we see struggle with fear of failure. They are reluctant to try new things or venture out of their safety zone because they don't want to subject themselves to criticism and rejection. Now look at the symptoms of most budding therapist-writers who compromise their own fluency and productivity. They don't metabolize feedback well, being unable to separate the product from the self. They become defensive, even angry, when reading the reviews of their work. They fear being judged good enough, not only as writers, but also as professionals. The waiting period between drafts is often about building courage to submit the work again and risk rejection. Sound familiar?

If you are going to write and attempt to publish your work, then criticism and rejection come with the territory. Whether your reasons for writing relate to profit or pleasure, you have the necessary abilities for success; most therapists do. What holds you back is an inability to engage the struggles needed for growth, to make the necessary time commitment, or to maintain an accurate perception of how the process works.

Publishing is a game with its own unique set of rules, some of which are accessible to most anyone who cares to investigate the arena and others that are rarely spoken about aloud. Personal choice will dictate your commitment and willingness to engage in the process, while the information contained in this chapter and other sources can help you increase the likelihood of your success. The main objective is to gain a feeling of being more like a family member in the publishing world rather than an outside observer.

PUBLISHING AS A FAMILY BUSINESS

The insiders of the publishing world know what reviewers and editors are looking for, while the outsiders don't. Journals look for material that fits their audience just as book publishers seek manuscripts that can sell to specific markets. The process operates very much like a family business by encouraging and rewarding those who attend to family and business needs.

Imagine an entrepreneur who would like to add a new dimension to a long-standing family business. Skepticism is the first reaction of the owner, but a good businessperson looks further to see what the entrepreneur knows about the business and the family: "I don't recognize you, but perhaps you can tell me a little about what you know of our family and what you would bring to the business?" The entrepreneur who shows little knowledge of family history and business expectations is not going to get very far.

The editor of *The Counseling Psychologist* expects to see articles written to meet the needs of clinicians (family members) and not experimentalists, who will be reading other journals. Readers of the *Journal of Humanistic Psychology* expect thoughtful material on the human condition, not the latest behavioral approach. The *Journal of Experimental Psychology* is looking for solid research, not thoughtful experiential pieces. Even more precise are the target audiences of book publishers who have done extensive market surveys to determine exactly what will sell and what will not. For example, textbook publishers realize that although texts are written for students, it is really professors who decide whether to adopt them; such books are not actually sold to the consumers. Publishers know that the professional market is made up primarily of social workers and psychologists in their thirties and forties who purchase books primarily through direct mail advertisements; they do not expect to sell therapists' material to the broader audience who frequent chain bookstores.

Each journal or book editor has a different family of readers to please even though they all require neatly typed, double spaced manuscripts that follow specific submission guidelines. Although this point may seem rather obvious, you would be amazed by how often authors send their manuscripts to places that don't publish works remotely related to their own. The author did not investigate very carefully to see if what he or she created matched the style and scope of the particular publishing outlet. As one editor remarked:

It doesn't take a genius to know what's going on when someone sends you a "dear editor" letter or, even worse, they refer to an editor who has been gone for five years. This person is not likely to know what we currently publish.

A thorough understanding of family member desires, behaviors, beliefs, feelings, and common knowledge is what makes communication within families so natural and easy. Outsider opinions of the family are not accepted very well because they don't fit expectations. Publishing works in much the same way. Writers must understand the family of readers being approached as well as the heads of the families; the editors and publishers. The better you get to know the publisher, the journal, the readers, and the unique aspects of the editing process, the more success you will have at producing what is needed and wanted (Hazler, 1992).

There are several ways to gain inside knowledge about a particular publishing outlet. First of all, study previous publications. Make yourself a student of the content and style that has been used before. There is no sense in sending in an article or book on what therapists never learned in graduate school if the journal or publishers already produced something similar a few years ago.

You may also wish to consider working with a coauthor who already has a track record of successful publishing efforts. Book publishers, in particular, are not inclined to risk their money with someone who is, as yet, unproven. Even with article submissions that are reviewed blindly, readers can tell instantly whether the author(s) is a member of the inner club.

Whether you work alone or with a coauthor, it helps to talk with members of the editorial board, or even the editor, to find out about what they are looking for. Most editors are quite amenable to speaking with prospective authors about their ideas, letting them know if the plans fit their own agenda. This is not unlike the process we undertake when we work with families in therapy. We first study their patterns and rules before we try any direct intervention. Particularly with journal articles, when you are only allowed to submit an article to one place at a time and the turnaround time can take many months, you don't want to make the mistake of submitting a manuscript without being fairly certain that your piece fits what they are usually seeking.

FINDING WHAT YOU WANT TO WRITE ABOUT

Selecting the best topics for writing requires a combination of knowing what readers are interested in, what they need to hear, what you know, and what you can write about effectively. There is no way to identify the one right topic because it does not exist, so most writers publish in a variety of places and on several topics. This also helps to cushion the blow of rejection when those negative reviews come in. We (JK & RH) have both followed a policy throughout most of our writing careers of working on several projects simultaneously so if one isn't well-received there are other options being developed.

A search for quality writing topics begins with renewed exploration of yourself. The issues that hold your interest and make use of your knowledge, experience, and beliefs are the ones to look for first. Even experienced writers need to reexamine their direction periodically in order to maintain enthusiasm, keep current, and expand their sphere of influence.

We struggled mightily before settling on the topic of this book and shaping it into acceptable form. We wanted to write about something truly original and provocative, to stretch ourselves into new areas, and to fill a gap that we could identify in what was already published. Months of dialogue by phone, letter, and e-mail, left us no closer to settling on a viable topic. It was only after spending a week backpacking in the Grand Tetons that we finally found the seeds for this present idea. Even then, it wasn't until the last possible moment, as we separated at the airport, that the title jumped out at us. This unpredictable creative process between coauthors, or between different parts of yourself, is not unusual. In order to write about something original, you must be willing to explore the deepest parts of yourself, your relationships with your clients, and your most provocative beliefs.

The following statements are examples of ways to brainstorm about future writing projects. While these stem sentences are quite useful to muse about or write in a journal, you will find it even more stimulating to talk to colleagues about what comes to mind and heart:

- The professional issues I feel most strongly about are . . .
- What I know for sure is . . .
- What puzzles me the most is . . .
- Something I've always wondered about is . . .
- One thing that nobody talks about is . . .

As one example of this process of settling on an idea for a future writing project, I (JK) had been leading a therapy group in which one man had been talking about something that was quite important to him. In the middle of his most passionate statement, a woman in the group began quietly crying. Obviously, she was relating on a deep emotional level with something that was sparked by this man's disclosure. All attention in the group then moved away from the man to the woman, trying to offer her comfort and help her to articulate what her tears were saying.

After several minutes the man jumped in, enraged.

"What is it with women and crying? There I was talking about something very important to me, trying to talk about what I was experiencing. Then she [points menacingly at her] starts crying and ya'll drop me like a hot potato, leaving me boiling over here, while you give her all the attention. Do I have to cry in order to be heard in this group?"

Several minutes of discussion followed in which the participants talked passionately about the differences between the ways that men and women cry and respond to tears. And while one part of me was leading this group, trying to moderate things and keep them under control, a voice within me was whispering: "Yeah Jeffrey, why do *you* have so much trouble dealing with women who are crying? In fact, now that we're on this subject, how come you, who is supposed to be so sensitive, never cry?"

I quickly shut that annoying voice up, telling myself that I had to deal with the volatile situation at hand (I am quite good at denial). Yet the first glimmering of a new writing project had shown itself—the subject of crying. I began to wonder what crying was for, how it evolved. I thought about the ways that men and women are so different in the ways they cry and respond to others' tears. Most of all, I was curious about why I had long ago stopped crying except in the most dire circumstances.

It wasn't until several months later that I found myself in a life-threatening situation while hiking alone in the New Zealand bush. Faced with my imminent death, I found that I really could cry quite fluently when the situation called for it. Ever since that time, I have been crying quite a lot. So what the heck happened, I asked myself?

It was from these two experiences, one professional and one personal, that a book was born about the *Language of Tears* (Kottler, 1996). The creative process of settling on the idea is one that is familiar to most therapists. We spend hours in our office listening to clients talk about the most poignant, provocative, private subjects that exist. During times when we are stimulated by the discussion, bored by the proceedings, or frightened by the theme, we lapse into our own thoughts. Not a day goes by that you don't reflect on some topic that is worthy of its own article, if not a book. The hard part, however, is to convert an elusive idea, or even a well-developed line of thinking, into a focused manuscript.

FINDING THE RIGHT FORUM FOR YOUR WORK

Most therapists involved in professional writing develop a pattern of what they write about, as well as where they publish it. They tend to find a primary niche in journals, books, or newsletters, and less frequently, magazines. The pattern emerges as writers develop a thorough understanding of what it takes to match the needs of one specific family of readers better than others. Just as it takes one sort of mentality and set of skills to write novels or children's stories as opposed to nonfiction, so it takes a different focus to write scholarly versus popular articles, or trade versus textbooks.

Success is far more likely if you concentrate initially on one type of writing style for one type of publication (Thompson, 1995). The confidence gained through having greater success with research journal articles rather than books, for example, makes it more likely that you will look to journals again with your next publication idea.

Experienced and new writers alike can benefit by reminding themselves of the key differences between various forums for publications. Each vehicle meets different reader needs and requires different writing approaches. The more sources in which your work appears, of course, the greater your overall influence on the profession.

Newsletters

Newsletters are the most overlooked and undervalued vehicle for publishing, especially by those who are just getting their writing careers going. As the workhorses of communication in professional organizations, newsletters are produced more frequently in order to provide the most timely and practical information to readers. The emphasis on timeliness brings about particularly strong requirements for brevity and practicality, where professionals can get the facts fast and move on to the next article.

Newsletter articles are generally one of five types: (1) information on the business of the profession, (2) opinions about current issues, (3) reports of experiences in the field, (4) "how to" articles in which practical techniques are described, and (5) book reviews. You would also be amazed at how hungry editors are for submissions in any of these areas. In fact, as long-time newsletter editors ourselves, we are willing to share the secret that we rarely reject a manuscript. As long as the author is willing to rewrite the piece as many times as it takes (usually an average of 4 drafts), the article will eventually see publication. We are, therefore, amazed at how difficult it is to recruit professionals to write for newsletters, especially considering how vast the audience may be.

Experienced therapists often want to tell about their professional experiences, and newsletters are the easiest place do that. Stories that can be kept brief, interesting, and relevant to readers are among the most interesting columns. This is also the place to share those "Five Most Effective Techniques I've Ever Used." Newsletters are a great match between readers who love practical tidbits and therapists who want to share them.

Newsletter articles are shorter, less well-documented, and often held in lower esteem than their cousins in journals and books. What they lack in the professional graces they make up for in reader attention and writer opportunities. Busy students and therapists often remark that newsletters are the only professional publications they regularly read cover to cover.

Journals

Major professional organizations generally publish both a newsletter for currency, opinions, and greater flexibility of documentation, and a journal where evaluation of material is formalized and involves more reviewers. Two to four editors will generally review a manuscript submitted to a professional journal to assess its value, support for ideas, and the quality of writing. The process is slow and can take from eight months to two years or more for an article to make it into print. Even getting an article into a specific journal is no sure task for the best of writers. Journal editors generally have many more manuscripts submitted than they can publish so rejection is a regular occurrence for those who submit manuscripts.

Details, logic, and supporting information in scholarly journals replace the brevity and timeliness of newsletters. Extra professional credibility comes with the more scholarly approach to journal articles even if they are not read as quickly as newsletter articles. Strong support of ideas and peer evaluation are demanded because journal articles are the historical record of theory and practice of a profession (Jaeger & Hendricks, 1994). A well-written journal article on one small issue should demonstrate clearly how it adds to a line of thought and research. Potential applications of findings and suggestions for where the next steps might be taken provide others with directions to the next level of concept development and provide necessary closure to a quality article.

If we have not lost you yet because of the high rejection of journal articles, we'd like to remind you how important it is to do your research on various publications. Whereas some journals have a rejection rate of over 90%, some newer peer-reviewed journals may accept well over half the submissions.

Regardless of the outlet, it is highly unusual to have an article accepted by the first journal you submit to. If your article is accepted, usually with revisions suggested, then your only task is to follow the instructions carefully and include a letter detailing all the changes you made. More likely, your first submission (as well as second and third) will be returned with reviewer comments that may be highly critical. Evaluate this feedback carefully, incorporating the best ideas into your next draft. Of course, if none of the reviewers like much of what you've done, you may need to reconceptualize the piece.

There could be two reasons for negative feedback: (1) the article truly isn't very good, or (2) the reviewers aren't very good at their jobs. The second situation could be the result of some very personal bias on their part, or perhaps something in your article they found threatening. We are not trying to give you ammunition by which to ignore reviewer comments that aren't consistent with your own views; rather, we are reminding you that occasionally peers don't like work that is beyond their own levels of understanding. There are many cases in which truly innovative and excellent work was not appreciated during the author's lifetime.

At this point, we'd also like to say a few things about dealing with rejection. If you are going to submit your work for publication, then you had better get used to receiving rejection letters. What makes a good piece of writing is not what you've done on the first draft, but what you've developed by the third or forth.

You must be able to separate evaluation of your work from you as a person. You must be able to metabolize criticism in a way that you don't become overly frustrated and discouraged. The reality is that as a beginning writer, your work is going to be rejected a lot. Until you develop skills, learn the rules of the game, make contacts within the field, and develop a reputation, you are going to hear lots of bad news.

To make matters worse, rejection letters are often impersonal:

Dear _____

Thank you for your recent submission. You have developed some very good ideas and made a substantial contribution [so far, so good]. Unfortunately, [uh-oh, here it comes] because of the high number of submissions, and backlog of manuscripts already accepted [They always say this], we are unable to accept your manuscript.

We wish you the best and hope you will consider us for your future projects.

Sincerely _____

Frankly, many people struggle with rejection letters to the point where they give up. In some cases, that may be an intelligent move if it means accepting your limitations; not everyone is cut out to be a professional writer. The greater problem is that most therapists do have the ability but give up on the joys of being published out of a fear of rejection.

As difficult as rejection is to accept, it can also provide unexpected benefits when the emotion is overcome. Our (RH & JK's) relationship actually began several years ago when, upon a first meeting, Jeffrey introduced himself by saying "Hi, I'm Jeffrey Kottler. You rejected my article!" We had a good laugh and talked about our similarities, differences, what we do, and how we see things. What has evolved is a close personal friendship and professional expansion for both of us.

Our example is not a common one, for most rejected authors and rejecting editors would prefer to avoid each other and the potential emotional trauma involved. It does demonstrate, however, a possible benefit of fighting through those anxieties.

If you do decide to write articles in professional journals, you greatly increase the likelihood of having your manuscript accepted if you follow the accepted standardized format. After all, the most common reason why articles are rejected is not because of their content but because they are not organized properly (Dies, 1993). This is particularly surprising when you consider that most contributors have already completed a structured research assignment in the form of a dissertation or thesis.

Close attention must be paid to organization since all publications expect you first to tell readers what to expect, then give them what you said was coming, and finally summarize the essentials. There is great variety within this general structure, but that does not change the overall demands for a consistent beginning, middle, and end for every manuscript in every publication.

This basic three-part manuscript can be expanded to include additional subsections, which can be emphasized to meet a particular publication's needs. Readers and editors have a set of questions they expect to be answered at specific times during a manuscript. Answering the questions at the appointed times places the reader's full attention on the ideas presented rather than diverting attention to a study of the writing. Here is the generic structure of most articles:

Introduction. This is the place for providing a clear statement of the central issue and rationale for the manuscript. Demonstrating credibility and personal relevancy for the reader is essential, as well as addressing the following questions:

- What is this central issue you are discussing? (problem)
- What is the significance of this study? (purpose)
- How will this article benefit me? (personal/professional change)

Method. After the introduction, the writer must draw a brief but clear picture of the method(s) used to collect and present information. Readers will be more attached to the material if they know the connections between the format for presentation, the origins of the information, and how these meet their needs.

- How will ideas be presented and why in that particular way? (flow of ideas)
- From where did the information originate? (sources)
- Why is this the best way to collect and present the information? (validity)
- How could what you described be replicated by someone else who wanted to confirm your work? (reliability)

Results. This is the home of the details. Everything up to this point should have led the reader on a logical and structured path pointing directly to this information. The writer must present it as simply and clearly as possible.

- What did you find? (content categories and specifics)
- What is the relationship between aspects of the information? (logical order of data)
- How much and how good was the information? (quantity and quality)

Discussion and conclusions. Many readers turn here after deciding the manuscript is indeed important to them. They are searching for the meaning and practical value for themselves that you seemed to promise in the introduction. Fulfill that promise in ways that make direct use of the previously presented information which made up the bulk of the manuscript. This is not the place to say whatever you want. Instead, it is your job to show how your presented findings lead clearly to logical conclusions.

- What exactly was said? (brief summary)
- How should the information presented be judged? (consideration factors)
- How are the initial problem and collected information connected? (logical relationships)
- What can be done with this information? (practical applications)

References. The most thought-provoking pieces always leave the reader wanting more. References are the map to where that additional information can be found. Books and journal articles traditionally list other books and articles used while newsletters and magazines may only give directions for finding one or two main follow-up places or people.

- Are references in the form expected for this publication? (style)
- Is enough information provided to acquire the originals? (completeness)
- How extensive and current are the references? (number and age)

The preceding structure must sound very familiar to the reader since it so closely resembles the format for writing dissertations, theses, or term papers that you used in graduate school. It is surprising, therefore, that the large number of manuscripts crossing editors' desks don't come close to following either this general standard format or the specifics of format and style as set by the *Publication Manual of the American Psychological Association* (APA, 1994).

Even the most respected writers sometimes lose track of this model, a phenomenon that was a major surprise to me (RH) when I became editor of a national journal. Among the most difficult challenges was having to tell well-published authors that their manuscripts did not conform to the most rudimentary standards.

Magazines

The differences between professional journals and magazines are driven by profit. Magazines exist by their ability to convince as many readers and advertisers as possible to pay the price for reading and advertising. This is a far cry from most professional journals that focus on the professional validity of what they publish for organization members who pay no additional fees for the journal.

Catching and holding the interest of as many readers as possible is the key to attracting the buying public to a magazine article. Excitement, readability, and entertainment become the driving forces that replace the journal's emphasis on fitting into a line of research. Written well, these articles make interesting reading, but their validity is regularly questioned by the professional community.

A few other things you should know about this forum is that getting material accepted is even more difficult than a journal. The good news, however, is that they often pay for articles they decide to use. If this is a place you would consider submitting your ideas, you will need to familiarize yourself with the bible for professional writers— *Writers Market* (Garvey, 1996). This annual publication, that will also come in handy for submitting book proposals, lists all the publishers and magazines that are regularly looking for contributions. Under each entry you will find very useful information about what exactly they are looking for, the name of the acquisitions editor, the percentage of submissions that are accepted, and whether they accept unsolicited manuscripts. Many magazines will not accept works unless they are invited or come through an agent they are used to dealing with. It is for all these reasons that this is probably the most competitive of all markets and the one you would least want to consider early in your writing career.

Books

Writing a book is the most ambitious of all writing projects and definitely should not be undertaken until you have experimented with articles, or even chapters in edited works. It is not just the length of a book manuscript that may seem daunting, but also the clarity with which you organize and structure it.

Most books that are submitted for publication never have a chance for the same reason that most articles are rejected: They don't conform to the standard format. Most people don't realize, for example, that editors are not interested in seeing a whole book manuscript. They don't have the time to read the whole thing, besieged as they are by what is known in the industry as "slush" (unsolicited manuscripts by unknown writers). Besides, an experienced editor can tell from reading the outline and a few introductory pages whether the book idea has promise or not. Also critical is that most publishers want some say in how the book is developed. They have preferences as to structure and style, as well as content customized for their unique audience. It is for these reasons that book proposals are often quite brief and can easily do the job in a dozen pages or less.

Writing the Proposal

What you emphasize in your proposal depends on the particular sort of project you are developing and the audience you are trying to reach. There are small presses, medium-size houses, university presses, and increasingly in today's climate of mergers and conglomerates, megapublishers that are run like large corporations. In addition, there are so many different specialty houses that concentrate primarily on particular formats or content — art books, travel books, self-help books, religious books, cookbooks, humor books, textbooks, true crime, business, romantic fiction, books for children or young adults. In constructing a proposal for any of these outlets, you would be well-advised to consult *Writers Market* (Garvey, 1996), or other sources (e.g., Mandell, 1995) that list the particular requirements of each publishing world.

In general, a book proposal should state, succinctly and clearly, what you are doing and how you will do it. Specifically, the following elements should be included:

Title. A catchy and memorable title is nice, but perhaps more important is a title that describes what the book is really about. In all likelihood, the title will change anyway once the production and marketing staffs get hold of the manuscript.

Introduction. In this most critical part of your proposal, you must describe what your book is about and who it is intended for. Since editors receive dozens or more proposals every week, their time is very valuable; often they (or their editorial assistants) won't read beyond the first page if it's not compelling. We can't emphasize enough how important this first section is to capture a publisher's interest.

About the author. How are you qualified to write this book? A brief narrative is helpful to introduce yourself as well as demonstrate your expertise to undertake the proposed project. A detailed resume should be included with your proposal.

Unique features. What is the marketing potential? How is your book different from anything else that has already been published? More importantly, why will it sell? You must be utterly convincing.

In the words of one acquisitions editor of a major trade publisher, prospective authors make the major mistake of overselling themselves instead of providing a convincing rationale for why the book can compete in the marketplace. "Writers should realize that an editor is essentially an in-house advocate for a book. They should supply us with arguments, material, and the ammunition not only to acquire the book, but eventually to use while publishing it" (Saletan, 1995).

Publishers invest hundreds of thousands of dollars to publish a book. Your royalties are a pittance compared to the printing costs, marketing and publicity expenses, distribution, and cuts taken by retailers. Your job is to convince the publisher that your project is a sound investment. Keep in mind that editors are very skeptical and have lots of options.

Contents. In this section describe the structure, style, and contents of the book. A narrative outline is helpful in which each chapter is briefly reviewed. It is important for the editor to be able to see how each part fits into the unified whole.

Sample chapters. Include a sample of your writing, hopefully one that demonstrates that you are both a literate and skilled writer. Include one or two chapters with your proposal. If editors wish to see more they will contact you.

Make sure that the chapters you include have been reviewed by knowledgeable experts to make certain your grammar is correct and prose is clear. One complaint editors frequently make about therapists is that they muddle their language with too much jargon. Much depends, however, on exactly who you are writing for. Your writing style would obviously be different for a book written for the public or for other therapists, a text geared toward students, or a scholarly work addressed to researchers and university faculty.

Submitting the Proposal

Unlike journal articles, book proposals may be submitted simultaneously to several publishers at the same time. Rather than sending them in cold, you will target your efforts far more accurately if you first make some contact with the acquisitions editor or an assistant. Find out if he or she is interested generally in the idea you have developed. Don't get discouraged

when the vast majority of publishers you contact are not interested. My
(JK) first book proposal was rejected by over 40 publishers over 2 years
before I could convince someone to give me a break. Even then, the outfit
was a tiny operation with a lot of flexibility. You have to start somewhere!

Using an Agent

Books directed to trade audiences (the public) are often submitted by
agents who will do most of the work on your behalf in exchange for 15%
of your royalties. In fact, quite a number of publishers won't even consider
a book unless it is channeled through a reputable agent with whom they
already have a good working relationship. This ensures that not only will
the editors be using their time to review the highest quality proposals, but
also that during the production process they will be dealing with a professional who can guide the author smoothly through the process.

The bad news is that it is almost as difficult to find an agent who will
agree to represent you as it is to find a publisher. You can find leads for
selecting an agent through several sources: (1) *Writer's Market* (Garvey,
1996), (2) referrals from people who are already published, (3) recommendations from editors you have made friends with even though they aren't
interested in your book, and (4) personal contacts you develop at conferences.

Books directed to a more professional audience do not usually need to
go through an agent; you can handle negotiations directly with the editor.
One good plan is to circulate throughout the book display area of various
conferences to find someone who may be interested in your project. At
the annual conventions of all the professional organizations (APA, NASW,
ACA, AAMFT, etc.), editors attend not only to sell books but also to sign
new ones.

MAKING THE BEST FIRST IMPRESSION

Anything that puts the editor's mind at ease with your style, or otherwise
creates a good first impression, greatly increases the chances for a positive
review. As obvious as this sounds, it is amazing how many prospective
authors put themselves at a disadvantage by not attending to the few details
that make a good first impression. Wherever editors gather to talk, some
portion of time is taken up by incredulous laughter and the shaking of
heads as one or another tells of the bad first impressions authors make.

This lack of attention to making a good first impression is related to the
days, months, and even years writers spend developing their manuscripts.

The last thing you want to do when you're finished with all this work is to pay attention to submission details. Fortunately, it doesn't take much time or energy to attend to the items in the following table before you put an article in the mail.

FIRST IMPRESSION CHECKLIST

PERSONALIZE THE PUBLICATION TO THE PARTICULAR JOURNAL OR PUBLISHER

_____ All stated author guidelines for this journal or publisher are followed.
_____ Abstract matches other publications by this publisher.
_____ Content matches similar publications by this publisher.
_____ Length matches similar publications by this publisher.
_____ Designated reference style is followed.
_____ Title page provides information to access the authors.

PERSONALIZE THE SUBMISSION LETTER

_____ It is short, one page or less for the journal and two for books, so the submission can do the selling.
_____ The current editor's/publisher's name is used rather than "Dear Editor/Publisher."
_____ The journal's/publisher's name is used in the first paragraph.
_____ Your reason for submitting to this specific journal or publisher is stated briefly.
_____ The specific journal section or publisher focus that is designed for is stated.
_____ Anything unique about the submission is stated briefly.

VALUE EQUALS CREDIBILITY PLUS CREATIVITY

Pessimists might view the tips, techniques, and patterns identified in this chapter as little more than uncreative steps adding up to no value other than getting your name in print. After all, they might say: "Aren't scholarly publications just dull, boring, and generally insignificant ramblings written by someone isolated from reality in an ivory tower?" Unfortunately, some are exactly that, but they don't have to be. The best writing allows the author (especially one who is a practitioner rather than a theoretician) to demonstrate creatively the credibility of an idea in a way that readers find personally meaningful.

Think, for example, about the things you've read that have had the greatest impact on the ways you work and live. It wasn't just what was said, but how the author spoke to you that made a significant impact. Just like our role as therapists, if the author came across as knowledgeable and capable, then we listened to what he or she had to say.

People are influenced by an author's ability to find creative ways of advancing ideas that may have been around for some time, but in less accessible forms (Salomone, 1993). Perhaps the writer added new information that brought old perceptions together. Perhaps the author did little more than rephrase previously known information in a more meaningful way. How authors achieve this goal is of less importance to readers than the fact that new insights were achieved. This points to the key difference between a good reader and good writer: While both understand and use the information, the best writers must also present it credibly and creatively.

Writers who begin publishing in professional journals quickly recognize the most common ways to create scholarly credibility. The obvious reason for all the citations is to prove that your ideas are believable because others have said something similar. Even original data needs to be justified by fitting it into a line of viable research. The more difficult task is to find the creative mechanisms to make this formal credibility fit into the reader's experiential world. That is where practicing therapists can make a substantial impact.

There are two basic forms of creativity that have relevance to writers and their manuscripts (Isaksen, Dorval, & Treffinger, 1994). The first form, "innovative creativity," is seen most clearly in those people who come up with totally new ideas. Einstein's theory of relativity or Freud's development of psychosexual stages are examples of people devising revolutionary concepts. This creativity model is consistent with the views of Americans and most Europeans, but it is quite different from those emphasized in other cultures. For example, the Japanese are among the best in the world at "adaptive creativity"—taking the ideas of others and designing better ways of using them. It is therefore useful to ask yourself as you begin developing a manuscript which type of creativity will be needed and how well it matches what you have to offer.

The greatest number of manuscripts emphasize theory, experiences, and reviewed literature rather than expressing totally new ideas. They depend heavily on adaptive creativity in their attempt to help readers see previously unrecognized, unstated, or poorly understood concepts in a new light.

Innovative creativity tends to surface in either new research data or conceptual articles and books that are not so heavily referenced. They rely on new data, logic, reason, and creative presentation to demonstrate the credibility of new ideas which are often not easily accepted by the scientific community. Creativity in research clearly focuses on the design of an idea, while the carrying out and presentation of the research employ more traditional models. In any writing endeavor, the most difficult task is to find innovative ways of explaining new ideas so that they tap into previous reader knowledge and experience. Again, this is a task for which therapists are especially well-suited since we do this for a living every day of our lives.

WRITING FOR YOURSELF

There are hundreds of book proposals and dozens of articles rejected for every one that is eventually accepted for publication. The reality of writing for publication is that most often you will feel frustrated, rejected, and unappreciated. Of course, as therapists we are used to this!

Even with developing skills, inner knowledge about what is involved, and lots of patience, you will still face a number of setbacks.

One of the reasons I (JK) became a therapist in the first place is that I hate being subjected to other people's whims and decisions. Not only did I choose to become self-employed as a way to avoid others who might control my destiny, but I've long reveled in the one-way intimacy that characterizes therapeutic relationships. I am the one in control, the one who decides how we proceed. I have the power to decide when I'll work, where I'll work, and how I will operate.

Writing for publication, however, ultimately involves being at the mercy of others' judgments. Editors decide whether they believe your contribution has merit, whether it is good enough. This is a most unpleasant, helpless position to be in.

One way to get around the situation of faceless editors being the gatekeepers who determine whether a wider audience will read your stuff is to write primarily for yourself. Write because it gives you pleasure, because it helps you clarify your ideas, because it stretches your thinking, because it forces you to be more disciplined. Write because you wish to do so for yourself.

Should you be fortunate enough to have your product published, that is an added bonus, not a necessity. You may be thinking, "That's easy for *you* to say; after all, your words do get in print." We worked diligently for over a decade, sometimes writing every day, before a first article was finally accepted for publication—in a small, state journal that only one hundred people will ever read.

It is truly lovely when a piece is published. It feels wonderful to know that many others will be reading our words. But this is a luxury rather than a necessity. If this book had never seen the light of day we would have still profited as its authors. Setting our thoughts to paper helped us to focus on hazy ideas we had been wrestling with for some time.

Write because it makes you happy. Write because it makes you a better therapist and a better thinker and a better communicator. Share what you've written with those whom you most respect and like. Circulate your manuscripts among your friends and colleagues. Create position papers for your clients. Most of all, to be a writer means that you have to write. Every day. Whether what you create becomes published is not within your control. First and foremost, you must write for yourself.

CHAPTER 9

Surviving Organizational Politics

They never told you in graduate school that the hardest part of your job would not take place in your sessions: It's the politics that will kill you! You spent all that time learning what to do with cases, how to plan your sessions, work through impasses. Little did you realize that compared to how your clients will test you, your colleagues may give you the greatest trouble.

You would think that as human relations experts we would be more than a little sensitive and skilled at dealing with interpersonal conflict. You would think we would be more tolerant and flexible than most folks, more willing to compromise and support one another. You would also expect that we would be especially able to recognize power struggles as they are occurring and intervene constructively, just as we do in our client's family systems.

So, why are human service organizations—schools, mental health centers, hospitals, universities, community agencies, group practices—just as notorious for their infighting as any other group? And why do academic departments that train therapists seem to be the most conflicted of all? Why do we have such trouble getting along?

This chapter was among the most difficult for us to write. One reason for this is because the subject is so personally painful; after all, we are talking about things that have been rarely spoken about publicly. Second, the two of us are not altogether in agreement about just how disturbing and destructive organizational politics can be. Although we will be talking about some of the more unsavory aspects of our profession, we do want to emphasize our strong belief that: (1) it doesn't have to be this way, (2) we are capable of doing so much better, and (3) you can make organizational politics in your office more constructive through your own behavior and interventions.

SIMON SAYS

People imitate what they have seen modeled. Look at the climates of most departments that prepare therapists. They may be academically rigorous. They may even turn out superlative clinicians. But whether we are speaking of departments of psychology, social work, counseling, psychiatry, nursing, family therapy, or human services, faculty members don't often demonstrate with one another, much less with students, the levels of empathy, respect, compassion, and caring that they say are so important. By and large, we are hypocrites, unable to practice what we preach, or unwilling to apply the same principles that we teach in our classes to our own lives.

If it is not the norm for professionals to bicker, undermine one another, and triangulate colleagues into their battles, then it is certainly not uncommon. If ever there is a dysfunctional system that is impervious to the most determined efforts to set things on an even keel, it is an academic unit. While you would consider it reasonable to assume that therapists who become trainers and supervisors would be true experts at working through disagreements, this does not always appear to be the case.

Perhaps there is some strange interactive effect that takes place when you mix together otherwise competent professionals in an environment that is designed to be cut-throat and competitive. In many institutions, success and rewards are directly proportionate not to how nice and cooperative you are, or even to how well-liked and respected you are by students, but rather to how many refereed articles you publish. Unfortunately, it is not the journals that need the referees but the departments themselves.

One department of a dozen faculty seems fairly typical of what we have witnessed. Well-known throughout North America as one of the premier institutions for training therapists, the faculty enjoys the reputation as being one of the most productive around. A few of the faculty have high visibility in the field; another handful are also first-rate scholars. Even the so-called "slackers" still manage to churn out the requisite two articles per year that is considered standard output.

Not only is the faculty highly competent in their research efforts, but their teaching evaluations are among the highest in the university. Among them, there are innovators who use cutting edge technology in their classrooms, the most valid measurement instruments to assess learning, and the most creative methods of pedagogy. Furthermore, the staff is also quite active in the realm of service to their university and community. They have representatives on the most prestigious committees—University Senate, Tenure and Promotion, Intercollegiate Athletic Council. They play very active roles as consultants to the movers and shakers in the State Department, the local mental health system, the schools, and other human organizations in town. In short, by any standard, these faculty members are absolutely first-rate.

You are waiting for the punch line, the "but" at the end of this story, and here it comes: Rarely have you seen a group of folks who work so poorly together. Although they appear to be getting business done in an exemplary fashion, they are really only successful in accomplishing their personal agendas. There are two major coalitions in the department that pretend their disagreement is ideological in nature, but it is really based on the passionate hate that the two ringleaders feel for one another, an animosity that nobody can recall its origin. If only the battle lines were so simple, students could figure out how to align themselves. Unfortunately, the boundaries are ever-changing, depending on who has struck a deal with whom.

Faculty meetings are singularly tense and unproductive. The same two or three people recite their same speeches. A few of the senior professors have an inclination to be verbally abusive at times; the untenured staff cower during such times, rarely making eye contact with others in the room. Hours go by and things rarely get done. Committees are formed. Heated discussions lead to position papers that will be studied at some future times. Votes are taken, rarely decisive. The meetings adjourn and then the battles resume in other arenas. It is always the students who are caught in the field of fire.

NECESSARY CASUALTIES

Many of us do not recall our days in training as being especially pleasant. One of the reasons for this was related to the political maneuverings going on all around us. We learned that mixing certain instructors together on the same committee was potentially explosive. In some instances, it wasn't even safe to mention one professor's name in the presence of another or we would risk being judged guilty by association.

During sincere attempts to make sense of discrepant feedback from different faculty, students are often caught in the middle. As one example, students are required to take a basic therapeutic process course that introduces them to the core helping skills and stages. The instructor operates in a highly structured fashion, helping students to learn a cognitive-behavioral, brief therapy model. While this is a reasonable and appropriate format for the class, the teacher is unusually dogmatic and opinionated about the "right" way things should be done. Any other staff member who does not share these beliefs is unceremoniously written off. The students learn their lessons well and exit the experience quite able to help clients define goals, commit to homework assignments, and measure outcomes. They are also a bit shell-shocked, having been drilled repeatedly in a method that leaves little room for their own unique style.

The next class they will take is a beginning practicum in which they are expected to see their first live clients in a laboratory setting, complete with one-way mirrors and videotaping. They are understandably apprehensive, filled with doubts about their abilities to actually help someone. The instructor is quite different from the previous one. Contradicting what they had just finished learning, she tells them that while structure, goals, and techniques have their place, their initial task is to simply relax, to concentrate on connecting with their clients and build a solid alliance. She is aghast at their insistence that every client must do homework, regardless of what they came for. She asks them to put the rigid model aside for a session or two, and to concentrate on developing their own unique, personal style of practice, one in which they can establish a good relationship with their clients.

The students revel in their freedom, feel confident and effective in their work, but also leery because they know what is coming next. The following semester they have internship, supervised by their previous teacher, the one who fully expects them to be experts in the system that he had introduced to them.

Of course, when team members are working cooperatively, discrepant feedback can be valuable in helping them to integrate what they are learning. In this case, however, the two professors are constantly at each other's throats, and the students know this. When this stable conflict is intensified by the coalitions that each is part of, the potential for systemic dysfunction is even greater.

When students are exposed to the kinds of power games, one-upmanship, coalitional battles, and backstabbing that are often so much a part of academic life, they come to accept this behavior in their mentors as almost normal. They hear their heroes bad-mouthing one another. They observe the intricate patterns of engagement that take place between warring camps. They join in the battles themselves, playing active roles as scouts, messengers, sometimes even firing off a few salvos of their own against the designated targets of the other side. Worst of all, most of us still have the scars to prove our courage, wounded in battle for what we imagined was an honorable cause.

What, then, do we learn in graduate school about the inevitability of factionalism, with its accompanying political games? We internalized far more than what our mentors said; we imitate the ways they act. If they presented themselves to us as noble crusaders fighting against the infidels, we learned to view hurtful actions as necessary casualties in a holy war.

LESSONS LEARNED WELL

Before we ever began our first jobs as therapists, and entered an environment that might already have been highly toxic, we had been shaped and molded as warriors, ready to add fuel to the flames of discontent. In earlier chapters, we discussed at length what we learned and did not learn in graduate school. In the case of surviving organizational politics, we also learned a set of lessons that were certainly not part of the organized curricula.

It is interesting to consider what it takes to flourish, if not excel, in graduate school. Students may have been screened based on their GRE scores, grade point averages, goal statements, and reference letters, but probably the predictors for success are rarely mentioned aloud.

Competition over Cooperation

Students are rewarded for individual success rather than working well together as team members. In fact, we have deliberately chosen prospective therapists who are already good at achievement as measured on tests and writing papers. We continue to reinforce this behavior by assigning the highest grades to those who perform better than their peers.

Students live in continual fear that they will be weeded out, that their professors will discover their deepest, darkest secret—that they are really quite ordinary and have been faking competence all their lives. They see some of their comrades giving in to the pressure and vow that they will rise above the fray, attain the highest honors, and therefore the choicest jobs.

These are bright people. They are folks who have been successful most of their lives playing academic games. They have learned their lesson well: You make yourself look better when others look worse.

Gender Confusion

A competitive learning environment is consistent with traditional male values that have dominated higher education for centuries. A Samurai mentality of defeating others on the path to glory is certainly inconsistent with what therapists are expected to do. Practicing therapy has been long identified as a "female" profession, not only because its ranks are made up primarily of women, but because its basic culture of caring emphasizes compassion, healing, and verbal expression of innermost feelings (Fancher, 1995).

Okay. If you are with us so far, we have an essentially "female profession" being trained in a "male environment" that emphasizes values that are at odds with the actual work. To complicate matters further, upon graduation these practitioners will be expected to work in what has become an increasingly corporate culture, one that stresses once again male values of competition, dominance, and achievement as measured by secondary rewards such as money and symbols of status. This brings us to the third lesson learned well.

External Validation

We have mentioned previously how graduate school teaches us not to trust ourselves but rather to put our faith in what authority figures tell us about how we are doing. You could write the best paper of your life, convinced you have integrated the research on the subject and articulated your ideas with such clarity you feel dizzy with pride, and yet if some professor gives you a B+, your self-assessment will be diminished. You could make the most brilliant comment in class that you have ever thought, much less said aloud, and yet if the teacher doesn't get the point, you assume it was some shortcoming on your part. You could make an absolutely flawless execution of an intervention, yet while viewing the videotape with your supervisor, you are easily convinced that your efforts were misguided. In other words, you learned over and over again that it is others' opinions of your performance that matter most. By "others" we are not referring to who really matters (clients), but to authority figures like teachers and supervisors who are continuously judging whether you are worthy of remaining part of this exclusive club.

Each of these lessons, while compromising our personal confidence and initiative, did its job well in preparing us to work in an environment where being competitive, political, manipulative, dominant, and achievement-oriented would be valued over values that lead to cooperation and mutual support. This, however, is only a few of the ingredients that help account for why the political squabbles in our work can be so vicious.

AN EXPLOSIVE RECIPE

Imagine what would come out of the oven if you mixed together the following ingredients and stirred vigorously. First, you have a half dozen or more individuals who:

- make a living convincing others to do things they don't want to do,
- are used to getting their way and not taking no for an answer,
- have been trained, molded, and drilled to be exquisitely sensitive to other people's weaknesses and vulnerabilities,
- are attracted to relationships in which they can be in control and in charge of the proceedings,
- are more than a little narcissistic and self-centered, with an inflated sense of importance,
- make a living pretending to know more than they really do,
- are used to being in conflict,
- gravitate to positions where they are used to being in dominant roles,
- have strong personalities and charismatic interpersonal styles, and
- spend most of their work day in the company of other people who pay them (directly or indirectly) for their wisdom, defer to them as special beings with supreme powers, and agree that what they have to say is helpful if not brilliant.

Add to this population of participants, the status of a profession that can't agree on:

- which discipline is best qualified to do this work,
- which approach to helping is most effective, or
- what setting is best designed for this work.

Stir in a cultural climate in the larger community that:

- shows increasing skepticism and disrespect for what therapists do and how they do it,
- puts more and more pressure on practitioners to defend their activities, prove their effectiveness, and justify their existence, and

- implements fiscal cutbacks that create more competition and less cooperation among clinicians.

Add to that an organizational structure of most institutions where therapists work that:

- is authoritarian and hierarchical in a professional context that is supposed to be democratic and
- looks at product rather than process, results rather than quality of experience.

Consider a value system that:

- invites disagreement and dissent and
- tolerates wide ranges of opinion.

Then, add an unknown element consisting of:

- a group of folks who love to gossip and analyze every nuance and underlying meaning to everyone else's behavior,
- an oversensitivity on the part of staff members to rejection or getting feelings hurt,
- one or more individuals who enjoy pulling other people's strings and watching them behave as predicted, and
- one or more individuals who exhibit gross interpersonal pathology well-masked in a seemingly appropriate professional demeanor.

Taken together, we have a group of therapists working together in an environment that seems perfectly suited to variations on themes of dissension and chaos. It is no wonder that this is ground for spawning such noncolleagial behavior.

MONSTERS AMONG US

It is our dirtiest secret. We speak about it in whispers with our closest friends. We ruminate about it constantly. It invades our sleep in the form of restlessness, nightmares, even insomnia. It dominates our most private discussions with staff members.

We are speaking about those among us whose behavior is not only disruptive but also borders on being pathological. If this field attracts the

Joan of Arcs, the Florence Nightingales, the Martin Luther Kings who want to be healers and saviors, to set things right and make the world a better place, then we have also attracted the forces of darkness. What a great place to hide, even blossom, for those who thrive on manipulating and controlling others.

Indeed, look around you. The odds are pretty good that if you work in an organization with more than a dozen people, there is a monster among you, one masquerading as a healer who really goes about hurting people—not only clients but also colleagues. We are not saying that therapists have more than their fair share of sociopathy within their ranks, just that we do have some dangerous colleagues and they are far better equipped and positioned to do damage than others might be. These dysfunctional professionals are predators in the sense that they hunger for chaos around them. They like being around other people in pain; even better, they enjoy causing it. It gives them a sense of power and potency. It helps them to feel in control.

It is too bad we were not provided with a diagnostic guide to identify such dysfunctional colleagues in graduate school. Not to sound too conspiratorial, but one reason this critical information was withheld, of course, is that such monsters lurk in the hallways of academia in disproportionate numbers. And why not? If you get off on dominating and humiliating people, what better place to do that than with students?

People who have been trained as therapists are far more skilled at disguising their disabilities. We all realize this; it is another of our secrets—that we entered this field in the first place as a way to hold ourselves together and hide better our imperfections. Some people are far better at this than others. Nevertheless, if you look carefully around you, you will easily recognize the same symptoms you see in your clients in a few of your colleagues. (Of course, *you* are exempt because you are reading this book. Unless, of course, you are doing so to equip yourself with even more devious strategies. . . .)

THE SPOILS OF WAR

At least with overt hostility you know what is happening even if you don't like it. In the case of those who are manipulative behind the scenes, sometimes you never know what hit you until it's too late. These are the sneaky ones, the colleagues who will be so cordial and considerate to your face but look for every opportunity to stab you in the back if it meets their needs. In the jargon of our profession, we would call these people passive-aggressive, or perhaps practitioners of a different sort of sociopathy than direct intimidation. Then again, they may be just extraordinarily well-schooled at playing the political games that are part of human organizations. If that involves deceit, deception, manipulation, so be it. If other people get hurt along the way, that is their problem. It is survival of the fittest.

According to evolutionary psychology, the strongest bond of friendship is predicated on a common enemy (Wright, 1994). In his book on political strategies of chimpanzees, de Waal (1982) provides a fascinating glimpse into the coalitional affiliations that take place as individuals wish to attain power and status and enjoy the fruits of those conquests in terms of greater resources. In the world of chimps, or a group of therapists, nobody can rule without the consent of those who are governed. A member who is skilled at using any means available, especially deception and manipulation, is likely to be rewarded in terms of the spoils of war.

What is it that therapists are maneuvering for, such that they would be willing to invest energy and effort in political pursuits? What is at stake that makes it worthwhile to spend time trying to win friends and influence people?

Savage political struggles are part of the therapist's existence because the rewards are perceived as worth the emotional risks. For one thing, those who are best connected get the choicest referrals. Like the chimpanzees who are part of the dominant male's social circle, there is status by association. We may not be after the best bananas or selection of mates, but we are very interested in having access to "insider" information that makes it easier for us to do our jobs. Obviously, those who have managed to maneuver themselves into the "in" group also have a greater likelihood of being promoted.

All politics is about cultural influence, that is, maintaining ideological dominance so that your favored platform becomes established policy (Sowell, 1994). On a practical level, this means having the power base to protect your right to act the way you please and the ways you think are in the best interest of your clients. For example, two therapists each think differently about their work in the same agency. The first has practiced psychodynamically for a decade or more, continuing to evolve a style of practice that incorporated contemporary movements of self-psychology, time-limited treatments, and eventually a responsiveness to the market's demand for brief interventions. He still stubbornly asserts his right to continue practicing a more insight-oriented therapy with a handful of his cases who express an interest in this type of treatment, despite the criticism from a new administrator who insists that he conform to the new party line.

By contrast, the second therapist attended the same local graduate school as the new supervisor. She is also in basic harmony in terms of espoused beliefs and operating style. Her experience is considerably different from the previous therapist, who feels stifled. She is given virtually free reign to do as she likes. Clearly, she is politically well-connected, a circumstance that allows her to serve her clients in the best way possible.

These external rewards are certainly reason enough to get involved in political action, but there are internal motives as well. The unfortunate reality is that some people like to become embroiled in political struggles because they need the action. They wish to distract themselves from the emptiness of their lives. They feel powerless in other areas and so thrive on the exhilaration that comes from knowing they played a role in stirring things up. Like gambling addicts, they get high on the thrill of the action, spinning the roulette wheel while their hearts pound in anticipation. Finally, they like the way it feels to be in the thick of things, action stirring every which way. They no longer get as much a kick from their therapy sessions. Like an addict who graduates to increasingly more powerful drugs, they need a bigger rush, the kind that comes from not only manipulating a helpless client or two, but also a whole room full of therapists.

BRANDS OF TOXICITY

So far, we have been talking about political squabbles as if they emanate from a single source, as if one or even two individuals are responsible for the work climate that we live in. We know better than that. We have listened to enough stories of placing blame on a scapegoat to realize that most conflicts are far more complex than we prefer to recognize and most often embedded in systemic patterns. It would be no different in the places where we are employed.

In the taxonomy of toxicity, there are a number of different systemic dysfunctions that we have come to recognize among groups of therapists. Surely you will recognize a few in your own experience.

Hierarchical Oppression

This organization is run like a single parent with a bunch of delinquent children. The administrator rules with an authoritarian style, which in turn sparks the rebelliousness of therapists who, by and large, resent any intrusion into their lives. After all, they became therapists to escape parent figures telling them what to do.

Although they complain incessantly about being treated like children, about not being given respect or responsibility, on another level many of the staff members enjoy their conspiratorial ploys to undermine the administrator and assert their independence. The more they act out, of course, the more the administrator feels justified in cracking down further, exerting more control, and thereby eliciting more dramatic acting out.

Surface Cordiality

You would think that this organization is the antithesis of the previous one, and in some ways you would be correct. Staff members are very respectful to one another, almost painfully polite in their dealings.

During a staff meeting you would be struck not so much by what they talk about as what they don't talk about. Things pretty much stick to safe areas of business and avoid anything resembling emotional risk taking. This strikes you most dramatically when one therapist is discussing a case she feels stuck with and everyone jumps in with helpful suggestions but carefully avoids dealing with some of her feelings toward the client.

Although this group functions quite well on the surface of things, especially in completing appropriate forms and generating client contact hours, the morale of the staff members is quite low. Digging beneath the surface, you find much hidden discontent. There are "family secrets" in this agency, long buried by mutual consent. They conspire to pretend their problems don't exist, satisfying themselves with a minimal level of collegiality that includes little intimacy or trust.

Gross Ineptitude

A government-funded department within a larger organization consists of four members, three of whom have worked there for more than twenty years. Whereas once upon a time they may have been quite good at what they do, the newer team member muses about what that must have been like: He finds it difficult to imagine that any of them were ever competent.

Prior to his arrival on the scene, this group functioned together in an uneasy truce of live and let live. Their level of job performance was marginal by anyone's standards, but with so much seniority there was no way that any of them could be fired or transferred against their will. Adding the fourth therapist only aggravated an already difficult situation.

Although his clinical work was flawless, the younger therapist inadvertently sparked a lot of conflict with his colleagues by undermining their authority. When people from other departments began to come to him for answers instead of his more senior staff members, they all banded together for the first time in years to protect themselves from a perceived assault to their integrity. In less than six months, the younger therapist moved on to another job, the third time this had happened in as many years.

Denial and Enabling

The only thing worse than ruminating constantly and complaining incessantly about the incompetent practitioners among us (without doing anything constructive to help them or their clients), is to pretend that they are not really impaired. Collective denial, or even enabling the dysfunctional behavior, is a common coping strategy among alcoholic or addicted families. The same holds true for groups of therapists.

In an institution that specializes in the training and supervision of therapists, two members of the staff demonstrate clear signs of major depression. Both are taking antidepressant medication and seem to take turns spinning out of control. They were hired in the first place by the benevolent and accepting administrator who believes in supporting his staff no matter what they are going through. Even though days sometimes go by in which each of them might not speak to anyone, make eye contact, or do anything but shuffle from their offices to the coffee pot or to fetch the next supervisee, the other staff members cover for them as best they can. They wonder how they manage to get any of the therapists to return for supervision and conclude that they must feel sorry for them, just as the staff does.

Most of the staff members in the institute feel embarrassed by the degree of dysfunction in their two colleagues and never confront the idea that they, along with the administrator, are part of the problem. The only way such impaired professionals could continue to practice is with the assistance of everyone else who is protecting and covering for them, including their own clients.

Islands in the Stream

In a group private practice, each therapist seems almost compulsive about issues of autonomy and freedom. They share rent for their office space but otherwise contract for their own phone, secretarial, and support services. This, by itself, is hardly an indictment of dysfunction as much as it may be a preferred business operation. However, most of the practitioners would hardly speak to one another besides a mumbled hello, much less ever talk in a meaningful way.

Most of the practitioners do not exactly enjoy the isolation they feel; in fact, the majority are exploring other practice arrangements as soon as their lease expires (only 21 more months!). For reasons that are guessed at but never discussed, mistrust is rampant between them. It is impossible to know who is in or out on any given day since their doors are inevitably kept closed, regardless of their occupancy.

Acting Out Behind Closed Doors

In another clinic, composed of a dozen or so practitioners of various disciplines, an ethos of camaraderie prevails. The administrators work hard to create a spirit of family among them. Biweekly case conferences offer not only guest supervisors, but also gourmet catered lunches. Regular retreats are scheduled. All policies and decisions are made democratically, by group consensus. New staff members are not brought on board until everyone, including the secretarial staff, has their input. In many ways, it seems like a utopian setting in which to practice therapy, one in which both morale and productivity are high.

But if you look closer, you'll discover the shenanigans going on behind the scenes. One therapist was convicted of fraud for double-billing an insurance company. Another therapist was found to be having sex with his clients, then another was actually doing so in the office while charging for his services! As things unfolded, what appeared to be a model office of decorum and professional conduct was actually a hidden jungle of deceit and immoral behavior. We therapists kid ourselves about our powers to ferret out truth, and yet it is frightening how often we have no idea what is really going on.

I (JK) recall doing a workshop in a small town on the coast of New Zealand's North Island on the subject of "Working With Difficult Clients." As part of the presentation, I asked the participants to gather in small groups and tell one another about their most difficult clients.

When I overheard a chorus of gasps from a group of four therapists, I stopped by to eavesdrop on their conversation. It seems that one of the practitioners was describing her most difficult client, when another therapist in the group interrupted her to ask a few questions. The case sounded suspiciously similar to one that he had been working with for a number of months. From my angle, I was the only one who could see the look of shock on a third therapist's face. Stuttering, he admitted that he had been working with a client who resembled this case as well. Upon sharing their experiences, it became immediately evident that all three of them had been seeing the same client for some months without any idea that she had been simultaneously consulting with at least two others. Since that humbling episode, I have never forgotten that things are often not what they seem, even with those we think we know quite well.

Chaos Abounds

This final example of toxicity in action occurs in those organizations without any leadership at all. A group of therapists can't agree on who should lead them, whether someone should emerge from within or whether they should find someone outside the setting. So they settle on a compromise position of trying to function without any leadership at all, doing everything by committee.

They find that no matter how much time they spend talking about issues they never get around to settling anything, much less taking any constructive action. In frustration, they disperse to conduct their own agendas, oblivious to the ways they are contradicting and undermining one another; or, if they are aware of their mutual interference, they don't seem to care.

It is a miracle that anything is ever accomplished in this atmosphere of ever-present chaos. Decisions are never deliberately made; policy is established through simple neglect. Nobody is quite aware of what is going on or where things are headed. In this spirit of inertia, the place seems to run itself on stored energy that is slowly running down.

Like each of the toxic environments we have mentioned as examples, this one permits therapists to function at minimal levels of competence even if morale is severely compromised. We have become so accustomed to these instances of dysfunction we hardly seem surprised any longer when we encounter them. It is, after all, what we have gotten used to.

THE NATURE OF HUMAN ORGANIZATIONS

An office takes on both the best and the worst characteristics of the people who work there. Organizations are not theoretical concepts we can manipulate in the ways most logical, reasonable, and beneficial for all. Instead, they reflect every one of the strengths, weaknesses, fantasies, fears, and appropriate or inappropriate behaviors that are a part of any group of humans. Organizations that include therapists are not relieved of these human frailties just because of the noble nature of the work.

Chapter 2, Walking on Water, examined how we, as individuals, want to do right and are desperately afraid of doing wrong. These same pressures push us to try and replace our most human weaknesses with idealized concepts of professional perfection. Some of us find success at denying our fallabilities for a time; but the longer we carry on the charade, the more damage it does to ourselves, clients, colleagues, family, and friends. We carry these same unhealthy desires and self-protective and self-destructive behaviors designed to eliminate any sign of weakness into the office with us. Our offices become reflections of our efforts to show the things we like best about ourselves and to hide, ignore, or deny the things we like least.

We came to believe that when we walked out of a particularly traumatic series of sessions, or when our home lives were in disarray, our colleagues would be there for us with all the strength, compassion, and necessary tools to keep us whole and healthy. It never occurred to us that everyone on a staff might need help for their own set of difficult sessions and personal problems.

We all hurt and we all need support. The personal and professional problems that go beyond our therapeutic relationships with clients cannot be eliminated from our office lives. Being highly trained therapists does not eliminate the human needs that push us to respond in ways we might not choose. Consider how much the conflicting needs listed in the table below affect the ways you interact with your colleagues.

These are just some of the human needs that interfere with our ability to operate consistently at the highest levels of personal morality and professional competency. They struggle for dominance inside each of us and

NEEDS IN CONFLICT

a need to feel safe, secure, and unthreatened	a need to challenge and to be challenged
a need for stability	a need for growth and change
a need to be accepted	a need for independence
a need to defend our abilities and hide our weaknesses	a need to test our abilities and locate our weaknesses
a need to demonstrate our knowledge	a need to show what we don't know in order to learn
a need to help others	a need to get help for ourselves
a need to get our way	a need to take others' needs into account
a need to win	a need to help others win

overflow into the work place, making their appearance as organizational struggles. No one side ever seems to win continuously in this psychological balancing act within us and the results can appear as the best or the worst of our characteristics.

WE'RE ALL IN THIS TOGETHER

The most noble of our therapeutic beliefs, values, skills, and behaviors can be identified in what Bolman and Deal (1991) refer to as organizations that operate from a human resources frame of reference. The same client-directed focus we employ in therapy is closely related to the goals and practices of human resource management; the focus is on understanding and meeting the physiological, social, and psychological needs of workers in much the same way as we do for clients. As therapists, we believe that clients who better identify their own needs and then work to meet them will lead more useful lives. Likewise, human-resource focused organizations believe that satisfied and motivated workers make the most productive workers over the long run.

This model would provide a place where you, coworkers, and formal leaders would all be acting to provide a mutually supportive environment. People would take time to get to know each other, to listen, be attentive when you are speaking, reflect on what you have said, ask for clarification of your meaning, and help you explore options knowing that you must make the final decision. Perhaps just as important, the people in this workplace would not avoid you during your times of struggle. Instead you could count on them being with you every step of the way. There would be no fair weather friends in this organization where commitment to be supportive during good times and bad is similar to what we provide our clients.

This theoretical model suggests a great place to work, but other realities make it a difficult model to implement in practice. One important difference from the therapeutic relationship is that the roles of helper and client are stable in therapy, but they must be quickly reversible in a human resource–focused organization. Whose tensions, weaknesses, desires, needs, and motivations will be given top priority is always an issue needing attention when no one is formally designated as client. Help upon demand cannot be guaranteed because there must be decisions made about who gets priority, when, for how long, and under what conditions.

Effective organizations bring people together on a regular basis to provide formal support and to make the hard decisions. Sometimes these processes are given formal recognition with terms and procedures like participative management (Katzell & Yankelovich, 1975), self-managing work teams (Bolman & Deal, 1991), or organizational democracy (Thorsrud, 1984). Other times they exist as a part of the informal structure of an organization. Groups that wind up gathering on a regular basis for lunch, drinks after work, coffee breaks, or Friday afternoon bull sessions often do so to provide the personal attention and support that their formal office structure may not offer.

Clearly, the essential knowledge and skills to create highly supportive organizations are available within us. Even though we may not always put these skills to the best use, and despite all the complaining we do about the people and conditions, most of us still want to be in organizations where colleagues and administrators are professionals like ourselves. Our commitment to human resource management as a model for our offices may not be 100%, but it is still stronger than many organizations we choose to avoid.

We are not the consistent saints we might like to be and much of the political maneuvering within our organizations reflects our inconsistency in approaching professional and personal needs. The environments that result similarly reflect that inconsistency, at times displaying healthy professional interactions with others in a mutual give and take, and at other times the unhealthy politics where war, victory, and getting your way are the only goals.

STRATEGIES FOR SURVIVAL

Can't we stop many of our conflicted interactions and begin to practice more diligently what we teach to others? How can we look our clients in the eyes, urging them to be what we are unable or unwilling to be ourselves? In the suggestions that follow, we offer a few reminders of things you already know, in that you recommend similar things to your clients, even if you are less than consistent in applying these principles to your own life.

Examine Your Role in the Conflict

It is so easy to blame others for the conflicts, to point the finger at the evil "monsters" who are making life so difficult. Far more interesting, and also in line with what we tell our clients, is what role *you* play in the struggles.

There is a marked tendency, not only on the part of our clients who are always pointing fingers at someone else, but also for ourselves to blame others for our troubles. We know, from both research literature and our own experience in sessions, that assigning blame to others may temporarily provide some relief but that ultimately it creates more difficulties. We know, for example, that the more victims of accidents blame others for their misfortunes, the less likely they are to adapt successfully (Tennen & Affleck, 1990). Paralyzed accident victims adjust much better to their disabilities when they believe they were in some way responsible for what happened (Bulman & Wortman, 1977).

Denying responsibility for conflicts at work creates a number of other negative side effects. First, such a condition creates more animosity and alienation through a paranoid outlook that others find unappealing. Second, this mentality contributes to a sense of a helplessness on the part of the victim that something was done to him or her without having any control in that matter and thereby perpetuating the belief that one has little power in the future. Third, being in an excuse-making mode tends to create more stress, worry, and a more negative mood. Fourth, blaming others limits the range of options you have to adapt to changing circumstances. Finally, making excuses and blaming others leads to other distortions and denial of reality, producing challenges to self-esteem.

Okay. We told you this would be familiar. We just wanted to remind you that by attributing vicious political struggles only to those around you while leaving yourself out of the picture, you engage in the same strategies of your most conflicted family cases. By turning your attention inward rather than outward, you empower yourself to consider that which is within your control to change.

Now to the hard part:

- How are you aware that you are denying a significant role in the conflicts that you face?
- What have you done most consistently throughout your life to create conflicts with others?
- When embroiled in disagreements, what have you been inclined to do to exacerbate the problems?
- Which buttons of yours are most easily pushed by others (i.e., need for approval, fear of failure, etc.)? How do you let others know where you are most vulnerable?
- In your present circumstances, what are you doing to fan the flames of discontent?

Not a pretty sight, we admit. It feels far more comforting to feel like a victim of others' abuse than it does to own our part in interpersonal struggles. However, as we so often tell our clients: You may not be able to change other people's behavior but you sure can change your own.

Diversify Your Life

One of our colleagues was literally on his deathbed. Although a relatively young man, his body was riddled with cancerous tumors. He knew that his life was limited to a matter of weeks and so wished to record his last thoughts and reflections, not only for his profession, but also for his family and friends.

I wish that I had spent less time so concerned with the things I thought were so important at work, and more time doing the things that really matter," he whispered in a soft but determined voice. After looking back on his life, he felt regret that he had allowed himself to get so caught up in the politics of his work setting, of devoting so much time to being productive. He wished that he had spent more time skiing, more time flying his plane, and most of all, more quality time with his wife, his children, and his friends. "I was so good at being productive, accomplishing things, succeeding in my teaching and my practice, that I let myself become seduced by my own competence. I forgot, though, that there were other things that were really more important.

In a strange, perverse way, this therapist almost felt grateful for his cancer in directing his attention to areas of his life he had been neglecting. In the few weeks he had remaining, he found to his delight that he was able to build a level of intimacy with his friends and family that he had never thought possible. It took impending death to get his attention.

When we keep things in perspective, the political squabbles at work mean so little in the grand scope of things. We exist to help people; everything else is secondary. One thing that we ask ourselves when we see people who are so involved in the goings-on within their work settings is, What else are they ignoring in their lives? The truth is that if our family lives are rich and satisfying, if we are surrounded by friends who support us, if we have interests outside our roles as therapists, then any conflict at work becomes a minor annoyance rather than a major upheaval.

Accept Reality

How often have you heard yourself tell clients to accept that which they cannot change and devote their energy working on what is within their power to influence? One of the realities of clinical practice is that we get together and complain a lot. We whine about how we are being treated so poorly, how unappreciated we are, how others are being mean or unfair to us. We gossip about all the weird things we think that others are up to. We mobilize support for our positions and attempt to influence others to see things the ways we do. A lot of the time, we simply feel sorry for ourselves, and listen to others do the same.

Enough is enough! There are certain conditions that are unalterable. If you put a bunch of bright, sensitive, independent people together, and make them work in concert, there are going to be disagreements. There is no sense complaining about the politics of our organizations; they come with the territory. Accept it and get on with the things that really matter.

Confront Injustices

This is a direct contradiction of what we just said. By simply accepting the way things are, we give up the chance to change systems that are inefficient or inhumane. Getting indignant does have its merits in terms of confronting wrongs, if you can do so without upsetting your equilibrium for very long. Some of us are just built differently. The two of us, for example, pay a heavy price for our involvement in political action. We lose sleep. We ruminate incessantly about things we wished we had said.

Sometimes, however, there is a price worth paying for fighting the good fight, that is, for taking a strong position in support of an issue that really matters.

Communicate Openly

Devious and unfair office politics require hidden agendas and closed-door rumoring to maintain their success. Important beliefs and problems often go undisclosed in public forums out of a fear of conflict, hurt feelings, and retribution. The more you give into these fears and do not communicate your concerns in the open, the less faith there will be in the concepts of openness, honesty, and fairness throughout the office. Greater openness on the other hand provides for the potential to directly deal with difficult issues and limits the influence of rumors, backbiting, and unscrupulous behaviors.

Combine Inquiry and Advocacy

Good political interactions require having a position to advocate and taking actions to learn more about the needs and positions of those who see things differently. Standing up for what you believe is important, but used alone it will get you no further in office politics than does lecturing a client on how to live life. Balance "I believe/I know" statements with questions about what the other person believes/knows. Add reflections of both their verbal and nonverbal answers and you will improve the relationship and increase the chances of finding the common directions necessary to foster cooperative relationships.

Doubt Your Own Infallibility

If you believe you can grow and improve, then you believe your ideas and behaviors can be in error. Allow those possibilities to be a highly visible part of your work with colleagues and supervisors. Explore the potential for your growth more often than defending who you are, what you do, and what you believe. You'll learn more and people will be more likely to see your ideas as being based in reality.

Separate Long-Term Goals from Short-Term Satisfaction

It may provide immediate satisfaction to hide from office politics, to do something you don't believe in to get your way, or to take the opportunity to "blast someone back" for their hurtful manipulations, but the feeling doesn't last for long. You're stuck with problems that are larger than when you started. People and politics don't change overnight and the better you are at doing what you know to be right over the long haul, the greater eventual impact you have.

Seek Common Goals and Mutual Support

Individuals and groups can disagree strongly and still find common goals to work toward. Give as much recognition to these common goals and the mutual support needed to meet them as you give to your differences with others. This will improve working relationships and increase the chances for eventually overcoming or moderating differences.

Emphasize Visions for the Future

Good office politics requires common directions and ways to make them happen. Unclear visions of where an organization is headed leads to every-one going separate ways. A lack of agreement on implementation strategies to achieve even a clear vision also leads to discouragement, disappointment with the system, and greater self-serving political behaviors. Seek a joint understanding of a common vision and don't consider the job done until the strategies people are expected to use in order to approach that vision are accepted.

Broaden the Base of Ideas

Actively seek new ideas from the people in your office that can continually be added to traditional ideas from the past. This action encourages growth, initiative, and involvement from both the oldest and newest members of an organization. It discourages ideological and behavioral staleness, a "who is right" mentality, and the devaluing of some more than others that "good old boy" politics requires to maintain control of an organization.

Give Stars Their Stage Time

Every office has one or more professionals who either deserve more credit for the work they do or have a greater need to be given credit. Allowing them to make a speech, go first, get an extra award, or have the last word in a discussion may at times be needed to keep them as working members of a group. Giving them the recognition they feel they deserve often makes them much more approachable to new ideas, tasks, and relationships.

Celebrate Hidden Achievements

Look for the little things that people do to provide support for colleagues and the organization's goals. Who does the dirty jobs that never get visibility? Who sees the clients no one else wants? Who is regularly willing to stay late when someone needs to talk? Take this person out to lunch, thank her at a staff meeting, give her a gift in public—don't let her go unrecognized.

Trust and Be Trustworthy

Creating a productive human relations focus in an organization requires you to believe in others and show it by giving them every opportunity to prove or disprove their worth. Giving responsibilities to those who are already trusted confirms a two-tiered respect level among staff. For yourself, you need to complete in the expected manner those tasks you are responsible for doing and behave in the ways you agree to behave. Trusting others and continually proving your trustworthiness increases the level of confidence within an organization that colleagues can truly depend upon each other.

Keep the Focus on Progress

Rome wasn't built in a day and you're not going to create the ideal organization in a day, a week, a year, or probably even a lifetime. What you can do is make things better for yourself, your colleagues, and those who come after you in the years to come. It is easy to be disappointed by feelings of "We'll never get it right" or "The changes that happen are so little they don't count." The fact that you probably never will "get it right" just because you are human only serves to strengthen the need for employing the series of small steps necessary to make things better over time.

Consciously choosing to use the best aspects of ourselves on a regular basis is essential to promoting a positive approach to office politics. You cannot have an effective group if you don't do your part. The next step is to recognize when others are not using the most healthy aspects of themselves and learn to deal with the problems that result.

Go Somewhere Else

When all else fails and you are unable to live with the daily political battles of your work setting, it is time to take a deep breath and plunge into the great unknown of other opportunities. We have many excuses why this isn't feasible just now. In other words, we are just as reluctant as our clients to give up a known constant pain for an unknown future where anything is possible.

If the place in which you currently work is rife with turmoil, a toxic culture that all but destroys your feeling of good will toward your colleagues and your clients, then it is time to move on. Make all the excuses you want for why you can't do this, why the timing isn't right, why the other options are limited. The reality, however, is that by continuing to participate in a dysfunctional environment that seems impervious to change, you are not only hurting yourself but also those you are most committed to helping.

In the next chapter, we move on from interpersonal problems for which we were unprepared, to those that are more intrapsychic in nature. In both cases, we stress that only by confronting these challenges directly can we ever hope to become models for what we teach to others.

CHAPTER TEN

Therapist, Heal Thyself

$\mathbf{F}$ew of us are as healthy as we appear to others, or even as we would like to be. There is a dark side to each of us, a part we keep hidden from view. Late at night when we are unable to sleep, or at other times when we are daydreaming, we are haunted by unresolved issues of our past, by things we have done for which we feel regret or shame, by our secrets long buried, by our weaknesses, our failures, and our imperfections. This is how human beings are, even when they are therapists.

Yet in spite of our flaws and limitations, most of us function reasonably well on a daily basis. We go about the business of helping people, doing the best we can. Through self-monitoring, workshops, growth experiences, peer consultations, professional training, supervision, and personal therapy, we confront our demons and can usually hold our most unsavory or self-defeating impulses in check. Sometimes, however, our efforts do not work that well and some among us may hurt ourselves or our clients.

Each one of us knows another professional who is, or has been at some time, seriously impaired. There are also times when each of us offered our clients far less than they deserved. This could have involved instances when we were suffering from boredom, burnout, clinical depression, incapacitating anxiety, or any number of other diagnoses that we readily bestow upon clients.

We know therapists who drink too much or lead self-destructive life-styles, therapists who are undergoing major life transitions, suffering finan-

This chapter is an expanded version of an article by the authors that appeared in the *Journal of Humanistic Education and Development*, 34(3), 1996.

cial strain, divorce proceedings, child custody battles, legal disputes, and a host of other problems that can substantially reduce personal and professional effectiveness. We also know therapists with full-fledged personality disturbances—those who are emotionally abusive, who thrive on having others dependent on them, who are overcontrolling and manipulative, or who demonstrate extreme levels of narcissism or sociopathy. We know them and we know deep inside that each of us has the potential to be one of *them*.

The professional work of every therapist undergoing a life transition or experiencing personal problems is not necessarily impaired. Diminished? Certainly. After all, how could any of us be expected to operate at optimal levels of performance when we are unduly distracted or distressed? It is certainly possible for us to be helpful to others even when we are struggling with our own difficult issues. Yet we can all identify individuals in our midst who we know, beyond any doubt, are hurting people more than they are helping them because of their impairments. How can these observable problems continue to go unattended? After all, we learned in graduate school that ethical problems are relatively straightforward: You simply do what the codes of our profession instruct you to do.

Indeed, there is a whole collection of such codes—by social workers, psychiatrists, psychologists, counselors, family therapists, and other groups—and they all say basically the same thing: We have an obligation to intervene when either ourselves or other professionals may be harming clients. This action may take the form of self-monitoring, confronting an impaired individual directly, or reporting suspected problems to state licensing boards. However, only a small fraction of the problems are actually dealt with in such an organized manner.

Before our fingers start pointing elsewhere, each one of us needs to consider how well we are personally functioning and who we know right now whose professional functioning seems to be impaired. It sounds easy enough, but there are many reasons we give ourselves for not dealing with our own problems:

- *I've got to handle this on my own.*
- *I'll get over it in a little while.*
- *I can keep it from affecting my work.*
- *Someone would have told me if it was really a problem.*
- *It's not as bad as it seems.*

Then there are the reasons we use to explain why we don't get involved in the impairment of others:

- *It's none of my business. Someone else should do something.*
- *It wouldn't do any good. Nobody would believe me.*
- *Even if I do report it, nothing good would happen from it.*
- *I'd just be setting myself up for some sort of revenge.*
- *Maybe things will improve if I just give it some time.*
- *Everyone else knows what is going on and they aren't doing anything either.*
- *What could really be gained by stirring up trouble?*

The truth is that these excuses for inaction are sometimes appropriate reasons to avoid taking aggressive action in sticky situations where we are not really certain what is going on. We are hardly advocating that everyone should report to "big brother/sister" everything that seems suspicious and strange in our own or our colleagues' behaviors. Rather, the suggestion is that we become more responsible for one another's welfare and take better care of each other, including ourselves. When someone among us is wounded and limping along, even when denial is rampant, we should be doing so much more to help that professional regain a sense of balance. Burying your head in the sand and hoping the problems go away has not proven to be helpful. Someone needs to take the risk of acting in order to improve difficult situations. The first place to look for that action is to yourself.

TAKING THIS PERSONALLY

This chapter comes from our desire to help move you closer to recognizing and dealing with the personal frailties of mental health professionals. Our individual experiences with the personal nature of impairment is what provides our motivation here. It therefore seems only fitting to begin with a brief look at our own experiences with impairment, and subsequent efforts to heal ourselves.

I (JK) have written extensively about my own struggles with being and feeling impaired throughout most of my life (Kottler, 1993; Kottler, 1995; Kottler & Blau, 1989). This has been my greatest weakness as a therapist. There isn't a day that goes by that I don't feel impaired in some way, hopefully not to the point that I hurt others, but at least to the point that my levels of competence are diminished. I am a voyeur, a perfectionist, an approval seeker, an obsessive-compulsive achiever, a do-gooder, a meddler, a reckless risk-taker, and each of these urges has compromised me in some way.

Yet these qualities have also been among my greatest strengths as a therapist and teacher. They have helped me to understand other people's pain through my own struggles. I have been committed to learning from my clients, as well as my therapists and supervisors, so that I have brought my impairments under sufficient control that I can function quite well. Along the way, there have been a number of colleagues, my coauthor among them, who have been instrumental in offering the caring, support, and honest confrontation that it takes to make me face my own demons.

I'd (RH) like it to be different, but the fact is I'm mediocre and fearful, and always have been. I'd like to be smarter and learn things more easily. I'd like to run away from my problems and those of others, and at times I've done just that. I'm afraid that failure at so many personal and professional things is just around the corner for me. The fact that people believe in me and appreciate me is wonderful, but it also creates a pressure that seems unbearable at times. What about all those I'll mislead and disappoint if my ideas for this book don't work? What if I don't read enough of the professional literature and a client is hurt or dies? What if I give in to weakness and hurt another? Can I be forgiven? Can I forgive myself? Should I run away from people and problems to avoid failure? Perhaps I'll change jobs. Perhaps I'll be more formal and less real to protect myself. Perhaps I'll drink more to make the world stop for awhile.

I've struggled with these issues in the past and continue to try and hold them at bay today. My success in the struggle varies and the people around me are treated differently during those variations. People don't get the same quality from Richard every time. My variations are major weaknesses, but perhaps blessings as well. I've not yet met a quality therapist who doesn't struggle with similar issues. The recognition and daily attention to the fact that my struggles are legitimate and comparable, if not exactly the same, as everyone else's is what I believe helps me communicate with clients, students, friends, victims, criminals, and even the lost child in the store. My mediocrity, self-doubt, fallibility, and commonness limit me, but they have also assisted me in understanding and helping others who are struggling. Perhaps just as importantly, they have moved me to allow others like Jeffrey to enter my life and help me as well.

We disclose our own vulnerabilities not because we enjoy admitting our weaknesses, but because we wish to emphasize the very personal nature of this subject. It is easy to shake our heads in disgust when a colleague commits some ethical transgression or otherwise acts inappropriately. We wonder how on earth a professional could take advantage of a client, engage in dual relationships or sexual improprieties, miss obvious cues, violate the customary standard of care, or breach boundaries and rules enacted to protect client safety. We speak about such individuals as if they are a breed apart, members of another spatial dimension. The truth of the matter is that any one of us can become impaired to the point where we hurt someone.

Any one of us can lose control, become depressed, abuse alcohol, or suffer a tragedy from which we cannot recover. None of us is immune from the potential to lose our way, slowly, so slowly we don't even realize what is happening. We all have the ability to so distort our view of a personal disability that we fail to recognize the damage we are doing. Any of us can hurt so badly that we can become threatened by others' attempts to be helpful. We are not just speaking about "them"; we are talking about *us*.

One therapist tells in her own words how sanctimonious and judgmental of others she was about lapses in conduct—until she found herself in over her head without any clear idea of how it all happened:

I always thought that the absolute worst thing that anyone could do in this field was to have a romantic relationship with a client. I have known colleagues, all of them men, who were predators in this regard. There! See how easily my feelings slip through? Actually, some of them were predators, but others were just like me. You see, I was going through a messy divorce. It had been years since I'd felt loved by a man. I guess my guard was down, or I wasn't thinking straight, or something. But anyway, I got involved with this man who was my client. I made excuses to myself that this was different; after all, I loved him and he loved me, but I knew that somehow, some way, I ended up doing what I found so abhorrent in others.

Another therapist tells of going to work in a substance abuse facility with a hangover for the third day in a row. Confronted by a client, he feels trapped by the accusation: "You've got a hangover again, don't you? I've seen this before." Should he lie, tell the truth, or change the subject? None of the choices seem right. What is the right choice when you are found out to be wrong and the consequences are severe?

The vast majority of therapists are good people. We almost always know and believe in the theoretical right and wrong ethical choices involved in work with clients and running our own lives. We learned the importance of this lesson in graduate school. What we learned since those days, however, is that thinking and planning about potentially difficult situations is not the same as actually facing them. The theoretical concepts of values, beliefs, ideals, and the future were our focus as students, while the human factors of emotions, commitment, practicality, consequences, and immediacy are the greatest influences we face now as therapists.

IMPAIRMENT AS A BASIC HUMAN FACTOR

No matter how hard we try, we are not flawless machines. The uniquely human characteristics that allow us to invent and produce creative solutions in our work are the same ones that make us susceptible to greater error and misjudgment.

- Confidence leads us to influence others when they feel no hope, yet it blinds us when we are heading off course.
- Sensitivity helps us read nuances in client behaviors, while it taps our emotions in ways that can spark distortions.
- Compassion allows us to nurture clients, and yet can also blur the strict boundaries that are vital in our work.
- Risk-taking promotes those creative innovations so necessary for the complexities of our work, but it can also lead us to act recklessly.
- Healthy egos permit us to model personal effectiveness to clients, but can also lead to feelings of narcissism and entitlement.
- High energy levels give us the freedom to extend ourselves for others, while at the same time promoting overextension and inability to continue helping.
- Control of ourselves, situations, and others is necessary to provide consistency in client outcomes, yet it can easily also lead us to abuse others.

It is not the presence of these qualities that creates difficulties; rather, it is our lack of awareness about their impact on ourselves and others. Instead of presuming our goodwill and ability can overcome any weakness, we must become more aware of the signs of stress that can bring on our disability.

SIGNS OF STRESS

It has been estimated that professional therapists average only about ten good years before the signs of stress and burnout become inevitable

(Grosch & Olsen, 1994). The signs can be as familiar as boredom, fatigue, loss of interest in work, and lessened productivity.

There are many sources for this stress we experience (Kottler, 1993): pressures in our work environment such as organizational politics, supervisory incompetence, time pressures, nonsupportive colleagues, excessive paper work, or torn allegiances; interactions with clients—those who are manipulative, angry, abusive, withdrawn, or suicidal; personal transitions and events such as financial or legal problems, job relocations, or life transitions. Stress may also be self-induced, resulting from feelings of perfectionism, need for approval, emotional depletion, self-doubt, of excessive rumination, or an unhealthy lifestyle. Each of us can identify with at least a few from each category, yet we may not give enough attention to where they can lead.

"Burnout" has received wide attention in most professions, in part because of the negative stigma it creates. A picture comes into focus of a stream of individuals leaving a chosen job or career because of an inability to manage the related daily pressures. It doesn't draw a very attractive employment picture for potential therapists, but the effects go well beyond the outcome of a career choice. Burnout may be better pictured as "rust-out"—a degenerative process where a variety of symptoms emerge. It is these symptoms that cause much more damage to therapists and clients than the potential of therapists switching careers.

Periodic depression is a common problem and those in the helping professions are no more immune than anyone else. One estimate suggested that 60–90% of psychiatrists could be identified as depressed, although their symptoms might not be clearly observable (Swearingen, 1990). Over half the therapists in another study even took the step of self-diagnosing themselves as having been depressed (Deutsch, 1985). It should be no surprise, then, to see withdrawal, loneliness, sadness, reduced communication, diminished affect, lowered self-esteem, a lack of interest in work, and suicidal ideation in our closest colleagues or ourselves.

We all have experiences with human disasters like the death of a loved one, a disability, an unwanted pregnancy, or being victimized. We expect them to cause pain and suffering. Loss of a job, an investment gone bad, or office infighting over a difficult issue may not seem so devastating, but we know that they too can have a severe impact on how people value their lives. Society presumes that people will not have it together for a period following such disasters, but our clients are not so understanding, since their needs continue regardless of our problems.

There is no exhaustive list available describing the full range of inappropriate therapist behaviors. However, those samples of impairment that we see most often include:

- meeting personal needs rather than addressing the concerns of the client
- undergoing some life transition or crisis that distracts us from the therapeutic tasks at hand
- ignoring "holes" in our conscience that allow us to refuse acknowledgment of the consequences of personal immoral, unethical, or inappropriate behavior that is clearly harmful to others
- addictions to drugs or alcohol that distort judgment
- suffering from certain personality characteristics, underlying organic problems, or other predispositions that limit our ability to function appropriately
- experiencing the same psychological difficulties as our clients who seek treatment for depression, anxiety, or a host of other emotional problems

Many times, no one event or reason can be clearly attached to a particular therapist's problem behavior. Instead it is an accumulation of stressors that come together in some critical mass. Even though the source may be in question, the changes in behavior that mark the problem's evolution remain visible if we look hard enough. One therapist discussed how she came to realize the signs of a colleague's impairment that had grown over time without her realizing it:

I explained to a client in the waiting room that her therapist, Jean, must have been held up after lunch. As soon as the words were out of my mouth, I realized how often I had been making these excuses for Jean of late with no real idea where she was. She was late in the morning, after lunch, and was regularly finishing early with afternoon clients. I knew by rumor that the manager was complaining about her productivity and the supervisor was griping about her records. Then I remembered how I had discounted the complaints from two of Jean's clients about not attending to their needs.

This therapist is caught like many of us between not wanting to overreact to one strange action and the possibility that all the events together add up to a major problem. Indecision delays judgment so that the problem is often not realized until it is too late. Individual occurrences of isolation, unrealistic self-expectations, enmeshment with certain clients, avoidance of professional responsibilities, missing appointments, and deviations from previous professional behaviors can be either anomalies or become dangerous when they intermix and continue over time.

The fact that the worst effects of these problems occur in combination and over time makes them much more difficult to handle. Dealing with an immediate, time-limited emergency is where individuals and organizations are most effective at pouring all available resources into the task. The necessary motivation, abilities, and attention span needed to give ongoing attention to difficult situations is much harder to create and maintain.

HEADS IN THE SAND

We all know the recognition of therapist impairment problems is nothing new. A 1991 American Counseling Association task force on impaired practitioners reported that it would be reasonable to assume from research that at least 10% of professionals at any given time suffer from some form of impairment that reduces the quality of their own lives and their ability to provide services (Borders, 1991). These figures just scratch the surface by giving recognition to only the most obviously impaired from a limited segment of the profession.

Just look over your shoulder at the colleagues with whom you work. You need not look far to see candidates—professionals who are impaired, hurting others through their own neglect, incompetence, or insensitivity. We see these people all around. We know about them by reputation, by complaints from people in the community, and even by direct observation. Yet rarely do we take direct actions to help them, or the people they are hurting.

Following are several probable reasons why the profession as a whole, as well as ourselves as individuals, have neglected to address one of the most important problems in the field.

The Profession's Priorities

We are at a stage in our development where increasing public confidence, expansion of services, and holding on to gains of the past are critical goals. Drawing attention to those among us who are most dysfunctional does not endear us to legislators, consumer groups, and third-party organizations that are already looking for excuses to put us out of business.

Systemic Dysfunction in the Profession

It is the nature of all professional groups to close ranks when a member is under attack. Neither doctors, lawyers, nor any other guild are interested in "tattling" on others. On the contrary, professionals in most groups enable dysfunctional behavior by the ways they protect their colleagues. One extreme case in Las Vegas had an esteemed radiologist in town misreading x-rays and misdiagnosing patients for over a decade because of his own degenerative neurological disease. In some cases, he recommended removal of the wrong breast or organ without any sanction or intervention. When his colleagues who protected him were queried afterward, they shrugged: "He was, after all, so well-regarded." Before we shake our heads in astonishment, consider the dysfunctions within our own profession.

Denial

As long as we pretend not to have a problem, we will never deal with it. This, of course, is exactly what we say to our clients, also with little dramatic effect. Nevertheless, until we recognize that we do have to do something, nothing will happen.

Shame

This is an embarrassing subject to be speaking about. It is also extremely uncomfortable to face a colleague who we believe might be impaired. Even worse, for those who are out of control it is extremely hard to admit it. Are we not the ones who are supposed to be so perfect and high functioning? If others only knew of our hidden weaknesses, they might never speak to us again.

Co-dependence and Enabling

A family system often has a designated client. The same might be said of professional families (e.g., schools, universities, mental health systems, industry, community agencies, or private groups) where one member becomes the scapegoat as the one who develops the symptoms and gets the attention. Just as acting out for some clients makes perfect sense, or as rescuing one family member provides a distraction for a dysfunctional family, so too does this phenomenon operate in our "professional families."

Ignorance

Some professionals just do not know any better. That is not an excuse, but simply a statement of reality. One therapist was recently confronted about bartering arrangements he made with some of his clients in which he exchanged services for credit on a jet ski. He was genuinely astonished that he was doing something wrong. Many therapists, especially those who are impaired, will not be aware of the latest professional standards of care.

Lack of Responsibility

Maybe it is best to mind your own business as long as a colleague's behavior is not in your neighborhood or harming someone in obvious ways. This seems to be commonly encountered reasoning when we observe behavior that seems a bit strange. After all, would you want colleagues pestering you every time they observe you doing something out of the ordinary? Quite simply, many of us do not easily accept responsibility for other professionals' conduct. Right this moment, we know by reputation at least a half dozen individuals and by personal experience another half dozen, who are impaired by any definition. So, why don't we do something about it? Why don't we take more responsibility? The internal dialogue goes something like this:

*Most of what I have heard or seen is inconclusive. Who am I to be judging someone else? Besides, I don't really have enough direct evidence to do something quite yet. But I will. **Really**, I will! Also, I don't have much of a relationship with these people. I hardly know them. I can't just call them out of the blue and say I heard you are into some weird stuff, better stop it or I'll tell. Frankly, I don't know what to do about the matter. I don't feel good about ignoring things and I don't feel very good about dealing with the issue.*

Hypocrisy

People have been attracted to our profession for a number of reasons that sometimes have more to do with personal motives related to power, control, and manipulation than with helping people. There are those among us who hurt people, not only clients but also other therapists, because they are not very nice individuals. They preach compassion and empathy while exploiting others mercilessly. They speak eloquently about the importance of being direct and honest while they are being manipulative and self-serving. If you think about it, what better job is there for someone who enjoys watching other people squirm and then dangling them like puppets at the end of a string? That such individuals find their way into our profession should not be a surprise; that we allow them to stay, or do little to help them change their ways, is inexcusable.

Fear of Retribution

We would be less than honest if we failed to mention that there are consequences to taking action. What are the personal payoffs to intervening with an impaired professional? Do we honestly think this person is going to be grateful when we express our concerns? Do we imagine that we will be applauded by colleagues for our courage? It may very well be the "right" thing to do, but it also has its price. We could be wrong or be overreacting. What if the person seeks to exact some sort of revenge? "You ruined my life, so I'll ruin yours!"

Considering the consequences of taking action, some might conclude that it will do little good anyway, maybe even make things worse. This is the last in a series of very good excuses that allow impaired therapists to continue hurting others, the profession, and themselves. These good excuses may soothe us and our fellow clinicians, but they do nothing to promote the necessary healing.

RECOGNIZING THAT IT'S TIME TO ACT

There is no shortage of ethical guidelines for us to follow. They include quality information, at least of a general nature, about what you should and should not be doing. We are left to follow these guidelines and make our own decisions as to what defines impairment and when it calls for some sort of intervention. It is a difficult challenge with so little direct guidance available. We know something more is needed and professional organizations have been making tentative steps to respond.

State licensing boards and major professional associations offer policies, standing committees, and procedures to deal with the identification, sanctioning, and in some cases, removal of the most obviously impaired individuals from their roles as helping professionals. However, those boards and professional organizations offer little guidance for the prevention, early recognition of symptoms, or support for those therapists who are floundering.

The pattern is a common one for growing professions such as ours. First we focus attention on developing the knowledge base and skills needed to provide quality services. Success at this first task leads to acceptance by well-served clientele and a recognition that some professionals are not living up to rightfully expected standards. Committees and licensing boards then form in order to stop problem members from providing services and thereby safeguarding the public and the reputation of the profession. A quality product and protection of the public are promoted by eliminating harmful providers. It is a logical and reasonable professional survival model, but it is also one that ignores the human frailty of its members.

Official recognition of therapists' frailty and calls for organizational support systems have slowly been emerging. The American Psychological Association (Kilburg, Nathan, & Thoreson, 1986), the National Association of Social Workers (Reamer, 1992), the American Association of Pastoral Therapists (Fisher, 1993), and most recently the American Counseling Association (Hazler & Kottler, 1996a) have each given formal recognition of the need to expand the professional knowledge base and seek better ways to deal with the issues. These actions have spurred the development of scattered publications, a sample of which includes an overview book (Kilburg et al., 1986), a resource book for the impaired (National Association of Social Workers, 1987), a practitioner's guide to ethical decision making (Forester-Miller & Davis, 1995), and a journal special edition directing organizational and personal actions (Hazler & Kottler, 1996b).

Starting is a good thing, but not as good as a strong finish. The proof will be in the impact these actions have. The question for the many communities of mental health workers is: Will they invest the energy and resources necessary to deal with the human needs of members, or will that energy and resources be placed elsewhere? Past experience tells us that the large-scale commitment to these issues given by professional organizations tends to be short-lived. One result is that little outcome data is available and few coordinated, active, or successful programs can be used as models. Will our profession follow a similar pattern or take the necessary steps to deal with the long-term problems? We offer a number of concrete suggestions that could take place, rather, that *must* take place if we to continue to survive, if not flourish:

- Provide practical encouragement to devise and implement prevention and treatment models.
- Promote research by seeking grants from professional organizations and related businesses that are affected by therapist impairment.
- Establish outcome studies on impairment prevention and rehabilitation programs.
- Create standing committees with responsibility to develop and evaluate

internal programs that identify and support the rehabilitation of impaired therapists and encourage a healthy work atmosphere.

- Give the issues of professional impairment an integral role in all aspects of training and practice.
- Form more working coalitions between professional organizations, certification and licensing authorities, and therapist education programs to create and implement programs that encourage professional wellness and provide for rehabilitation of impaired therapists.
- Insure a continuing focus on the progress of therapist health, impairment research, and program development by creating regular columns in organization newsletters, making these issues regular agenda items for staffing, supervision, and consultation meetings.

There are many things our profession has yet to learn. What we know for sure about people, their needs, and how to support them is dwarfed by the information we are missing. Decisions must continuously be made regarding where to put our efforts, resources, and energies because there are not enough of these to meet all needs. The issues of impaired professional therapists demand a definitive portion of those efforts, resources, and energies. We must find the courage to better care for our colleagues and ourselves with much the same purpose and professionalism that we provide to our clients.

BEING THERE FOR A COLLEAGUE

A group of therapists was asked the question, "What should you do when you believe a colleague to be impaired?" The discussion that followed focused on the legal and reporting dimensions:

- *You've got to turn the person in to protect clients.*
- *Tell the supervisor. It is her job.*
- *You've got to figure out whether you are right before reporting.*
- *If it is bad, report it to the state licensing board.*
- *Keep them away from anyone they can hurt.*

There was much discussion of making judgments and legal consequences, while the topic of how to provide supportive assistance to a colleague never arose. This discussion is a direct reflection of the way our profession as a whole deals with the issues. Most ethical publications deal with how and when to protect clients and remove offending therapists from practice. Few deal with what help is needed by impaired therapists, and even fewer describe how to provide the needed support.

Herlihy (1996) presented a reasonable five-step ethical plan of action for dealing with impaired therapists as a means of bridging the gap between reporting needs and supportive needs. The five steps for concerned colleagues include:

1. Identify the problem and your relationship to it.
2. Apply current applicable codes of ethics to the circumstances.
3. Determine the nature and dimensions of the dilemma.
4. Generate potential courses of action.
5. Consider potential consequences of all options and determine a course of action.

This model provides a reasonable process to follow in order to assure your own personal ethical behavior. What it does not approach is a sense of how to interact with the colleague as you work your way through this emotionally trying process. We believe there are some specific factors that also need to be considered related to your personal involvement.

Give Conscious Recognition to the Problem

Other professionals are rarely surprised when the impairment of a close colleague is brought into the open. We see the signs and symptoms, but often don't allow ourselves to give them formal recognition. We are afraid that by admitting to what we know, even to ourselves, we make ourselves judge and jury, creating decisions that become immediately unalterable. Yet it is only by giving conscious recognition to our concerns and questions that answers and supportive actions have the opportunity to be found and implemented.

Learn More about the Problem and Your Colleague

The questions raised by giving recognition to what you see and hear need answers, and it takes work on your part to find them. Many professionals quit at this stage simply because they are not willing or able to put in the time and energy required. Quitting can only bring about two results and neither is productive for your colleague or your ability to help: The problem will be ignored or judgments will be made based on inadequate information.

Two kinds of information need to be sought about the problem and your colleague. First, you may need to seek professional information about problems such as substance abuse among professionals, professional burnout, personality disorders, or ethical guidelines. You will also need additional information about your colleague as a person and professional in order to answer questions like: How long has this been occurring? Have there been sudden changes? What is happening in this colleague's life beyond work? What other psychological, physical, or behavioral symptoms might be occurring that you haven't seen in casual observations? What is the impact on clients, other colleagues, and family? Only when you have sufficient information should you move on to the high-risk stage of confrontation.

Arrange a Confrontation between the Right People

The skills of productive confrontation are ones we have all studied well, even if we are sometimes reluctant to use them. What the literature and classes provide less often is the importance of choosing the right people with the most appropriate relationships for a given confrontation. Different relationships may be called for depending upon situational needs and desired outcomes.

- Collegial relationships are best used when you want to give plenty of leeway for the potentially impaired colleague to reject the approach and the individual doing the confrontation. Going alone to confront a colleague provides maximum safety for your colleague while it also leaves you much more vulnerable than any other relationship. It is risky, but then the best of friends or colleagues are expected to take those kinds of risks for each other.
- Supervisors add the dimension of authority to the intervention and shift the risk factor much more to the side of the potentially impaired therapist. Once the issues are presented by a supervisor they cannot be easily discounted either now or in the future. Mistakes in judgment here are much less easily reversed and much more likely to result in formal decisions being made.
- Experts with experience and knowledge of a therapist's specific impairment can sometimes provide a level of pressure that falls between colleague and supervisor relationships. Expert advice can be more easily discounted personally, because no friendship is involved, and professionally, because experts are not necessarily in a position to make judgments

that have formal consequences. It is the knowledge they possess that is hard to discount. This role is most effective when a colleague can benefit from new information as much as or more than personal support or formal pressure.

- Family and friends might be the best people to approach a problem that is having equal or greater impact away from work. You might think that this need is none of your business as a colleague, but there is no doubt that major problems in one's personal life directly influence the ability to do quality work. Enlisting family and friends in the support of a colleague can sometimes be the only realistic way to help.
- Combinations of confronters is sometimes appropriate when the problem is serious and the impact is diverse. The extremely high stakes in this model may be just what is needed to deal with a problem that needs immediate and drastic attention.

Offer Support During the Struggles

Confronting someone is risky business, but staying with a colleague throughout the struggles that follow is hard work as well. Once impaired therapists recognize their problem, their work has only begun and they need support more than ever. No professional ethical obligations force you to actively provide support during recovery. It is the caring and moral aspects of yourself as a person and a professional that will be needed to make this commitment.

Take Care of Yourself

Making the commitment to be a part of another professional's struggle for recovery does not extend to allowing yourself to become impaired. You must make continuing and conscious analysis of your status and decide to do whatever is necessary to keep yourself healthy. There is only so much you can give of yourself before you become a burden rather than a supporter. Recognizing and working within your personal limits is an essential aspect of your responsibility that must not be overlooked for everyone's sake.

LOOK IN THE MIRROR

Understanding others seems to fall into our laps many times by simply looking, listening, and observing. We take in all the information and analyze it, using all the knowledge and experiences we have accumulated.

The process seems natural and the information so clear that we wonder how anyone could miss such obvious problems and solutions. Observing and analyzing ourselves is a different story.

In order to see and hear ourselves, we need a mirror that allows us to see our lives from an external viewpoint. Only someone or something outside ourselves can provide the feedback to help us judge our actions just as a mirror on the wall helps us judge our looks. Whether it is a friend, family member, stranger, or therapist, we need others to help us see ourselves more clearly.

You cannot buy human mirrors in a store, but they can be found in places that are surprising. Sometimes it is even our clients who inadvertently reflect back our own images. I (RH) was working with a depressed male who told a story not so different from many others:

I am respected at work, make a good living, don't hurt for material things, and have a good family. So why am I depressed? Why do I want to quit work? Why do I want to run away? Why do I feel so tired? Why do I feel inadequate? Why do I feel like a failure? And why is everyone saying I need a shrink to help me? Why can't I do something about this myself?

The questions were ones I'd heard many times before, yet today they had a different meaning. I wanted to get a note pad, ask the client to repeat them, and then write them down word-for-word. My reaction had nothing to do with the client, it was just that these were the same questions I had been asking myself late at night when I couldn't sleep. These were the ones I was trying to avoid by watching the news, reading, and having a drink as soon as I came home late. These were the ones I couldn't talk to anyone about because of all the work I had to do; the ones I shouldn't tell anyone about because I should be strong enough to deal with them alone. These were my questions and it was my depression whether I wanted it or not. I was handling them just as poorly as most people; it was time to call my own therapist.

The main difficulty in dealing with our own impairment is not a lack of knowledge about what to do. It is not a lack of skill, ability, or even motivation. It is an avoidance of the mirrors in our lives that allows us to ignore the problems or blame their consequences on things outside ourselves.

The Therapist's Therapist

This chapter would be much less vital if mental health check-ups were as common for therapists as medical check-ups are for physicians. We know the value of therapy and the dangers it poses for therapists. We accept human frailties and believe they need to be supported. It seems like a no-brainer—we should all go to a therapist on a regular basis.

Listen to Your Clients' Healing

As your clients get better, they will tell you about how their lives are changing, what convinced them to change, and how they got through it. While you are taking time to feel good about the work you've done, also listen closely to what they are telling you about the healing process. Compare their healthier new thoughts and lives to your own. Commit to do no less than what you asked of them and you'll probably improve the way you treat yourself.

Invest in Colleagues

The more physically or mentally isolated you find yourself from your colleagues the more likely it is that you may be avoiding dealing with important problems. A lack of conversations on personally relevant issues, avoiding contact outside the office, staying in your office rather than meeting colleagues in the hallways, and finding more and more ways to work alone are clear signs that you need to make a greater investment in your colleagues. These are the professionals who should be most familiar with your work and your actions on a day-to-day basis. The more contact you have with them and the more you request their input on yourself, the greater the possibilities are that they can provide the mirror you need to see how you are really doing.

Let Friends and Family See You from Other Angles

The consistency we strive so hard to obtain in our relationships can also become the intransigence that holds us back from learning new things. Friends and family can better act as a mirror to our behavior when we show ourselves to them from a greater variety of angles. From time to time, try some of the following with your friends and family:

- Talk about aspects of work you don't normally share.
- Bring colleagues home with you.
- Take a non-colleague to work.

- Act the way you want for once rather than the way you should.
- Take a friend to dinner for the first time.
- Be serious, silly, caring, and obnoxious all with one group.

The idea is to do something different, break out of the mold. Give these people a chance to see and talk about a side of you not frequently available to them. The contrasts will help bring out a clearer picture of who you are, how you act, and allow you to do more with what you discover.

Write it Down

Some of the things we do for clients seem so simple and yet they are so effective. Elementary paraphrasing of what a client said about themselves often brings a response like, "It sounds crazy, doesn't it?" The same idea that seemed reasonable when it was closed up inside often makes no sense whatsoever when it is seen in reflection. Talking to ourselves often does not give the degree of honest reflection we need; writing can do a much better job.

Some of the most objective feedback you can obtain about yourself can come from writing your ideas down and then reading them later. An even more powerful tactic is to give your writings to a trusted friend to read. We don't like to put things in writing that we don't want to admit, so this is no simple task. The results are worth it though, as they can help you see those errors in thinking that are not so apparent in our normal ruminations.

OUT IN THE OPEN

Throughout this chapter we have tried to highlight the fact that therapist impairment, be it your own or another's, can only continue to exist to the degree it is allowed to remain in hiding. We tried to act on this belief by starting with ourselves. The personal disclosures of our own struggles with fallibility and impairment are not so different from anyone else's. They cause us the most pain when we keep them hidden; when they are out in the open, they seem much more manageable and more normal.

Our professional organizations are slowly coming to the same realization that open discussion of therapist impairment is the only real way to begin treating the problem. Businesses know it, agencies know it, families know it, and we know it as individuals: Hiding problems promotes their festering and deterioration, while dealing with them openly creates the potential for healing.

Unfortunately, what we know to be true is not necessarily what we choose to employ in our own best interest. Our first reaction is generally to hide the issues and to then create extensive defense mechanisms designed to keep them hidden. At the same time we are protecting ourselves from embarrassment, we are also fostering the growth of the very problems that are causing our embarrassment.

Solving our problems is not the greatest danger we face as individuals and as a profession. We have the skills, ability, and knowledge to deal with most of the things that hold us back or keep us impaired. Our greater challenge is to find the courage and the mechanisms necessary to bring our problems out into the open. It is only there that we can apply all the resources available to effectively treat the problems. It is past time that we attend to ourselves in the same honest and caring ways we attend to our clients and it is certainly time for us to do so out in the open.

We must keep alert to the seduction associated with being seen as an expert and the pride that is on the line as we try to fulfill the expectations of others. It feels safe to know we can say things that others expect us to say and dangerous to say what is not expected. Our discomfort and anxiety levels rise when we attempt to press supervisees to step outside the expected boundaries of the traditional tutorial relationship in order to explore more threatening issues. Only when we get directly in touch with these reactions inside ourselves can we gain control and modify them to create a more balanced offering of expert advice and support for supervisee self-identified needs. It is a difficult task in which success will be determined by our professional abilities and our personal commitment to serve others in the most growth-oriented ways.

CHAPTER ELEVEN

Getting the Most from Supervision

Nobody ever asked us how we wanted to be supervised; our teachers and mentors already had very definite ideas on the subject. We so desperately wanted their approval and a good recommendation that we readily complied with their preferences about whether we should talk about therapeutic skills, planned interventions and outcomes, transference dynamics, family coalitions, or personal issues triggered by the sessions. Rarely did we entertain the idea, much less mobilize the courage, to say, "Excuse me, but this is what *I* want and how I learn best."

Once we left graduate school and got a real job, we were ecstatic about the possibility that now, finally, we could get the kind of supervision that would take us to the next level of competence. No longer would we have to worry so much about figuring out what our supervisors wanted to hear and then give it to them in the exact language they mandated. We could talk about the issues that bothered us most, ask the questions that most befuddled us, and structure our consultation sessions with the same freedom and self-responsibility we bestow on our own clients. What a surprise it was to discover that in some ways little has changed.

HIERARCHICAL RELATIONSHIPS AND TRADITIONAL SUPERVISION

The staff meeting began when the clinical director cleared his throat. Gosh, he looked impressive, decked out as he was in all the accouterments that he imagined his position demanded—immaculately trimmed beard, smug smile, tweed jacked *with* elbow patches, and a pile of case folders stacked neatly before him in all their color-coded splendor. Except for the no-smoking policy now in force, he surely would have been lighting a pipe, or at least using its stem as a pointer to recognize the next person to speak.

The clinic administrator sat on the director's left and the staff psychologist on the right. It made a formidable impression. Sprinkled around the table were a dozen other mental health professionals—psychologists, social workers, counselors, a psychiatric nurse, a medical resident, and a few interns. Then, of course, there was you, the new kid on the block. Nervous anticipation built as you checked out the posturing and apparent confidence of all the professionals present—here is a group of people who really seem to know their stuff, at least if their nonverbal behavior signals are any indication of inner wisdom.

Working through the cases under review, it was all too apparent that many of those present had very strong opinions about what should be done. Unfortunately, there was a direct relationship between how much staff members spoke, how stridently they made their points, and how they fit in the pecking order. A hierarchy of authority and seniority had been established, not unlike what you had experienced in graduate school. This time, however, it was not just the faculty who had absolute control—there were gradations in power depending on how close the professional sits to the ultimate seat of authority.

This situation represents an extreme version of what many therapists experience in their supervision, but it nevertheless highlights some of the aspects of traditional supervision that are based on hierarchical relationships. Even if you work in a setting with a looser, more informal structure, it is likely that supervision is characterized by the following features:

A Paradoxical Relationship

The supervisor expects full disclosure of your doubts, fears, failures, and mistakes, yet is in a position to evaluate your performance based on what you say and do. Depending on the judgment formed, you may or may not be recommended for licensure, a promotion, expanded responsibilities, or a future position. The mixed message you get is, "Tell me everything about what you are doing. Be honest. Leave out nothing. I will not only offer you support and guidance, but I will evaluate what you have said and done afterward."

A Limited Sort of Confidentiality

Some of the personal details of your life may be kept private, while the nature of what you reveal about clients, how you handle cases, and how you respond to suggestions offered will be shared with others. Furthermore, what the supervisor tells administrators and other colleagues about the sessions will be accompanied by critical judgments about where you are in your development in relation to where he or she thinks you should be.

A Dependence on the Expert

The tutorial model of supervision reinforces the notion that the supervisor knows the truth, or at least the way to find it, and the trainee had best follow the wisdom of superior judgment and experience. This may very well be the most appropriate model to follow for beginning therapists who need a lot of guidance in the early part of their careers. Unfortunately, tutorial supervision is often continued with more experienced practitioners, because it is often the only model that is familiar to them.

A Reactive Therapist Mode

The judgmental and expert-based nature of the traditional supervisor role focuses attention not on therapist assertiveness, but instead on trying things in anticipation of your supervisor's wishes. What will the supervisor want? Have I done what will be expected of me? These are the questions that begin to drive your actions, rather than: What do I believe would be good to do? What am I expecting of myself? How would I evaluate myself?

Supervisor-Focused Creativity

Your most creative thinking is often directed toward the supervisor rather than the client in this model. Generating ideas through brainstorming is done only when the supervisor considers it necessary and the final selection of "best ideas" is generally based upon supervisor criteria rather than your beliefs. This might be a very effective use of creativity if you were being paid to help supervisors feel good about their supervision. It has little value as a mechanism for developing your ability to find new, productive insights about the actual clients who do pay the bills.

WHAT YOU REALLY WANTED FROM SUPERVISION

We don't wish to imply that tutorial supervision is not helpful, because it is, in fact, the preferred model to use in many cases. Rather, its usefulness depends to a great extent on the clarity of boundaries that have been established, the degree of flexibility in the supervisor's role, the amount of safety the therapist feels, the way confusion is handled, the manner in which disagreements are worked through, and the conduct of evaluation

(Bernard & Goodyear, 1992). It is the implementation of this traditional relationship rather than its formal description that will best determine its effectiveness.

What was first learned in graduate school, and reinforced in practice, is often more similar to approval-seeking in supervision than truly seeking how to get the most from the experience. We can get so busy trying to impress mentors with our brilliance and to convince them we are made of the right stuff that we neglect the issues that are troubling us the most.

Consider what you talked about to faculty members, internship supervisors, or perhaps your current supervisor, compared to what you really wanted to bring up. Had you been completely open and honest, you would have probably emphasized several issues that remained unspoken in your actual experience. In all honesty, how many times were you able to say any of the following during supervision?

I am scared that deep down inside I don't have what it takes to be a good therapist. I'm just faking it most of the time. I don't really know what I'm doing. I feel stupid and incompetent. Furthermore, I don't think I'll ever know enough.

I sure blew that one! I really misjudged things, and as a result of my error, I don't think the client will ever come back. I didn't write that in the progress notes but that is the reality of what took place.

Much of the time, I find it hard to concentrate on what my clients are saying because I am personalizing the issues too closely to my own life. Almost everything clients bring up I think to myself, yup, I struggle with the same thing. I wonder about who the hell I think I am trying to help these people when I am really no better off.

No, I know nothing about that theory/technique/strategy you are mentioning that you say is so widely used. Actually, I've never heard of it before. I don't know if I missed that class, I was sleeping, or they just left that one out of my education.

Frankly, I don't have any idea what to do with this case. I don't even know where to begin. I'm not sure what you are really asking me, whether you are testing me to see if I know what to do, or whether you are just stalling because you don't have any idea either. I wish you would just say what you really want.

I can't believe how attracted I feel to some of my clients. They are talking to me, and I'm sitting there pretending to listen. All the while, though, I am thinking about how attractive they are. Do you ever do that, or am I some sort of pervert or something?

You're wrong! You are so certain that you know all the answers but this time you've missed it by a mile. You don't understand what I'm saying because you are listening to yourself rather than hearing what I am saying. With all your experience, you still don't know everything all the time. You act like you are so flexible, and sometimes you even pretend to give in, but we both know that you believe that you are really seeing things clearly and that I'm not.

These examples highlight that sometimes the things that we most need to talk about in supervision are pushed underground because it doesn't feel safe enough to bring them up. Instead, we follow the lead offered by the supervisor, reasonably satisfied that although we are not getting everything we want, at least we are getting other stuff that may be useful. This attitude is probably a healthy adaptation to a difficult situation, reminding ourselves to focus on the positives about what we can be learning rather than what is being omitted.

GETTING THE MOST FROM TRADITIONAL SUPERVISION

We will present some alternative models of supervision that may address more readily the crucial issues mentioned previously. At the same time, there are other strategies that can be used to create a very different type of experience. Obviously, it makes a difference which type of therapy you are practicing and which supervisory philosophy is operating in the sessions. A training model of supervision used to teach brief therapy skills promotes a very different process than the experientially oriented sessions embedded in a psychodynamic or existential mode of practice. Nevertheless, regardless of the therapy style and the kind of supervision being practiced, there are still some universally effective ways to get the most from the experience.

We know that success in therapy occurs most often when the relationship has been structured to obtain mutual agreement on methods and goals specifically tailored to client needs (Kottler et al., 1994). Supervision, as well, works best when the particular structure and process has been negotiated to the satisfaction of both participants. Of course, the problem with the tutorial model is that the supervisor holds the formal power that can dictate what directions things should take, how far-reaching they might be, and whether negotiations will even be allowed to be a part of the relationship. Lacking the influence to make demands or to direct negotiations, there are other assertive techniques for seeking your needs that may fit the less powerful position of supervisee. You may wish to introduce some of the following techniques into your sessions to promote your agenda within the tutorial relationship.

Make Role Inquiries

It is reasonable and relatively nonthreatening to occasionally ask about the best roles for you to play and how they might match those of the supervisor. Most supervisors have not thoroughly considered what roles should be played by themselves and their supervisees in a given session. They fall into patterns that have gotten minimal complaints in the past. These patterns may need to be shaken up by questions about roles in order to bring the issues into conscious awareness.

Role-appropriate behaviors are among the most commonly buried topics in supervision. When you ask supervisors to clarify roles and responsibilities, you make them more likely to take responsibility for the choices they make rather than assuming mutual agreement. Even the supervisor who cares nothing about your opinion will at least provide role descriptions to guide you in deciding how to make the most of the situation.

Express Inquisitiveness, Not Doubts

Questioning the supervisor's ideas, role decisions, directives, or evaluations is part of any supervisory relationship, whether they are handled directly or not. When you can bring these questions into the relationship through a self-focused inquisitive approach, you stand a greater chance of having them resolved productively. This self-initiated yet noncombative approach allows for assertive behavior without the drawbacks of more traditional argumentative options.

Total avoidance of questioning your supervisor, and the potential confrontations that might follow, is not productive for the long-term relationship. Each question you hold inside reduces the truthfulness of your interactions and increases the chances that problematic hidden agendas will develop. On the other hand, directly expressing your questions in the form of doubts and potential weaknesses in your supervisor is even worse. The practical reality of the situation is that while supervisors are expected to express doubts about you, your expressing doubts about the supervisor verges on supervision mutiny.

Traditional models of supervision accept the threatened position of the supervisee, while rejecting such threats for the supervisor. The only real choice you have is to either find ways to bring your doubts into the conversation accompanied by a low level of threat, or bury them inside knowing they will eventually cause problems that you cannot control.

Expressing your concerns as personal curiosity rather than supervisor-focused doubts is a good starting place for getting difficult issues into the conversation. You might begin by simply asking what the supervisor has said, follow it with a comment reflecting your experiences, and end with your self-focused inquiry. There is a big difference, therefore, between saying to a supervisor, "You're not making much sense" and "I'm not understanding what you're saying," or "You're not listening to me" and "I'm not making myself very clear."

Convey Humble Knowledge

Power imbalance in traditional supervision models does not account for the fact that you will at times know something the supervisor does not, recognize the supervisor has said something that is contradicted by information you have, or realize that the supervisor's beliefs or actions are way out of line. You have a professional obligation to share the information for the benefit of the supervisory relationship and for your clients' best interests. Of course, sharing the information also leaves you vulnerable to potentially severe consequences if a threatened supervisor responds negatively. One way to meet professional responsibilities while keeping the likelihood of insulting the supervisor to a minimum is offering your knowledge in as humble a manner as possible.

The secret of providing information beyond, or in contradiction to, what a supervisor knows is to do so in ways that emphasize how the "power" of the relationship continues to be with the supervisor: "I wonder if you could help me to clear up some confusion I have about this issue? I had a different impression."

The power aspect of supervisory relationships is most likely to result in negative outcomes when the supervisor's ego is threatened. Some supervisors will have more fragile egos than others and the longer you work with a supervisor the easier it will be to judge the best means for being direct while also allowing the supervisor to maintain a necessary level of self-respect.

Seek Examples

Supervisors can offer endless hours of words that may sound great, but leave you with no real ability to visualize them in practice. Asking for examples is the most common way of requesting practical clarification of all those words, theories, and cited authors.

Using examples in supervision does more than just help clarify verbal descriptions and theory. Examples provide a common practical context in which both sides can compare and contrast reactions, knowledge, beliefs, and techniques. Common examples recognized by both learner and mentor are often missing in graduate school in which the supervisor's theory and the student's lack of experience may find few points where examples have common interpretations. Supervision of practicing therapists, on the other hand, should be much more amenable to finding numerous meaningful examples recognizable by and useful to both parties.

Request Demonstrations

The most direct way to move a supervision session from theory to practice is to ask the supervisor to show you how to do what she is suggesting. Such a request can be offered as a genuine compliment of her abilities, which can strengthen the relationship as well as get you more of what you need.

Asking the supervisor to role play the therapist while you are the client allows for immediate application of theory. It provides an opportunity for the supervisor to get an immediate, close approximation of your situation while you get to experience how another professional might handle things differently. Role-plays provide the conversations that follow with a wealth of immediate, first-hand information to consider, which is likely to make them some of the most direct and practical supervision times.

Another way to get a better first-hand picture of the supervisor's implementation of theory and techniques is to request the opportunity to observe the supervisor doing therapy. What we say about how we do therapy is rarely a direct representation of how it looks and feels in person. Even if a supervisor's explanations become no better following such observations, you are much more likely to understand them given this new and more realistic context.

Invite Direct Intervention

Gaining the opportunity to watch supervisors work with their clients will create further understanding of how well and in what ways theory and actual practice coincide. However, the most direct way to assure common understanding between you and the supervisor is for both of you to become directly involved with a client.

There will be those times when no matter how much sense the words make nor how well the role-plays go, none of it seems to work when you try them with a particular client. No matter how right everything sounds and feels, you recognize that the supervision is missing some critical aspect of therapeutic reality. These are the occasions when you want to create as many opportunities as possible for you and your supervisor to directly interact with clients together. Asking to have the supervisor work with the client for a time while you observe or for the two of you to work together are legitimate additional dimensions to occasionally request in most supervisory relationships.

The preceding actions can help you to get the most out of traditional supervision in which the supervisor has primary control of content and style. Used judiciously, they can help you to take a more assertive position without challenging the authority and abilities of the supervisor. However, no matter how much these actions might improve a traditional supervisory relationship, they will not eliminate all the problematic aspects. Another form of less threatening and more self-directed supervision is needed to supplement traditional approaches.

PEER CONSULTATION AS AN ALTERNATIVE

Traditional supervision is hierarchical in the sense that the supervisor is seen as an expert, a person in a position of authority. Peer consultation is an alternative form of supervision based on the principle of equality in the relationship. It is a model that emphasizes individually directed growth in which the difficulties associated with the power structure of traditional supervision are eliminated. As inviting as this less threatening model might be, it can only add additional dimensions to therapist development; it cannot replace traditional supervision.

Something important is lost when you give up the greater potential for influence that takes place in traditional supervision; after all, that is the basis for the work we do in therapy. The reason why people come to therapists in the first place is because they are likely to pay attention to us and follow our direction in ways they would never do with friends or coworkers who might offer the same guidance. It is, in part, the power invested in the role of therapist or supervisor that promotes a number of the dramatic changes that can take place. In fact, some would conceptualize the whole process of supervision as a form of social influence in which explicit attempts are made to alter trainee attitudes and behavior (Claiborn, Etringer, & Hillerbrand, 1995).

Clearly, then, there is a trade-off when attempts are made to provide professional guidance in a context that no longer includes a sanctioned expert. The greater wisdom and experience relied upon to create the light through a horrendous storm is no longer available. If anything, it could be said that the blind are leading the blind. It is for this reason that we are not advocating these alternative supervisory structures as a substitute for traditional models. Rather, we are offering these ideas as adjunct structures that can fill an important gap that may have been missing in your growth.

Some practitioners have organized themselves into peer group supervision formats that follow structured agendas (Borders, 1991; Greenberg, Lewis, & Johnson, 1985; Hamlin & Timberlake, 1982; Marks & Hixon, 1986; Nobler, 1980; Wendorf, Wendorf, & Bond, 1985). Participants in these structures take turns presenting cases, specifying what they need in the way of input; this might include any of the following:

- *Support.* "I've been struggling with the same problem for a while. I just want you to know that I'm here for you if you need me."
- *Criticism.* "I don't agree with the way you are handling that situation. I think you're setting yourself up for some greater difficulties later unless you deal with the problem now."
- *Confrontation.* "On the one hand, you say that you are in control of things, but on the other hand you've just described a number of ways that you feel very much out of control."
- *Constructive feedback.* "I really like the way that you decided to bring the whole family into the session, but I'm not sure you maximized the advantages of that decision unless you decide to include everyone in the process."
- *Conceptualization.* "This may not be so much a case of dysthymia as it is a matter of this woman being told for so long that she is depressed that now even she believes it."
- *Treatment planning.* "First, I would attempt to stabilize the situation, then I would contact possible sources of support for him. Make sure you get him to sign an agreement not to hurt himself before you let him go."
- *Specific direct actions.* "You might try using an externalization as a way to prevent further self-blaming and scapegoating."

- *Remedial instruction.* "Why don't we practice doing some externalizations in here. I just learned how to do this myself."
- *Discussion of ethical issues.* "This girl is 15. She's dating and having sex with a guy who is 19. Am I required to report this to protective services? And if I do, I'm certainly not going to be able to help her much."
- *Exploring feelings.* "I just don't feel the same enthusiasm for this kind of work that I used to. I don't know if I'm bored or tired or just burned out. How do the rest of you deal with this?"
- *General discussion.* "I wonder if we could talk for awhile about how a constructivist framework might alter the ways we think about ourselves as change agents?"

The variety of options available in peer consultation groups makes this a popular alternative to traditional supervision. Researchers in one national survey of psychologists in private practice found that almost one-fourth of the 480 therapists sampled were currently participating in a peer consultation group and another one-fourth of respondents had participated in the past. Among those who were not currently involved in such a group, 60% expressed a strong interest in being part of one (Lewis, Greenberg, & Hatch, 1988). Clearly, there is a need on the part of therapists that is not being satisfied by traditional supervision alone.

Practitioners want very badly to feel accepted, respected, and understood in ways that can't be met through more hierarchical, tutorial structures. Allen (1976) describes one of the earliest systematic efforts on the part of a group of therapists to develop their own peer supervision model. Eschewing the tutorial, one-on-one model, this group evolved into a supervisory group of co-equals as a way to avoid the usual pitfalls associated with the dominant supervisory model. There was to be no dependence on an expert and avoidance of those unsavory details that might invite censure by an outside authority.

Based on two years' experience working together without a designated leader, this group of therapists recommended several things that would be valuable for all of us to keep in mind:

1. The quality of supervision is based on the responsibility of the participants.
2. There must be a matching of experience among those who are participating in the process or there ends up with a hierarchical arrangement with the most experienced members being the authorities.
3. Exchanges should always be respectful in order to maintain the atmo-

sphere of safety and openness that is sometimes lacking in other supervisory venues.
4. Seeking outside consultations is encouraged as needed.

It is interesting that the group did not mention the importance of being honest with one another and the consequences of not doing so. Case consultation is valuable only to the extent that feedback is accurate, specific, and clearly presented (Blocher, 1983; Friedlander, Siegel, & Brenock, 1989). Peers who are reluctant to provide truthful, sometimes confrontive feedback short-change everyone involved in the process.

One problem scenario that often develops in peer consultation is that people being painfully honest with one another can create hurt feelings in which irreparable damage may be done to relationships. Far more likely, in our experience, is that people become so polite and cautious in order not to hurt anyone's feelings that they avoid telling one another those things that most need to be brought out in the open.

There are other problems that arise when professionals get together to try and help one another. For one thing, a lot of complaining and whining takes place in which therapists compete with one another over who is most unappreciated and worst-treated by their clients:

Therapist A: I've been seeing this one guy. He comes into my office each time, proceeds to tell me how much worse he is feeling, and then spends the rest of his time telling me what a lousy therapist I am. When I tell him that there is only so much that I can do, that the rest is up to him, he . . .

Therapist B: You think *you've* got it bad? I've got this client who's seeing two other therapists besides me. At the same time! The only way I found out was that I was talking to a friend at . . .

Therapist C: You guys have no idea how bad it can really be. There is this woman who I've been seeing for over four months. Just like clockwork she shows up for her appointments. Then, this week, no show, no phone call, no nothing. I call her to find out what happened and her phone has been disconnected. No forwarding address. Just gone. Not even a good bye, much less a thank you.

This type of complaining often continues when therapists get together during a break. Ostensibly, we are trying to help one another, but what really happens is that we often end up feeling worse by only stating our woes. As in many self-contained groups, nobody is likely to confront the group with ideas that they may be adopting a victim mentality where we blame everyone else for our problems. This type of group has the potential to replace its sense of professional growth with an overriding concern for self-protection.

Advice is liberally dispensed in peer supervision, but it often comes too late to do much good. Weaker groups have a tendency to focus on past occurrences rather than future actions. Members can end up feeling stupid, believing they should have thought of the advice being given beforehand. Now that the information is brought to their attention, they realize the situation will have changed dramatically by the next session, rendering most of the suggestions obsolete.

It is for these reasons that we are introducing a particular kind of peer consultation as a supplement to traditional supervision methods. This peer consultation model is particularly helpful during times when you have reached an impasse with a client, things appear to be headed nowhere, and you have run out of ideas.

Teaching People to Help You when You're Stuck

Although peer support groups can be very attractive, they can carry some distinct problems. Finding a time for so many busy professionals to meet in one place can be annoying at best and an insurmountable obstacle at worst. There are also very real concerns related to confidentiality in these therapeutic communities—the consequences of sharing our deepest concerns and issues is that we risk losing credibility among our peers. One practitioner describes the dilemma this way:

I've been in a peer support group for years. It helps me in a lot of ways, but there are limits to what I can talk about. I get referrals from these people. If I expressed to them the extent of my doubts, they'd never send anyone to me again. So I just keep my mouth shut about some things.

Like any group format, little time is available for each participant to explore their individual needs. Some members will dominate and others will quietly wait their turn, which may at times never come. Pressing issues that cannot be brought up in scheduled supervision may have even less opportunity for sensitive discussion in a group where people are fighting for time.

The alternative peer supervision format we are suggesting here involves working with a single partner during times when you feel stuck with a case. It is designed to avoid the power- and expertise-based issues of traditional supervision as well as the time and confidentiality issues related to peer group formats. This model provides a framework for creating a professionally supportive session at almost a moment's notice and dealing with each of the stages in a single session of less than an hour.

This strategy can prove useful in a variety of circumstances. It works equally well with *any* conflicted relationship found to be at an impasse. Although a particular client will most often be the focus of a session, the strategy is also productive for dealing with conflicts related to a supervisor, colleague, or friend. No matter what the specifics of the problem situation, there are eight basic steps that should make the system work for you.

1. *Find a partner you can trust.* The choice of the partner may be the single most important decision that determines the effectiveness of this method. Make a mistake and you risk betrayal. Choose someone you work with too closely and you can jeopardize a friendship during those times when you must be painfully frank. Find someone who will always choose answers to make you feel good and growth will be stunted. A good compromise is to pick someone you trust to be flexible in following your direction and honest enough to make you aware of your cognitive and emotional blind spots.

   The selection of a partner based on trust level is much more important in this strategy than in other forms of supervision. It isn't necessary in this process to reveal any more than you desire because most of the work takes place inside yourself as a direct result of the structured dialogue. The partner's role is to confirm the safety of the relationship, follow your lead, and provide honest feedback at the times and in the ways that you determine are necessary.

2. *Describe your most difficult case right now.* The starting place is to briefly provide necessary background of the one case that is giving you the most trouble. Don't dwell on the details. Focus on *one relationship* rather than a complex web of influences associated with numerous relationships. Limit your presentation to just a few minutes. Resist the temptation to whine, complain, and seek sympathy. The focus will be on you so your description of the problem individual(s) should take up as little time as possible.

I am having trouble with a couple who, while polite and respectful during sessions, refuse to talk about anything or do any work once they walk out the door. I have been seeing them for a few months, but they don't seem to be improving. After 15 years of being together, they are on the verge of splitting up. These sessions are their last resort.

I've tried everything I know how to do. They act like these ideas are absolutely brilliant and surely will make the difference, but nothing changes. They come in every session feeling hopeless. Now I'm feeling that way as well.

3. *What things does the client do that you find frustrating?* This is the time to be specific; generalities will only confuse the issues and delay the process. Describe a few examples of the type of behavior you find most irritating, the situations in which this is most likely to occur, and the consequences to you and the relationship.

Well, there are several things they do that drive me nuts. For one, they don't listen to one another, nor to me. It is as if each of them has already rehearsed what they want to say and it is the telling of this story that is their first priority. When I reflect what is going on, they both smile, thank me for my brilliant observation, and then proceed to continue doing the same thing.

Then they keep bringing up stuff from the past even though we've already agreed that isn't helpful. They take turns, like a wrestling tag team—one of them accuses the other of some misconduct, while the other acts like a victim of some minor misunderstanding. I watch them go at it, always painfully polite. I feel like I'm at a tennis match where my head keeps following the ball back and forth across the net.

4. *What feelings are being elicited in you?* Stop talking about the client and speak about yourself. Tell your partner about all the feelings that come up as a direct and indirect result of your interactions with the client. As much as you feel willing and safe to go, dig deep inside yourself for what is being triggered by these interactions. You are searching for those most human parts of your being that operate beyond your regular conscious control rather than the formal professional parts that are more consciously accessed.

These people make me feel hopeless and foolish. Left unsaid is the accusation that I don't really know what I'm doing, which in this case, is mostly true. I *don't* know what to do with this couple. I have exhausted all my favorite techniques.

I feel sad as well. I really like these people and so badly want to help *them. Yet I feel inadequate because I am up against the limits of what is possible. I tell myself over and over again that there is only so much I can do, that the rest is up to them, but I guess I don't believe that. There should be something else I can do.*

5. *Conduct a professional assessment of what has been going on, along with a corresponding list of your personal reactions.* Your partner may have been reflecting your ideas and seeking some understanding up to this point. Now it is time to directly request significant involvement from your partner. Ask your partner to help you answer the following questions honestly and sincerely (Kottler et al., 1994):

- What are the ways this relationship is not working?
- How am I overreacting to what is taking place?
- How might I alter my working diagnosis?
- How have I distorted the picture?
- What is the client doing that is getting in the way?
- How has my humanness been withheld or diluted?
- What is the client accomplishing by avoiding issues through resistance?
- How am I punishing the client for not cooperating with my agenda?
- What have I done most consistently in my life to create or exacerbate relationship conflicts?
- How is what is happening here go on elsewhere, in *each* of our lives?
- How are issues of power and control getting in the way of us relating to one another in more helpful, authentic ways?

These are only a portion of what could be a list of a hundred questions. The importance of asking the questions is to promote thinking about your personal role in the struggle and how this fits in the larger context of your life. This approach accesses those critical areas of information and insight needed for your development that are rarely a part of traditional supervision.

6. *List what you have tried that hasn't worked.* Similar to any strategic or problem-solving method, you now need to figure out what you are doing that is consistently ineffective. The very nature of being at an "impasse" in a relationship should confirm for us that ineffective reactions need to be identified and discarded. Write out a list of all the things that have been tried unsuccessfully, and the number of times you tried them.

Okay, I really like accentuating the positive myself and then getting clients to do it. That's one of my favorite things to do. It almost always works. But not with these people. I'm sure I've tried it at least once in every session, but they can never do it for very long.

I get them to agree to some specific assignment after each session, but they never complete them. It's gotten to the point where now they ask me for something to do if I don't offer first. We then go through the motions of coming up with something that we all know they will never get done.

They've seen through my paradoxical directives, another of my best techniques. I've told them about what I'm feeling and what they trigger in me and all that does is elicit an apology for being so difficult, which was never my goal. They don't actually hear what I'm saying to them. I've tried . . .

7. *Commit to no longer doing the things that haven't worked.* This is the hard part. Just like our clients, we don't like to give up our favorite strategies, even when they're not working. They're familiar to us. They are comfortable. They almost always worked in other cases. We feel extreme pressure to hold onto these techniques at all cost and when they don't work, we are likely to blame the client.

   This commitment phase is particularly crucial because it appears to demand so little new information, thought, or energy while the reality demands a much higher personal price. It is a deceptively simple sounding act to say, "Yes. I will not do the things that don't work." Of course we know that making good on those simple words is much more difficult. The troubling issues of self-doubt, fear of failure, potential exposure of our hidden inadequacies, and venturing into stormy therapeutic waters with untested techniques provide the turmoil that can stop even the best of therapists from carrying through with their commitment.

I'm not sure what I have left to do if I stop doing these things. Our sessions have settled into a routine now where they come in, each complaining about the other one, and then I listen carefully, reflect what I hear them saying, and then make them relate to one another in alternative ways. If I give that up, I don't know what else to do.

But okay, I promise for one session to experiment with something different, although I have no idea what that might be.

8. *Brainstorm a list of other options.* It doesn't really matter what you come up with as long as it breaks you loose from the dysfunctional patterns that are already keeping you at an impasse. A flexible and creative partner is invaluable at this stage. You were stuck and that is the worst possible framework in which to creatively develop new ideas on your own. An effective partner will help you generate a long list of possibilities from a wide assortment of frameworks.

The intention at this point is *not* to come up with a correct solution to the problem, but rather to spur thinking along more innovative lines. A relationship impasse by definition is when two or more people are stuck in a frustrating, dysfunctional pattern characterized by each of them blaming the other. Once you let go of who is at fault, abandon strategies that are not producing desirable outcomes, and begin a creative exploration of new strategies, then it is only a matter of time until you discover one combination of ingredients that breaks things loose.

This is just one systematic structure that can be employed with a partner in peer consultation. Other possibilities may come to mind, depending on your own theoretical orientation, the setting and circumstances in which you practice, the strengths and weaknesses of your partner, and your particular needs at the time. The greatest value of this type of process is that it provides a framework for working through issues that may not be possible in sessions with a traditional supervisor with whom you are being evaluated as well as being helped.

This chapter was presented from the viewpoint of the therapist as supervisee in order to emphasize our belief in the importance of directing your own growth as a therapist. Graduate school, professional organizations, ethical standards, legal cases, licensure laws, and traditional supervision all focus attention on how others will guide and judge us. While each of these is necessary to guard the rights of the public, none give sufficient attention to the healthy self-directed growth model we feel is also essential. You must take direct control over your own development in order match those strengths, weaknesses, and needs that are most unique to you with the resources that can best serve them.

CHAPTER TWELVE

Being Mentored

Graduate school may have failed us in many sectors, but not in the area of providing support. For many of us, being a student was a time of camaraderie in which we came together to aid one another. We studied together. We worked on group projects. We sat together over coffee or beer, complaining about how unfair our professors were. During times of difficulty or special challenges we supported and helped one another.

Then, there were the other sources of support available to us: financial aid, graduate assistantships, computer laboratories, study skills centers, social events, counseling services, student organizations, and faculty advising—both through an assigned mentor and also through informal relationships. In spite of how badly we wanted to graduate and get back into the real world, we didn't realize at the time how much we would miss the spirit of camaraderie. We didn't realize how much of the time we would feel so alone.

One of the most frequent complaints voiced by practitioners everywhere is how little support we receive from the organizations we work in and the colleagues we work with. In the way that time heals all wounds, we even feel wistful about our days in graduate schools, longing for those special times when we felt supported. Furthermore, we absolutely need this support in order to survive, if not flourish.

There are three things involved in transforming ourselves in such a way that we can meet the challenges of a rapidly evolving profession: a clear vision of where we are headed, retooled skills for adapting to these changes, and a support system for carrying through with our intentions. Among those sources of support that are available to us from family and friends, colleagues and peers, is the able assistance of a mentor who is concerned for our welfare and in a position to do us some good.

ROLES OF MENTORING

Trina couldn't have been more pleased with the way her weekly supervision session had gone. She received some very specific guidance from the clinical director about what to do with a few of her more perplexing cases. They watched one video of a session that she had made a point to record because her use of metaphor had not been having the effects she had hoped. During verbal replays of the proceedings, both Trina and her supervisor had been unable to identify where things had gotten bogged down, that is, until they watched the video together. Trina thus felt quite good about being focused on a few aspects of her therapeutic technique that she intended to refine.

Trina enjoyed this formal supervision with her administrator, a woman who was both very knowledgeable and highly skilled. Unfortunately, because of the nature of her other clinic-wide responsibilities, the clinical director wasn't available much except during regularly scheduled sessions. It was for this reason that Trina also met regularly with a number of her colleagues in a kind of peer supervision that was focused less on her cases and more on providing mutual support.

Even with this support and excellent supervision, Trina felt lost. Her friends at work, while well-meaning, knew only a little more than she did about the inner workings of the organization. She often wondered whether she should attend a particular meeting, go to a workshop in town, affiliate with certain individuals, but without any mentoring, she was left to her own naive judgments.

There was certainly no shortage of advice among her peers, but this guidance was based more on subjective opinions than it was supported by wisdom and experience. There was a lot of gossip about who among the administrators could be trusted and who could not, but there was no definitive opinion among her friends. Trina had a number of questions and concerns, but nobody she could turn to who could offer *informed* guidance. For example, should she begin a doctoral program, and if so, how could she get into one, and which ones should she consider? She also hoped, someday, to move into another specialty area but she wasn't sure exactly how to do that. She was ambitious, hoping to eventually serve in a supervisory role herself, but she didn't have a clear idea about how that evolution took place. In summary, Trina was getting plenty of case supervision. What she was missing, however, was systematic nurturance, both as a person and a professional. She hadn't realized that once she left graduate school, she was on her own as far as her continued development, unless she could find a mentor.

WHAT MENTORING CAN DO

Supervision is only one facet of the development of therapists. While it is a critical component of the evolutionary professional process, the bigger scheme of things includes a kind of intellectual, emotional, and career sponsorship that is conducted by those of higher rank and experience toward those who are just beginning their careers.

Mentors function in a number of different roles for the newly minted professional. Among those highlighted by a number of authors on the mentoring process (Brinson & Kottler, 1993; Murray & Owen, 1991; Phillips-Jones, 1982) include the following:

- *Being an advocate.* In order to make your way through the maze of confusion that surrounds most work settings—the politics, the power struggles, the organizational process, the unique ways of doing business—it is absolutely crucial to have a sponsor looking out for your best interests. Ideally, this is someone of senior standing in the organization who can speak out on your behalf, introduce you to the right people, gain you entry into the most advantageous subgroups.
- *Being a confidante.* A mentor is someone you can trust, someone you can go to for advice, who will help you to make sense of events within the organization, and who will help you to interpret situations accurately. Providing emotional support is just as important as logistical support in order to help boost confidence. This is especially the case during critical incidents in which something goes wrong or when the therapist is undergoing some developmental transition.
- *Being a role model.* Just as therapists are models for everything their clients wish to be, so too do mentors serve this role for the developing professional. Mentors are symbols of success. Naturally, they are good at doing their jobs; even more so, they are highly skilled at operating efficiently. They know how to work the system. They know how to metabolize stress. Most of all, they know how to get things done, even in the face of challenging obstacles.
- *Giving useful feedback.* Unless you can hear the truth about what you are doing well, and what you are not doing up to par, there are few

opportunities to improve your therapeutic and organizational competence. It is sad how often experienced therapists talk among themselves about another colleague who consistently makes mistakes and misjudgments. They know exactly what this person is doing wrong, what should be improved, and how behavior should be altered. Unfortunately, nothing is said directly to the individual so there is no opportunity to improve performance.

Mentors give feedback to developing clinicians on how to work the system better, how to cultivate helpful relationships, how to handle critical meetings. They tell therapists what they are doing well in their sessions, as well as which skills they need to upgrade. Most importantly, mentors offer guidance and suggestions for how to deal with the many stressful and confusing aspects of this type of work.

- *Being a tutor.* When it has been determined that a therapist is in need of remedial instruction in specific areas of conceptual thinking, case formulation, skill development, or interpersonal comportment, mentors teach their proteges what they need to know. This may include some crucial methodologies that had been neglected in graduate school, or even some skills that are simply in need of upgrading.
- *Guiding a career path.* It has been the way of the world for thousands of generations that the role of experienced people is primarily to help those who are less experienced to find their way toward desired goals. Mentors help developing therapists to make sound decisions related to: where and how they should continue their training, opportunities for promotion and advancement within the organization, and when it is desirable to switch jobs. While it is certainly important to gather information from among your peers, there is no substitute for consulting someone in a position of greater authority who not only sees the bigger picture, but who is empowered to recommend you for other opportunities.

FINDING A MENTOR

No single mentor can provide all the answers and support every one of your needs. Mentoring relationships go through stages (Hazler, Stanard, Conkey, & Granello, 1997) that reflect an increasing equality of knowledge and expertise on the part of both participants. The same mentors who once seemed to know all the answers and have all the power, begin to look more like everyone else as proteges become more similar in their own levels of knowledge, expertise, and influence. The result is that no one person is likely to fulfill a career's worth of guidance, nor can a series of mentors provide all the support needs of any therapist. Mentors can only provide the central thread in what needs to be a complex web of support systems.

We recruit our mentors from among a wide variety of sources. The authors of our favorite books provide us guidance and direction within the context of somewhat limited relationships in which we get from them only what they feel like offering in each chapter. We may talk back to them, ask questions, plead for elaboration, but then we must construct the answers ourselves from whatever we can deduce from their dialogue.

Senior colleagues and supervisors at work are other obvious candidates for mentors. In fact, such an individual is absolutely crucial to show us the ropes. Unfortunately, it takes a certain degree of luck to be placed in a work group in which there is someone qualified, interested, and available.

Hiring our own therapist is another obvious choice, although one that is all too often avoided by those of us who should know better. Certainly, we make lousy clients, by and large. We play games, second guess our therapists, critique their performances, intellectualize, hide behind our experience watching others do the same. Still, if we are honest and talk about our resistances, if we hire someone with experience working with other therapists, the protective facade will come down.

We don't look for mentors often enough outside our own field. If we are searching for people who are wise and experienced, who can teach us things we never learned in graduate school, then they are most likely those who are operating in a different arena altogether. In fact, most of us need more of such diversity in our lives. We spend altogether too much time thinking about therapy, talking about therapy, reading about therapy, doing therapy, that we leave little opportunity to expand our worlds from outside influences.

Ultimately, one of the things that crippled our growth the most in graduate school was the belief that the best way to become a better therapist was to read, study, practice, and learn more about therapy. This is true only to a certain extent. As we well know and understand with our clients, sometimes the best way to promote dramatic and lasting changes is to push people to move beyond the safe boundaries of what they already know, to delve into areas that are unknown, even a little frightening.

In graduate school, we learned to avoid risks, to play it safe, to do what is expected, to meet the approval of others. We learned to read accurately what others wanted from us, whether that was the correct choice on an exam, the perfect formula for a term paper, or the ideal comment to make in class.

Once we secured our first jobs, we continued this pattern of pleasing others. Since we were already well-trained as approval seekers, it didn't take much for us to do whatever we could to fit in, to get others to like us. Indeed, being likable and delivering what others want and expect is critical to getting clients to return.

Somewhere along this path, however, what has been lost is our own ability and willingness to mentor ourselves. Yes, it certainly helps to have mentors like professors, supervisors, therapists, wise and experienced friends, who can show us the way, just as we do for our own clients.

There comes a time when we believe that we have finally moved beyond the boundaries of graduate school. We no longer need mentors to guide us. We recognize that most of what we read in books and hear in workshops is already familiar to us. Less experienced clinicians begin to approach us because they recognize that we have something original and useful to offer. And we do. What we realize, finally, is that we never left graduate school, and furthermore, we never will.

References

Allen, J. D. (1976, March). Peer group supervision in family therapy. *Child Welfare,* 183–189.

Alperin, R. M. (1994). Managed care versus psychoanalytic psychotherapy: Conflicting ideologies. *Clinical Social Work Journal, 22,* 137–148.

American Psychological Association. (1994). *Publication manual of the American Psychological Association* (4th ed.). Washington, DC: Author.

Anderson, W. (1990). *Reality isn't what it used to be.* San Francisco: Jossey-Bass.

Baskett, H. K., & Marsick, V. J. (Eds.). (1992). *Professionals' ways of knowing: New findings on how to improve professional education.* San Francisco: Jossey-Bass.

Beck, M. (1994, June 6). Managing the mind. *Newsweek,* 30–32.

Beigel, J. K., & Earle, R. H. (Eds.). (1990). *Successful private practice in the 1990s.* New York: Brunner/Mazel.

Belar, C. D. (1995). Collaboration in capitated care: Challenges for psychology. *Professional Psychology: Research and Practice, 26,* 139–146.

Belenky, M. F., Clinchy, B. M., Goldberger, N. R., & Tarule, J. M. (1986). *Women's ways of knowing.* New York: Basic.

Bennett, M. J. (1994). Are competing psychotherapists manageable? *Managed Care Quarterly, 2,* 36–42.

Bernard, J. M., & Goodyear, R. K. (1992). *Fundamentals of clinical supervision.* Boston: Allyn & Bacon.

Blocher, D. H. (1983). Toward a cognitive developmental approach to counselor supervision. *The Counseling Psychologist, 11,* 27–34.

Bolman, L. G., & Deal, T. E. (1991). *Reframing organizations: Artistry, choice, and leadership.* San Francisco: Jossey-Bass.

Borders, D. (1991a). A systematic approach to peer group supervision. *Journal of Counseling and Development, 69,* 248–252.

Borders, D. (1991b). *Report: Plan of action for addressing issues related to impaired therapists.* Memorandum from Chair of the Special Task force on Impaired Counselors to the American Association for Counseling and Development Governing Council, June 12, 1991.

Boud, D., & Griffen, V. (Eds.). (1987). *Appreciating adults learning.* London: Kogan Page.

Breggin, P. R. (1994). *Toxic psychiatry.* New York: St. Martin's.

Brinson, J., & Kottler, J. A. (1993). Cross-cultural mentoring in counselor education: A strategy for retaining minority faculty. *Counselor Education and Supervision, 32,* 241–253.

Bulman, R., & Wortman, C. B. (1977). Attribution of blame and coping in the real world. *Journal of Personality and Social Psychology, 35,* 351–363.

Butler, K. (1994, March/April). Surviving the revolution. *Family Therapy Networker,* 28–29.

Butz, M. R. (1993). Practical applications from chaos theory to the psychotherapeutic process: A basic consideration of dynamics. *Psychological Reports, 73,* 543–554.

Butz, M. R. (1994). Psychopharmacology: Psychology's Jurassic Park. *Psychotherapy, 31,* 692–699.

Carson, R. (1962). *Silent spring.* Boston: Houghton-Mifflin.

Chapman, S. (1992). What is the question? *The Journal of Experiential Education, 15,* 16–18.

Chinen, A. B. (1991). The return of wonder in old age. *Generations, 15*(2), 45–58.

Claiborn, C. D., Etringer, B. D., & Hillerbrand, E. T. (1995). Social influence processes in supervision. *Counselor Education and Supervision, 35,* 43–53.

Clance, P. R. (1985). *The impostor phenomenon.* Atlanta: Peachtree.

Cowley, G. (1994, February 7). Culture of Prozac. *Newsweek,* 41–42.

Csikszentmihaly, M. (1990). *Flow: The psychology of optimal experience.* New York: Harper Collins.

Cummings, N. A. (1995). Impact of managed care on employment and training: A manual for survival. *Professional Psychology, 26,* 10–15.

Deutsch, C. J. (1985). A survey of therapists' personal problems and treatment. *Professional Psychology: Research and Practice, 16,* 305–315.

de Waal, F. (1982). *Chimpanzee politics.* Baltimore: Johns Hopkins.

Dies, R. R. (1993). Writing for publication: Overcoming common obstacles. *International Journal of Group Psychotherapy, 43,* 243–249.

Doherty, W. J. (1995). *Soul searching.* New York: Basic.

Ehlers, C. L. (1992). The new physics of chaos. *Neuroscience, 16,* 267–272.

Elkind, D. (1995, September). School and family in the postmodern world. *Phi Delta Kappan,* 8–14.

Ellis, H. C. (1992). Graduate education in psychology. *American Psychologist, 47*(4), 570–576.

Ericsson, K. A., & Smith, J. (1991). Prospects and limits of the empirical study of expertise: An introduction. In K. A. Ericsson & J. Smith (Eds.), *Toward a general theory of expertise* (pp. 1–38). Cambridge, MA: Harvard.

Etringer, B. D., Hillerbrand, E., & Claiborn, C. D. (1995). The transition from novice to expert counselor. *Counselor Education and Supervision, 35,* 4–17.

Fancher, R. T. (1995). *Cultures of healing.* New York: Freeman.

Farber, B. A., & Heifetz, L. J. (1981). The satisfaction and stresses of psychotherapeutic work. *Professional Psychology, 12,* 221–230.

Fisher, L. C. (1993, January). *Impaired professionals intervention: A working paper.* Memorandum from Chair of the Professional Concerns Committee of the American Association of Pastoral Counselors.

Fisher, S., & Greenberg, R. P. (1995, September/October). Prescriptions for happiness? *Psychology Today,* 32–37.

Forester-Miller, H., & Davis, T. E. (1995). *A practitioner's guide to ethical decision making.* Alexandria, VA: American Counseling Association.

Fox, R. D., Maxmanian, P. E., & Putnam, R. W. (1989). *Changing and learning in the lives of physicians.* New York: Praeger.

Frank, J. D. (1973). *Persuasion and healing.* Baltimore: Johns Hopkins.

Freudenberger, H. J., & Robbins, A. (1979). The hazards of being a psychoanalyst. *Psychoanalytic Review, 66,* 275–296.

Friedlander, M. L., Siegel, S., & Brenock, K. (1989). Parallel processes in counseling and supervision: A case study. *Journal of Counseling Psychology, 36*, 149–157.

Garvey, M. (Ed.). (1996). *Writer's market* (75th ed.). Cincinnati: Writer's Digest.

Gelatt, H. B. (1995). Chaos and compassion. *Counseling and Values, 39*, 108–116.

Gilligan, C. (1982). *In a different voice: Psychological theory and women's development.* Cambridge, MA: Harvard.

Gleick, J. (1987). *Chaos: Making a new science.* New York: Viking.

Goodman, M., Brown, J., & Deitz, P. (1992). *Managing managed care.* Washington, DC: American Psychiatric Press.

Gore, A. (1992). *Earth in the balance: Ecology and the human spirit.* Boston: Houghton Mifflin.

Greenberg, S. L., Lewis, G. J., & Johnson, M. (1985). Peer consultation groups for private practitioners. *Professional Psychology, 16*, 437–447.

Gregersen, H., & Sailer, L. (1993). Chaos theory and its implications for social science research. *Human Relations, 46*, 777–802.

Grosch, W. N., & Olsen, D. C. (1994). *When helping starts to hurt.* New York: Norton.

Guy, J. D. (1987). *The personal life of the psychotherapist.* New York: Wiley.

Hamlin, E. R., & Timberlake, E. M. (1982, February). Peer group supervision for supervisors. *Social Casework*, 82–87.

Harris, G. A. (1995, September). Fact from fiction. *Counseling Today*, 4.

Haynes, S. N. (1995). Introduction to the special section on chaos theory and psychological assessment. *Psychological Assessment, 7*, 3–4.

Hazler, R. J. (1992). Increasing your publishing chances by showing you are a part of the family. *Journal of Humanistic Education and Development, 30*, 98–99.

Hazler, R. J., & Carney, J. (1993). Student-faculty interactions: An underemphasized dimension of counselor education. *Counselor Education and Supervision, 33*, 80–88.

Hazler, R. J., & Kottler, J. A. (1996a). Following through on the best of intentions: Helping impaired professionals. *Journal of Humanistic Education and Development, 34*, 156–158.

Hazler, R. J., & Kottler, J. A. (1996b). Professional counselor impairment and renewal [Special issue]. *Journal of Humanistic Education and Development, 34*, 98–159.

Hazler, R. J., Stanard, R .P., Conkey, V., & Granello, P. (1997). Mentoring new group leaders. In H. Forrester-Miller & J. A. Kottler, *Issues and challenges for group practitioners.* Denver: Love.

Herlihy, B. (1996). When a colleague is impaired: The individual counselor's response. *Journal of Humanistic Education and Development, 34*, 118–127.

Hoffman, E. (1992). *Visions of innocence: Spiritual and inspirational experiences of childhood.* Boston: Shambhala.

Holmes, J., & Lindley, R. (1989). *The values of psychotherapy.* New York: Oxford.

Houle, C. O. (1980). *Continuing learning in the professions.* San Francisco: Jossey-Bass.

Howard, G. S. (1993). Ecocounseling psychology: An introduction and overview. *The Counseling Psychologist, 21*, 550–559.

Isaksen, S. G., Dorval, K. B., & Treffinger, D. J. (1994). *Creative approaches to problem solving.* Dubuque, IA: Kendall/Hunt.

Jackson, L., & Caffarella, R. S. (Eds.). (1994). *Experiential learning: A new approach.* San Francisco: Jossey-Bass.

Jaeger, R. M., & Hendricks, A. Y. (1994). The publication process in educational measurement. *Educational Measurement: Issues and Practice, 13*, 20–26.

Jaret, P. (1994). Beyond Prozac. *Vogue, 184*, 394–5.

Josselson, R. (1992). *The space between us.* San Francisco: Jossey-Bass.

Karon, B. P. (1995). Provision of psychotherapy under managed care: A growing crisis and national nightmare. *Professional Psychology, 26*, 5–9.

Katzell, R. A., & Yankelovich, D. (1975). *Work, productivity, and job satisfaction.* New York: Psychological Corporation.

Kilburg, R. R., Nathan, P. E., & Thoreson, R. W. (Eds.). (1986). *Professionals in distress.* Washington, DC: American Psychological Association.

Kottler, J. A. (1991). *The compleat therapist.* San Francisco: Jossey-Bass.

Kottler, J. A. (1992). Confronting our own hypocrisy: Being a model for our students and clients. *Journal of Counseling and Development, 70,* 475–476.

Kottler, J. A. (1993). *On being a therapist* (rev. ed.). San Francisco: Jossey-Bass.

Kottler, J. A. (1994). *Advanced group leadership.* Pacific Grove, CA: Brooks/Cole.

Kottler, J. A. (1995). *Growing a therapist.* San Francisco: Jossey-Bass.

Kottler, J. A. (1996). *The language of tears.* San Francisco: Jossey-Bass.

Kottler, J. A., & Blau, D. S. (1989). *The imperfect therapist: Learning from failure in psychotherapy.* San Francisco: Jossey-Bass.

Kottler, J. A., Sexton, T. L., & Whiston, S. C. (1994). *Heart of healing: Relationships in therapy.* San Francisco: Jossey-Bass.

Krippner, S. (1994). Humanistic psychology and chaos theory: The third revolution and the third force. *Journal of Humanistic Psychology, 34,* 48–61.

Lawless, L. (1995, January/February). Helping therapists take charge. *Family Therapy Networker,* 73–76.

Lett, W. R. (1987). A conundrum: Counselling and creativity. *Australian Psychologist, 22,* 29–41.

Levin, A. M. (1983). *The private practice of psychotherapy.* New York: Free.

Lewis, G. J., Greenburg, S. L., & Hatch, D. B. (1988). Peer consultation groups for psychologists in private practice: A national survey. *Professional Psychology, 19,* 81–86.

Lewis, L. H., & Williams, C. J. (1994). Experiential learning: Past and present. In L. Jackson & R. S. Caffarella (Eds.), *Experiential learning: A new approach* (pp. 5–16). San Francisco: Jossey-Bass.

Lipchik, E. (1994, March/April). The rush to be brief. *Family Therapy Networker,* 34–39.

London, P. (1986). *Modes and morals of psychotherapy* (2nd ed.). Washington: Hemisphere.

Mahrer, A. R. (1989). *The integration of psychotherapies.* New York: Human Sciences.

Mandell, J. (1995). *Book editors talk to writers.* New York: Wiley.

Margenau, E. A. (Ed.). (1990). *The encyclopedia handbook of private practice.* New York: Gardner.

Marks, J. L., & Hixon, D. F. (1986, September). Training agency staff through peer group supervision. *Social Casework,* 418–423.

Maslow, A. H. (1968). *Toward a psychology of being* (2nd ed.). New York: Van Nostrand.

Maslow, A. H. (1987). *Motivation and personality* (3rd ed.). New York: Harper & Row.

Matthias, M. R. (1991). *A comparative study of continuing competence among male members of selected professions.* Unpublished doctoral dissertation, University of Toronto, Toronto, Canada.

McClure, B. A., Merrill, E., & Russo, T. R. (1994). Seeing clients with an artist's eye: Perceptual simulation exercises. *Simulation & Gaming, 25*(1), 51–60.

McGoldrick, M. (1989). Ethnicity and the family life cycle. In B. Carter & M. McGoldrick (Eds.), *The changing family life cycle* (pp. 69–90). Boston: Allyn & Bacon.

Michael, D. (1983). Competence and compassion in an age of uncertainty. *World Future Society Bulletin, 17,* 1–6.

Minuchin, S. (1991, September/October). The seductions of constructivism. *Family Therapy Networker,* 47–50.

Morley, J. (1995, March/April). A PC guide to political correctness. *Family Therapy Networker,* 17–18.

Murray, M., & Owen, M. A. (1991). *Beyond the myths and magic of mentoring.* San Francisco: Jossey-Bass.

National Association of Social Workers (1987). Commission on employment and economic support. *Impaired Social Worker Program Resource Book.* Silver Springs, MD: Author.

Nobler, H. (1980). A peer group for therapists: Successful experience in sharing. *International Journal of Group Psychotherapy, 30,* 51–61.

Norcross, J. C., & Glencavage, L. M. (1989). Eclecticism and integration in counseling and psychotherapy: Major themes and obstacles. *British Journal of Guidance and Counselling, 17,* 227–247.

Omer, H. (1987). Therapeutic impact: A nonspecific major factor in directive psychotherapies. *Psychotherapy, 24,* 52–57.

Phillips-Jones, L. (1982). *Mentors and proteges.* New York: Arbor.

Prochaska, J. O., & DiClemente, C. C. (1984). Transtheoretical therapy: Toward an integrative model of change. *Psychotherapy, 19,* 276–288.

Reamer, F. (1992). The impaired social worker. *Social Work, 37,* 165–170.

Ridley, C., Mendoza, D. W., & Kanitz, B. (1994). Multicultural training: Reexamination, operationalization, and integration. *Counseling Psychologist, 22,* 227–289.

Rieff, P. (1961). *Freud: The mind of the moralist.* Garden City, NY: Anchor.

Roberts, P. (1995). Prozacville. *Psychology Today, 28,* 16.

Salameh, W. A. (1990). Critical equations in launching a clinical practice. In E. Margenau (Ed.), *The encyclopedia handbook of private practice* (pp. 48–66). New York: Gardner.

Saletan, R. (1995). Queries, proposals, manuscripts: What editors want and don't want. In J. Mandell (Ed.), *Book editors talk to writers.* New York: Wiley.

Salomone, P. R. (1993). Trade secrets for crafting a conceptual article. *Journal of Counseling and Development, 72,* 73–76.

Schon, D. A. (1983). *The reflective practitioner: How professionals think in action.* New York: Basic.

Schreter, R. K., Sharfstein, S. S., & Schreter, C. A. (Eds.). (1994). *Allies and adversaries: The impact of managed care on mental health services.* Washington, DC: American Psychiatric Press.

Shapiro, A. K. (1991). Placebo effects in medicine, psychotherapy and psychoanalysis. In S. L. Garfield & A. E. Bergin (Eds.), *Handbook of psychotherapy and behavioral change: An empirical analysis.* New York: Wiley.

Simon, H. A. (1973). The structure of ill-structured problems. *Artificial Intelligences, 4,* 181–201.

Sinacore-Guinn, A. L. (1995). The diagnostic window: Culture- and gender-sensitive diagnosis and training. *Counselor Education and Supervision, 35,* 18–31.

Smith, K. E., & McCormick, D. M. (1992). Translating experience into learning: Facilitating the process for adult students. *Adult Learning, 3,* 22–25.

Sowell, T. (1994). *Race and culture.* New York: Basic.

Stevens, B. A. (1991). Chaos: A challenge to refine systems theory. *Journal of Family Therapy, 12,* 23–26.

Sussman, M. B. (1992). *A curious calling: Unconscious motivations for practicing psychotherapy.* Northvale, NJ: Jason Aronson.

Sussman, M. B. (1995). Intimations of morality. In M. B. Sussman (Ed.), *A perilous calling: The hazards of psychotherapy practice* (pp. 15–25). New York: Wiley.

Swearingen, C. (1990). The impaired psychiatrist. *Psychiatric Clinics of North America, 13,* 1–11.

Sweet, J. J., Rozensky, R. H., & Tovian, S. M. (1991). *Handbook of clinical psychology in medical settings.* New York: Plenum.

Syme, G. (1994). *Counselling in independent practice.* Buckingham, England: Open University.

Tennen, H., & Affleck, G. (1990). Blaming others for threatening events. *Psychological Bulletin, 108,* 209–232.

Thomas, L. (1979). *Medussa and the snail*. New York: Viking.

Thompson, B. (1995). Publishing your research results: Some suggestions and counsel. *Journal of Counseling and Development, 73,* 342–345.

Thorsrud, E. (1984). The Scandinavian model: Strategies of organizational democratization in Norway. In B. Wilpert & A. Sorge (Eds.), *International perspectives on organizational democracy* (pp. 337–370). New York: Wiley.

Tosi Hosmand, L. L. (1991). Clinical inquiry as scientific training. *The Counseling Psychologist, 19,* 431–453.

Wallach, M. A., & Wallach, L. (1983). *Psychology's sanction for selfishness.* San Francisco: W. H. Freeman.

Wendorf, D. J., Wendorf, R. J., & Bond, D. (1985). Growth behind the mirror: The family therapy consortium's group process. *Journal of Marital and Family Therapy, 11,* 245–255.

White, M., & Epston, D. (1990). *Narrative means to therapeutic ends.* New York: Norton.

Wilbur, M. P., Kulikowich, J. M., Roberts-Wilbur, J., & Torres-Rivera, E. (1995). Chaos theory and counselor training. *Counseling and Values, 39,* 129–144.

Wright, R. (1994). *The moral animal.* New York: Pantheon.

Wylie, M. S. (1995, September/October). The new visionaries. *Family Therapy Networker,* 21–32.

Index

human resources frame of reference,
179–80
ideological conflicts, 172–73
individual functioning and, 180–82
individual recognition, 185
lack of leadership, 177
manipulative behavior in, 171–72, 177
organizational goals and, 184
participation in, 185
propensity for problems in mental health
care settings, 169–70, 177–79
prospects for improving, 163–64, 185–
86
recognition of unalterable conditions,
182–83, 186
as source of individual stress, 193
strategies for improving, 180–86
see also collegial relations
outcome review
agent for change, 40–41
current practice environment, 12–13
dealing with failure, 34–35
emphasis on, 46
limitations of, 33
in scientist-practitioner model, 58–59
techniques, 59–60
Owen, M. A., 228

paradigmatic thinking
emerging concepts, 83
external pressures for change, 78
pace of change, 95–96
role of, 76
shift in perception, 77–78
shifts in practice, 90–94
use of, 75–76
peak experiences, 70–72
peer consultation
alternative format for stuck cases, 220–
25
application, 217
current utilization, 218
group supervision, 217–18
honesty in, 219
potential pitfalls, 219–20
power relations in, 216–17
recommendations for implementation,
218–19
personal life
combining professional life with, 205–6
dysfunctional professionals, 187–88
family relations, 38–40

in private practice schedule, 108–9,
112–13
professional priorities and, 182
pharmacotherapy
criticism of, 79
implications for practice, 9–10
prescription privileges, 21, 84–85
therapeutic relationship and, 9
therapist education, 21
trends in help-seeking behavior, 8–9
political correctness, 14
postmodernism
application to practice, 88–90
conceptual basis, 87, 88
principal exponents, 87–88
relevance to practice, 83–84
private practice
advantages, 108
business management skills, 111–12
controlling schedule in, 108–9
economics, 107–8
implications of managed care, 117–18
marketing skills, 110–11, 112
opportunities for time off, 112–14
professional isolation in, 114–16
strategies for success, 110–14
structure and operations, 120–21
therapeutic relationship in, 114
therapist expectations, 107
therapist qualities suited to, 109–10
Prochaska, J. O., 98
Prozac, 8–10, 79
public perception
reluctance to intervene with dysfunctional colleagues, 195
scrutiny of therapist's private life, 32
of therapist effectiveness, 32–34
public speaking
attunement to audience, 126, 137–38
audience expectations, 129–30
becoming accustomed to, 122
benefits, 124–25
challenges, 122–23
closing remarks, 134–35
coordination of elements in, 138–39
goals of, 128–29
good qualities in, 125–29
growth as presenter, 139–40
informational content, 133
learning style of audiences, 126–28
opening remarks, 131–32
paid compensation, 125